The Miraculous
Powers of Love

ALSO BY CELIA HADDON:
The Sensuous Lie
The Sunday Times Book of Body Maintenance
(co-editor)

The Miraculous Powers of Love

Celia Haddon

Scarborough House/Publishers

Scarborough House / Publishers
Chelsea, MI 48118

FIRST PUBLISHED IN THE UNITED STATES IN 1990

Library of Congress Cataloging-in-Publication Data

Haddon, Celia.
  The miraculous powers of love / Celia Haddon.
    p. cm.
  Bibliography: p.
  Includes index.
  ISBN 0-8128-3064-4
  1. Love. I. Title.
BD436.H25 1990
177'.7—dc20

Contents

To my father, Darby Haddon

Acknowledgements

A book about the powers of love should begin with a full acknowledgement of all the friendship and support the author has received from others while writing it. I am particularly grateful to my husband Ronnie, my agent Mike Shaw, my editor Michèle Young, my geographically distant friend Michael Pye, and those closer at hand like Marie, Jenny and Bina. There are many others too, but I cannot name them all.

Institutions such as the Westminister Library in Great Smith Street, and the London Library, have been of great help. And the Group for the Study of the Human-Animal Companion Bond should be mentioned for their pioneering work.

I need also to thank the following publishers and authors who allowed me to quote from their books: Macmillan, *Solitary Confinement* by the late Christopher Burney – a remarkable book that is now regrettably out of print though it deserves to be a classic; Weidenfeld & Nicolson, *Breakdown* by Stuart Sutherland – another excellent book; Pergamon Press, 'The socialising role of pet animals in nursing homes' by Samuel A. Corson, E. O'Leary Corson, Donald D. De Hass, Regina Gunsett, Peter H. Gwynne, L. Eugene Arnold and Candace N. Corson from *Ethology and Nonverbal Communication in Mental Health*; the *British Medical Journal*, 'Changing attitudes to the management of severe head injuries' by Walpole Lewin – a very moving article; the *Spectator*, 'A ghost of Christmas past' by Peter Paterson.

Finally, I want to put on record my gratitude to those who did not charge any copyright fee at all, or only a small one. Generosity to authors should be duly noted, so a special thank you to the *BMJ* and the *Spectator*.

1

Our Want of Love

Consider the way we live now. Consider the American camera team, anxious for exciting footage to entertain their viewers. An unemployed man phoned the TV station in Anniston, Alabama, to say he was going to set fire to himself in the town square of Jacksonville. Both the police and a two-man camera crew turned up to wait. After an hour the police left, but the TV crew were still waiting when the man arrived. As he drenched himself in lighter fuel, they filmed. As he set it alight, they filmed. The flames began to spread across his legs, and they continued filming. Then one of them shouted, 'Don't do it!' The flames spread further. The man began to moan and cried, 'Put it out.' One of the crew still filmed. The other started to try to beat out the flames using his reporter's notebook, though it wasn't till a volunteer fireman came to the rescue with an extinguisher that the fire went out. Throughout this harrowing scene, the other cameraman had been filming away, getting eighty-two seconds of film in the can ready for the evening's news, a juicy harrowing film for the onlooker's entertainment.[1] Or consider an afternoon among the shoppers in Oxford Circus tube station in London's West End. A young woman screamed over and over again. She was being sexually assaulted in the daytime in a respectable part of London. 'What still haunts me is that hundreds of people walked past, ignoring my screams,' she recalled. 'One man with the build of a lumberjack actually shook me off when I grabbed his legs and pleaded for help.'[2]

This is not the way most of us want to live. At the very least, we do not want to be the woman screaming for help as scores of impervious shoppers pass by. Nor do we want to be the half-mad unemployed worker, allowed to set fire to himself unhindered for the sake of eighty-two seconds of burning human flesh on the TV news. Yet people like us walked by that woman, and people like us watch another's torments on TV for entertainment. This is the way we live, and the way we will continue to live unless we make a positive choice not to be part of that uncaring world.

Such behaviour is dangerous – for all of us, onlookers as well as casualties. For we are designed to live in a world of loving others. Babies who are not loved grow up unloving. Adolescents without love turn to violence and delinquency. Marriages without love breed more marriages without love. Divorce begets wounded children and wounded adults. All the orgasms of the sexual revolution cannot heal these wounds. Without love, we suffer. Stress and strain tear us apart and, broken-hearted, we end up in intensive care in hospitals. Some of us go a little mad, sunk in self-pity and self-centred torment. Others are so mad that they must be sheltered in hospitals. Still others try to blot out the unloving reality with drink, and drugs, and gambling, and sex. And some use guns and ropes and deliberate overdoses to mutilate or kill themselves.

Among these tormented people are children. In the United States the suicide rate for young people between fifteen and twenty-four years old has risen by three hundred per cent in the past twenty years. It is estimated that at least seven thousand teenagers kill themselves every year, and that a shocking four hundred thousand attempt suicide. One psychiatrist blames parents who do not give enough attention to their children. 'Parents sometimes are so busy working hard to provide the material things that they've neglected what the child really needs and wants – time, attention, love and affection.' Another suicide researcher says there is a link between falling church attendance and teenage suicide. Some of the children are even pre-teen. A six-year-old boy tried to hang himself because he thought he was a burden to his financially-stressed family.[3] In Britain this rise in teenage suicides has not yet happened. In 1982 there were seven deaths for children under the age of fifteen, about the same number as forty years ago.[4]

But there are signs of a rising number of suicides among men, after several years when the figures were falling. Researchers whose job it is to look at various possible causes, do not think that this has anything to do with the current recession and high unemployment. Instead, they think that one of the causes is the divorce rate. In the despair of divorce, men and some women are finding it difficult to want to go on living. 'The rise in the numbers of suicides of divorced persons . . . was partly responsible for the rise in overall numbers in men, and for a smaller decline in women,' reported a British Government publication.[5] Suicide is just one way that divorce takes its toll of people.

The break-up of marriages, or the war within the home of those not yet broken, drives children out into the world prematurely. In Hollywood's Hollywood Boulevard, scores of under-age girls sell their bodies; so do boys on Santa Monica Boulevard, stripped to the waist to attract the gay cruisers in their cars. In 1983 Los Angeles police estimated there were at least four thousand abandoned or runaway children roaming the city streets on any one night. In New York there may be as many as twenty thousand children living on the streets—some sharing destitution with their parents in cars and derelict buildings, others on their own. One New York priest, founder of a house for runaways, estimated that it only takes forty-eight hours for one in ten teenagers to turn to prostitution.[6] It is the easiest way to raise cash, as the teenage drifters in Britain's major cities soon discover. In the late 1970s the number of prostitutes under eighteen years old on Scotland Yard's prostitute index started rising sharply.[7] I have not been able to find up-to-date figures, but with teenage unemployment still high there is little reason to suppose the figures are now falling.

Many of these children are runaways from council homes and foster homes where they are meant to be 'in care'. For the past five years the proportion of children in England and Wales needing this kind of protection has stayed high. In 1982 there were 93,200 of them. Of these 2300 had been abandoned or lost, and 8900 had been deserted by one parent with no hope of the other parent looking after them. A further 18,400 had been taken from their parents because they were either ill-treated or neglected. It is worth remembering that these 93,200 children are born into a country where birth control and abortion are freely available and where there are provisions - basic perhaps, but at least they exist – to make sure families have a roof over their heads and something to eat. If we could feel that these children were going from bad homes into warm loving ones, perhaps these figures would not be so horrifying. But many of the children will not find warmth and love where they are going. Some will start the weary trek from one foster home to another; others in their teens may be put into bed-and-breakfast establishments. Government figures revealed that in 1982 1900 children, presumably teenagers, were in lodgings, not families. [8]

Of course there are still children who live in 'normal' families, with a father and a mother who love each other and love their children. But their number declines every year. In Britain there are now more than one and a half million children who live in a family with only one parent. [9] In 1971 there were 562,000 families with dependent children but only one parent; ten years later the number had very nearly doubled to 912,000. [10] Where once children had to live with the pain of being illegitimate, or orphaned, nowadays their pain is a more bitter one. They know that their father has left home – either of his own accord, or having been turned out by their mother. For these children natural sorrow at the loss of a parent is mingled with the bitterness of divided loyalties. In America the figures are similar. In the ten years between 1970 and 1980, the proportion of children living with only one parent rose from fifteen per cent to twenty-three per cent. [11] By 1980 roughly one in five children lived with only one parent – 12,162,000 children in all. And the numbers of children so affected would be even higher, if one took into account those who spend some of their childhood in a one-parent home, before their mother marries again.

The effects of broken or quarrelsome homes can be far-reaching indeed. As well as the risk that a child will turn to crime (and it is therefore little surprise that more and more children have been getting into trouble with the law over the last twenty years in Britain[12, 9]), there is even some evidence that a disturbed childhood tends to produce a lonely adult, who is at greater risk of coronary heart disease.

Of course, our children's suffering is nothing to compare with the suffering of children in the developing countries. In Africa, Asia and the Indian subcontinent adults and children alike are dying of starvation and of the diseases which prey on the poor. Their sufferings must outweigh anything we suffer in the West. Yet, rich as we are, privileged as we are compared with them, we have our own malaise. If we examine our lives, our societies, we can see everywhere miseries and despairs which our affluence has failed to cure. Sometimes our affluence even exacerbates them. These ills should be heavy on our consciences for they are in our own homes, next door behind the lace curtains of a terraced street, or lying in our own gutters as we pass by on the other side.

Where I live in the centre of London, there are always half a dozen or so people dressed in rags, sleeping rough in the doorways. I know their faces. I recognise the man whose face is one living scar, because burns have ripped the surface skin away. I know one of his friends, who stands in the doorway shaking when he has not been able to afford the meths, and when he has a bottle he stands there roaring and swaying as the meths burns in his stomach. Then there is the old lady with the respectable voice and three carrier bags, who falls in a drunken heap outside the off-license and who sometimes asks me to go in and get her a bottle.

The slow rise in the number of deaths by cirrhosis of the liver shows that these people are increasing in number as a tide of alcoholism runs through society sweeping away not just the meths drinkers but the wealthy company directors in their smart suits. Behind the posh front doors of the streets where I live is another kind of addiction – the housewives and elderly women who obediently take the tranquillisers and sleeping pills their doctors so lavishly prescribe. They blot out the reality of their lives in a more genteel way and because they do not fall over vomiting in the street, we do not see their pain. There are perhaps a quarter of a million of these addicts. Less respectable are the ten thousand 'hard-drug' addicts now registered with the Home Office – a fifty per cent rise in the numbers in 1983.[13] There are a further forty thousand of these buying their drugs on the streets, who never show up in the government figures. At least two or three out of every hundred will die each year of overdoses or drug-induced accidents. The youngsters in their ranks are increasing yearly. There are tales that children as young as ten years old are now hooked on heroin.[14] Hundreds more are sniffing glue and other substances – deodorants, hair sprays, patent medicines, petrol fumes. In 1982 twenty-eight children fifteen years old or younger died from these experiments.[9] We have ways of killing our children as sure as hunger and disease.

And in the United States these include guns and explosives. Taking the American population as a whole, the years of expected life lost through violence are now more than those lost *from any other cause of death*. Violence kills people younger than disease does; firearms are more efficient killers than infections. Looking at the problem as a whole, high unemployment seems responsible for some of the violence, as does the high proportion of young people in the population; the young are more prone to violence than the elderly. But there is another reason too. 'A third trend has been a rising divorce rate, with a resulting progressive decrease in the numbers and proportion of children living with both parents. Both of these latter trends – high unemployment and increase in single-parent families – have been more pronounced in the population groups that have born the brunt of increasing homicide and suicide rates, namely young, adult urban blacks.'[15] In Britain, where firearms are strictly controlled by law, we will not get an epidemic of violent deaths like that in America. But with a rise in crimes of violence, we too can expect to suffer from the disorganised society we have helped create.

The skein of causes and effects is almost impossible to tease out. What causes the suicide rate to increase, the number of drug addicts to rise, or the number of murders to soar? What makes one individual fourteen-year-old boy start sniffing glue? Why is that particular fifteen-year-old girl selling her body on the streets round London's King's Cross station. Why does a boy run away from home and sell his body in San Francisco? Are the murders 'caused' by the sheer number of guns on the US streets? Are they just the result of a baby boom two decades ago, so that there are more young men in society? Are children more often taken away from their parents because social workers notice neglect more efficiently? Or are more children being neglected by their parents?

The most careful researchers would hesitate to specify all the causes of these ills in society. Those who simply point at a single cause are usually those who have not thought very carefully. Yet

I think these problems have one thing in common – not so much the 'why' of their existence, as the 'how'. These ills are failures in love. Sometimes it is the failure of the victim to care for himself. Sometimes it is the failure of the perpetrator to care. No doubt there have been times when these failures were even worse – in the thirteenth century, in the Dark Ages, in Victorian slumland, perhaps. I find the historian's argument little comfort. For we live now. Whether they are better or worse than those of the past, these failures in love are *our* failures. They torment *our* lives. *We* perpetrate them.

Ironically, at least some of these ills are spawned by 'progress'. The relative loneliness of our lives is at least partly the result of our very affluence. Most of us can afford to live alone. We can afford to set up home in a little flat with one bedroom, one living-room and a bathroom all to ourselves. Teenagers can afford to leave home and set up house by themselves: unmarried or divorced people in their twenties and thirties often are rich enough not even to need flatmates. They do not have to go into lodgings where the lodgers eat dinner round a table with the landlady. Elderly people can pay their way, and need not depend on the charity of their children. They do not have to move into their son's or daughter's home; instead they can spend their evenings away from their family, staring at the TV screen in a living unit all of their own.

Steadily the proportion of single people living alone has risen in Britain, from twelve per cent of all households in 1961 to twenty-two per cent twenty years later. Most of this increase comes from the higher proportion of old people, of whom about a third live by themselves.[16] Indeed perhaps elderly people are wise to live alone nowadays if they can. Granny-battering is beginning to be noticed in Britain. One woman in her nineties was sexually abused by her teenage grandsons. Others are kicked, pushed or just locked up by their children.[17] These elderly victims, like battered babies, are still the exception in our society, thank goodness. But it does seem as if, for a variety of reasons, family ties are less close: elderly parents are more likely to want to live alone, children more ready to let them.[18]

There is the same proliferation of single households in the United States. There were 10.9 million single households in

1970, and ten years later this figure had risen to 17.8 million. But these new singles are not just the elderly. 'Most of the growth has been among the divorced or never-married persons and persons under thirty-five years old.'[10] Divorced people living on their own have more than doubled in numbers during that period. *New York Magazine* coined a new phrase for them – 'apartners'. These are the affluent men and women who have a sexual relationship but can afford to run separate homes. 'By maintaining their own residences, the apartners feel they can have it all. The sharing of responsibilities is kept to a mininum. Finances are separate; one partner's chores and children don't overconcern the other. They do share interests and vacations, and during an illness or a crisis they help each other out. But when the vacation is over, or the crisis has passed, they return to their own lives.'[19] The article went on to describe apartners – significantly allocating space to the description of their furnishings, and how they rate each other sexually. Some of them likened their arrangement to constant honeymoon, clearly believing that sexual excitement outweighs the benefits of more mundane affection: they have found a way to combine a longterm sexual relationship with freedom from responsibility. They do not have to make the effort to love. Their emphasis on the continuing sexual excitement of 'apartnerships' is symptomatic of society's values: we place sex above love.

Affluence separates us out into little living boxes, and it keeps us on the move. Love on the other hand takes time to develop, and affection thrives on the familiar. By changing houses and neighbourhoods we reduce our chances of friendships and neighbours. Four out of five British children will have moved home at least once by the time they are sixteen. About sixteen out of a hundred will have moved at least four times.[20] In the United States only 57.4% of families lived at the same address in 1970 and 1974, and the average person of twenty taking his first job can expect to change jobs at least seven times during his working life.[21] Our lives are a series of uprootings – changing neighbourhoods, changing schools, changing jobs – and perforce breaking off old friendships. But creating new ones is a slow business. It takes time. The longer you live in a neighbourhood, the more neighbourly you feel. Those who have lived in a place for ten years or more, know more of their neighbours by name.[22] So the changes that we inflict upon ourselves – the new houses and smarter districts – have a price tag on them.

We pay the price of ignoring the human need for love in loneliness and unhappiness. In Britain almost a quarter of all adults feel lonely at times. One in twenty-five feels lonely every single day, and about fourteen in every hundred feel lonely at least once a month. Mostly the lonely are the young, the elderly, single parents, and widowed people. Being divorced or unemployed also seems to make people feel lonely. The lonely suffer from lack of confidence; they are less sure of themselves; and they may find it difficult to get on with others.[23] Research into today's quality of life has found a similar pattern in the USA. 'People who are currently single generally report a good deal less satisfaction with life than do married persons and the lack of satisfaction shown by women and men who are divorced or separated is quite remarkable indeed,' reported one team of researchers.[24] Our happiness seems literally to depend on others.

With nowhere else to turn in their unhappiness, the lonely go to professionals for help. One in every five lonely people goes to see a doctor at least once a month.[23] 'An interesting and rather sad experience of treating both the old and not so old is the number of times I am told that he or she is grateful for having someone to listen to them,' says a psychiatrist. 'This is often after quite a brief interview of ten minutes or less. This is a non-listening society, but it is quite ridiculous that an individual should view a few minutes of listening to them as a unique experience.'[25]

People who have not married, and are thus more likely to be lonely, are more likely to fall ill. Loneliness takes its toll of their health. In the United States in 1972 those who lived alone spent 13.5 days in hospital, compared with only 8.5 days in hospital spent by married people[21] – so that our failure to love exacts a very literal price. Out of our taxes must come more and more hospitals, doctors' surgeries and social work departments to deal with the mental and physical side effects of the lack of love. Studies of mental illness have shown that the single, widowed and divorced have higher rates of mental illness than the married. 'Probably . . . the key difference between the roles of the married and the unmarried (whether single, widowed or divorced) is that the unmarried live a relatively isolated existence which lacks the close interpersonal ties that the data suggest are a key factor in maintaining a sense of wellbeing.'[26] Of those at risk, the widowed are least vulnerable to mental illness; and women are less affected by being single than men, perhaps because they seem better at keeping up family ties and friendships which can substitute for some of the warmth of marriage. All in all, though, it is the men and women who remain single into the middle years who are more likely to need hospital care for mental illness.[27] We need love to remain sane in the face of life's uncertainties.

We also need love to stay alive. Premature death comes more frequently to those who have not married, or to those whose marriages have broken up. Unmarried men, whether single, divorced or widowed, are more likely to die of tuberculosis, cirrhosis of the liver, pneumonia, syphilis, accidental fire or explosion, murder, accidental falls, suicide or car accidents. These forms of death are particularly likely among divorced men, next to the widowed.[27]

Heart disease is the other illness that strikes at the unloved and unloving. Our society is obsessed with proper diet, exercise, and generally with the outward appearance of health. Books are written about it. Fortunes are made on the advice. Yet – with a few notable exceptions – doctors and researchers have ignored what is equally obvious. Those who are loved and love in return stay physically more healthy. 'We must either live together or face the possibility of prematurely dying alone,' writes Dr James J. Lynch in *The Broken Heart*, which outlines the medical consequences of loneliness.[21] It may even be that the human heart is such a sensitive recorder of love or its lack, that it responds physically. Men whose marriages are unhappy seem more likely to suffer from heart disease. The broken or the wounded heart is not just poetic metaphor. It is a reality.

If the lack of love can so bruise the human spirit and wound the human body, then perhaps love can heal us as well. For a generation or more the medical profession has been obsessed with pharmaceutics. They have handed out pills which blot out reality, first the barbiturates, now the benzodiazepine tranquillisers—as well as drugs that provide rather more specific cures. But they have been slow in trying to offer love. For a long time hospitals refused to allow parents to clutter up the wards of hospitals when their children were being treated there. And many are still places with an atmosphere of formality, sometimes even of hostility.

I have visited an old lady in three London hospitals over several months, and in one of them the non-nursing staff were extremely unfriendly, not just to me, but to her too. They scowled. They refused to help with directions when I was lost in the miles of corridors. When in her dementia she told me that the staff had been beating her, I carefully checked her body for bruises. There were none. But in view of the unloving atmosphere, I could not assume that this was just her confusion. I believed it was possible she might be being abused. 'Loving and sexuality not only keep people healthier, but also help people heal more rapidly – even with conditions such as heart disease,' admitted a physician with the World Health Organisation. 'Modern medicine ignores the importance of loving with regard to staying healthy and getting well – hospitals are asexual, even anti-sexual.'[28] He complains of the lack of sexuality in hospitals, but the lack of love is much more serious: very few ill people want sexual intercourse.

'But what is love? Can you define it?' somebody asked me, while I was preparing this book. 'If you can't define it, how do you know what you're talking about?' Here indeed is my greatest problem. For I find it difficult to define, and definitions seem to confuse me rather than help me in my understanding of love. What I know is that I am not talking about romantic love, the passion between men and women which makes the knees tremble, the heart palpitate, and fires the body with sexual excitement. If this is a form of love, then it is so far away from the kind of love I am writing about that it does not require much consideration.

The love that I recognise as being essential to the health of my mind and body is the love which is described as kindness, loving kindness, friendship, caring, affection, warmth, tenderness, sympathy or empathy, concern. I can sometimes sense it in others very strongly, even if they do not put it into words. I can read it in the tone of their voice, in the way they may shake my hand or put an arm round me or just touch me. I can see it in their eyes, and in the way their face responds to me. In the same way I can sense lack of love.

Some writers have divided love into four different categories. C.S. Lewis distinguished between affection, 'the humblest and most widely diffused of loves'; friendship; eros, or 'being in love'; and charity, the Bible's word for the truly unselfish love of others.[29] I do not find such distinctions helpful, not least because I cannot see much in 'being in love' which has much to do with 'true' love. 'Being in love' is an accident of sexual attraction, of imprinting, which can lead to love, but seems to me has little to do with it at the outset. Nor do I find much sense in distinguishing between affection, friendship and charity. All include kindness to others, for instance. All include feeling with and for others. All include a kind of natural warmth – or should do, for a cold charity is to my mind no real charity at all. I will admit, though, that at its best, this kind of love, the charity of the Bible, allows people to love the unlovable.

St Paul's definition still holds good for me, as a description of the best kind of human love:

> Charity suffereth long, and is kind; charity envieth not;
>   charity vaunteth not itself, is not puffed up,
> Doth not behave itself unseemly, seeketh not her own, is
>   not easily provoked, thinketh no evil;
> Rejoiceth not in iniquity, but rejoiceth in the truth;
> Beareth all things, believeth all things, hopeth all things,
>   endureth all things.[30]

There is a modern translation which puts this more clearly.

> Love is patient with people; love is kind.
> There is no envy in love;
>   there are no proud claims;
>   there is no conceit.
> Love never does the graceless thing;
>   never insists on its rights,
>   never irritably loses its temper;
>   never nurses its wrath to keep it warm.

Love finds nothing to be glad about
    when someone goes wrong,
    but is glad when the truth is glad.
Love can stand any kind of treatment;
    love's first instinct is to believe in people:
    love never regards anyone or anything as hopeless;
    nothing can happen that can break love's spirit. [31]

All the kindness, gentleness, patience and optimism of human love are described in this passage. There are, I think, only two other aspects of human love which need pointing out. Love grows with familiarity, and it flourishes with fellow feeling.

If I single out the way love grows with familiarity, it is because I feel this is the most hopeful aspect of natural human love. We love what we know. The man who hates those of a different race may still learn to love the Jew or the African or the Pakistani who moves in next door. The very familiarity of his neighbour may do the trick. And from this one love may grow a greater tolerance, though it is not always so. A humble example is provided by the way in which animals can wind themselves into our hearts. When a black and white stray cat turned up to have its kitten in our shed, my husband wanted me to give away both mother and kitten. With extreme reluctance he allowed me to keep the cat. He had never owned pets as a child. He did not like them. He did not want them. He was not particularly fond of cats. Three years later he finds pleasure in caressing the cat, in feeding her, in watching her antics. Indifference has turned into love—not through any winning charm of our cat. She is a somewhat shy and charmless cat. Love has grown through mere familiarity. We are indeed more likely to love our neighbour, who is familiar and next door, than an unknown individual half a world away. But if we can learn to love through the effects of time and closeness alone, then there is hope indeed for all of us.

The art of loving, however, requires something of imagination. We need the ability to put ourselves in another's place. Without this act of imagination, which is almost an act of intelligence too, our love is irremediably warped. 'Never put down to malice what can be explained by stupidity,' goes the old saw. Much of the harm and unkindness humans do to one another arises from a failure of intelligent imagination. Those who are unable to imagine how others feel may wound without malicious intention. Sometimes this failure of empathy, of fellow feeling, is literally the result of a low IQ; sometimes it is the result of never having been taught this skill in childhood. For we learn to love.

More often, among adults, fellow feeling is driven away by self-obsession. The truly self-centred individual cannot think of others, for his mental horizon is so filled with his own interests. I have known self-obsessed people locked into a kind of permanent inner agony, a self-inflicted self-pity which they cannot escape because they cannot wrench their minds free from their own concerns. Thinking of another's welfare would literally unchain their emotions, free them from their inner torment, but they are unable to do so. There are also those who seem happier in their self-centred world. These bouncing egoists do not feel another's pain. They literally know not what they do. The pain of others means nothing to them. They are only half-living and most of the time I can pity them too.

For it is empathy or fellow feeling, which distinguishes human love from mere human infatuation or possessive desire. The stranger who insists on picking up a child who is shrinking away from her is not being loving. She has failed to read the child's distress. She has failed to make that imaginative leap which would have shown her that picking up the child – otherwise a friendly act – could in this case inflict more distress. Likewise the doctor who treats an elderly old lady as if she was a mentally disturbed five year old, is not being loving. Elderly ladies need their dignity kept intact, for I have noticed that even elderly ladies suffering from senile dementia have a kind of consciousness of who they are. They do not make sense, but equally they are not mad all of the time. And in their lucid moments, it is unkind to talk to them as if they were children.

The lover who pursues an unwilling girl with phone calls, propositions and caresses is not being loving. He has failed to imagine the unpleasantness of unwanted embraces. He has no fellow feeling for the girl, only the feeling of his own desire. Perhaps the best example of all is the animal lover who cages wild birds. He loves birds – the sight of them, the beauty of them, and he wishes to possess them. But he does not think of, or feel their pain in captivity. The flutterings they make at the bars mean nothing to him for he lacks the imagination of empathy to feel what they feel. None of these people loves. For if they did, they could not do what they do. The adult would put down the child. The doctor would speak sensibly to the demented old lady. The lover would stop pursuing the girl. The animal lover would open up the cage and set free his wild birds.

There are many who inflict pain without knowing, without caring or without feeling what they do. Truly we can look at human behaviour – our own as well as others – and despair. But looking at the worst in women and men takes us no further. The human jungle is not the only truth; in some ways it is not true at all. For human love exists in potential in all of us, and in most of us it grows in practice. We do not love all of the human race all of the time. But we love some people all the time, and we love almost everybody for some few precious moments. It is perhaps more natural for us to love than to feel complete indifference. And in that natural love could lie not just the salvation of our whole society, but the salvation of our own ordinary humdrum lives. Each of us, with our own and others' love, can make something from life, whatever our circumstances.

2

First Love

My first love was my mother. Nearly all my memories before the age of about eight concern her. My mind is still stocked with scores of baby rhymes she taught me – 'Here's the church and here's the steeple . . . '; 'Two little dickie birds sitting on the wall . . . '; 'One little pig went to market . . . '; 'Round and round the garden goes the teddy bear . . . '. This rich inheritance occasionally surfaces in my mind when I am faced with a baby to amuse, and I realise just how often she must have played those games with me. Though I am now in my forties, I still feel an absolute security in her love for me – no matter how bad, mad, or even evil I might become. I know that she will always love me – something that I do not feel about any other human being. For when every other member of the family has given up, when wives and husbands have left, sisters and brothers have turned their backs and fathers have cut off the relationship, mothers remain faithful. When we read of the utter downfall of a man in the newspapers – fallen from high position, facing imprisonment, bankrupt, disgraced – we often read that he is staying with his mother. There are thousands of mothers who are still caring for grown-up children suffering from severe mental illness, mentally handicapped children, downright impossible alcoholic children. Those mothers who are faithful to the bitter, the sometimes truly bitter end, are often widows. Those with husbands often find that their husband will not allow the sacrifice. They stay in secret contact with children who have been cast out of the family.

My own relationship with my mother has, of course, had its

moments of strain. I have occasionally hated, despised, or felt angered by her. I have often found her extremely irritating. And I know she has felt all these emotions towards me. Yet I cannot ever remember a single moment when I have doubted her love for me. Even as a child when she punished me by temporarily withdrawing that love – an agonising punishment – I do not recall thinking it was a permanent withdrawal. Now, some forty years after the relationship started, we are still extremely close to each other. On the surface, it seems as though she depends on me. Deep down, in an entirely irrational way, I still depend on her. It is not by coincidence that when my marriage broke down, I went back to my mother first, then to my father, like an animal takes refuge in the safest place it knows. 'A man who has been the indisputable favourite of his mother keeps for life the feeling of a conqueror, that confidence of success that often induces real success,' wrote Sigmund Freud, the favourite of his own mother. [1]

Extended mother love is a necessity for our species. Indeed all mammals need some kind of maternal care. Blind and helpless at birth, the young would not survive but for the mother who licks them, feeds them, keeps them from straying too far from nest or den, and cleans up their excrement. The male in the mammal world varies in his attention to his young. Where the males are completely promiscuous, his fatherly role may be non-existent. But where the species is pair-bonding, the male usually has a fairly important paternal part to play. There are a few mammals where the male plays the major role in infant care. The male marmoset carries its babies seventy per cent of the time, only giving them to their mother to be suckled. [2] If, in this chapter I speak only about mothers and mother love, it is not because I think only the mother can give love. Some human infants will be reared and cared for by women who did not give birth to them. A few may be mothered by their natural fathers or by a male taking over the role of mother. Much confusion has been caused by this particular misunderstanding, when writers have forgotten to remind their readers that a child's mother may be other than its biological mother. I should not like this chapter to be misinterpreted in that way. Nor should I like it to be assumed from my frequent reference to research on monkeys and apes, that I equate human with primate

behaviour. Our higher intelligence and different social organisation mean that comparisons must always be cautious. But
maternal dependency is one of the characteristics we do share
with our monkey cousins.

Children without mothers, or without good mother substitutes,
generally do not thrive as well as those with good mothering. In
the early years of this century orphanages were large impersonal
organisations where young babies and children were given
decent food and clothing, good hygiene and physical care.
Nappies would be changed in a kind of shift system, rather than
when the individual child was wet. Girls and boys were segre-
gated. Discipline was army-like.

An English writer, Peter Paterson, recalls Christmas Day in
a pre-War orphanage:

> Christmas day at the main orphanage in south London –
> at any rate on the 'boys' side', for we never encountered
> the girls at all – was quite different from any other day,
> particularly for those unfortunate boys who habitually wet
> their beds. It was the one day of the year when they were
> not obliged to rise before the morning bell sounded, make
> their way to the bathroom and rinse out their sheets.
> Failure to wake earlier than the rest of us meant running a
> gauntlet of punching, kicking and towel-flicking tormen-
> tors, egged on, it must be said in extenuation, by the house
> matron.
>
> Other rules and restrictions were also relaxed on Christ-
> mas Day. We were not required to parade before each meal
> for an inspection to ensure that our boots and fingernails
> passed the scrutiny of the ex-sergeant major who carried out
> the odd maintenance jobs around the place, and who then
> marched us four abreast along the drive to the dining hall,
> insisting that we stamped our right feet at every fourth step
> – a drill, I learned many years later, which had once been a
> ceremonial march practised by the Rifle Brigade. Failure
> to pass muster on these inspections meant missing the
> meal, and then spending the time between the end of
> school and lights out marching round and round the play-

ground 'marking the fourth', or spending hours brushing our cropped heads with a hard bristle brush, or cleaning our two pairs of boots without the benefit of the usual Day and Martin's spit-on blacking.

Nor were we obliged on Christmas Day to eat all meals in silence, as was the rule for the rest of the year, with the exception of Sunday tea, when the supervisory staff withdrew, leaving the dining hall to the bullies and gang leaders to exact their tribute from the smaller boys – forcing us to surrender the thick slice of currant cake which was doled out once a week at this meal. [3]

It is not surprising that when researchers examined children brought up by these impersonal regimes, they found some were warped and stunted in mind and character. From the orphanages and crèches of earlier generations came children with low IQs and an inability to love. In one survey, for instance, babies showed 'a catastrophic drop of developmental quotient' between the ages of four and twelve months. The reason was that they had only one nurse between seven of them and 'for reasons of hygiene, the children were kept restricted to cots and cubicles in what amounted to solitary confinement'. [4]

The man who drew forceful attention to this was John Bowlby. In a monograph for the World Health Organisation shortly after the last world war he wrote:

> . . . mother-love in infancy and childhood is as important for mental health as are vitamins and proteins for physical health." Collecting together the various studies, he warned: "It is submitted that the evidence is now such that it leaves no room for doubt regarding the general proposition – that prolonged deprivation of the young child of maternal care may have grave and far-reaching effects on his character and so on the whole of his future life. Although it is a proposition exactly similar in form to those regarding the evil after-effects of rubella in foetal life, or deprivation of vitamin D in infancy, there is a curious resistance to accepting it. [4]

There is still resistance to the idea that human love is of such importance. Some thirty years later, it is clear from reading Bowlby's original report that he knew that much of the detailed evidence was still missing. Even so, the results of grossly neglecting the emotional and intellectual needs of young children were clearly evident.

Since his report, controversy has continued. Bowlby's work was originally misinterpreted by many to mean there was a near-miraculous bond between an infant and its biological mother. Social workers and child guidance experts began to make great efforts not to separate the two. Children were sometimes left with mothers who were inadequate, neglectful and even cruel. There were good results too. Children's homes were reorganised into fairly small units. Fostering was increasingly accepted as a substitute for institutional care. (Not that fostering is miraculously successful, either.) But, as it began to be accepted that some mothers were capable of battering, even killing, their children, the pendulum began to swing back again. At the same time the behaviourists were beginning to question Bowlby's arguments.[5] Perhaps mother love was not irreducible, irreplaceable, but could be broken down into its component parts – into physical contact, verbal response and so forth. How a mother behaved – her gestures and facial movements, her speech – began to be examined. This sudden surge of interest stemmed partly from the new enthusiasm for ethology which had shown that the young of certain species go through a period of extreme receptivity during which they are imprinted with certain behaviour patterns. Human babies might experience similar periods, scientists hypothesised.

In the laboratories, work started with apes and monkeys. Mother love for these was not simply cupboard love. A baby monkey did not cling to his mother just because she gave him milk. When rhesus monkeys were given wire mothers which fed them and furry mothers which didn't, they would cling to the fur-covered mother substitutes. Fur-contact was obviously as important as food.[6] The same rhesus monkeys showed marked personality problems if they were brought up in complete isolation. As adults, these monkeys could not fit in with others. They, in their turn, became indifferent mothers, neither grooming, feeding nor retrieving their infants. Sometimes they became baby batterers. Often they would sit in their cages rocking backwards and forwards. Without anybody to love them in their childhood, they were unable not merely to love others, but to behave normally at all. (Some of these pathetic monkeys were given remedial treatment afterwards to help them recover.)

These animal experiments stimulated a more scientific interest in child-rearing. Researchers, instead of merely asking people how they had been brought up, began to look at what was happening before their eyes. Like natural historians, they began to look at human beings as if they were a different species. They started counting up and measuring the actions, the words, the noises, the eye contact, the stroking and the kissing. And this approach is producing some tantalisingly interesting hypotheses.

There may be, for instance, a 'natural' maternal response to a newborn baby. Characteristic responses are found in other animals. The female cat for instance starts by licking her newly born kittens, then she curls round them and rests for about twelve hours. Doctors have noticed that in premature baby units, when mothers are first invited in to touch their babies, there is a recognisable pattern to their behaviour. When they are allowed to put their hands into the incubators, they usually touch the babies' toes and fingers first – brief touches using their fingertips. Observations of women having their babies at home in California, and also of some Guatemalan women, show that both groups of women behaved in a rather similar way. The new mothers started by stroking their babies with their fingertips, then with the palms of their hands. They used a high-pitched 'baby' voice to the infant. They gazed deeply into the child's eyes. [7] Babies induce similar behaviour in most adults, not just their natural mothers.

The newly born exert a powerful attraction for most people. Just take a second look at the next person you see looking at a baby. Their eyes are alight, and their mouths are smiling as they peer into the face of the apparently helpless young human there. Even medical students who are not keen on babies, find their indifference changed after they have made eye contact and a relationship with one particular baby. [8] For much of my life I was the exception to this rule. Babies frightened rather than delighted me. Lately I have found this is changing – a mark, I feel, of my own growing emotional wellbeing. I am learning, at last, to love them.

Whatever it is about babies which exerts this attraction, we now know that babies are not the passive little objects they may seem to the onlooker. In the very first days of life they can distinguish the smell of the mother's breast. By the age of six days, they can tell the difference between the milky smell of their own mother's breast and the milky smell of a stranger's.[9] In the first ten days of life some babies seem to be able to suck more or less enthusiastically, according to what liquid they are being fed.[10] They can detect the difference between water and salt solutions, or between cow's milk and human milk. Some of them seem to breathe more regularly when they are sucking breast milk. Their vision is not as inadequate as doctors used to believe. Within the very first days of life, they will look at a black-on-white drawing of a face for longer than at a mere pattern of black dots. A ten-day-old infant seems able to distinguish between his mother and a strange caretaker. At two weeks the baby knows which face is his mother's, which that of a stranger, and can reach and grasp in a way which shows he can measure the size and distance away from him of what he is grasping.[11]

In fact, the medical establishment is now beginning to acknowledge what mothers have always known – that babies have distinct characters. My own mother always used to say that her three children were different in behaviour and character from the very first days of life. It seemed unlikely to me, a stranger to motherhood, but there is the research to confirm it. Some babies, for example, do not seem to enjoy the cuddling that most have pleasure in. They will actively resist and avoid the caresses that most infants enjoy.[12] Other babies have difficulties in sleeping – seem to be fussy, rather fretful babies. At a very early age, on day eight or nine, these babies had been given a sucking test, in which a teat is given for four minutes and taken away. The babies who were still wakeful at eight or nine weeks were those who had been quickest to cry when the teat was removed. 'This pattern strongly suggests that these babies have differed from the rest of the sample from the time of birth or earlier and that sleep problems are not the result of any particular style of parental handling, in contradiction to much medical folklore,' reported the researchers. [13]

Any conception of mother love, therefore, which sees it merely as the outpouring of love from an adult to a passive infant is incorrect. Between mother and baby, from the earliest moment, there is a two-way relationship. Just as the mother's behaviour and feelings can affect that relationship, so can the child's. [14]

In humans, 'natural' behaviour is easily overridden by the dictates of the society in which we live. One has only to think of the huge change there has been in child care in the last half century. I was brought up in the early 1940s on the fixed time regime. Babies, it was thought, should be fed to a strict time-table, never fed on demand or over-pampered. Dummies were forbidden. The great authority was F. Truby King, who wrote: 'Never give a baby food merely to pacify him or to stop his crying: it will damage him in the long run. Feed only at the proper feeding times . . . ' A list of don'ts included: 'DON'T feed baby more frequently than five, or at the most six, times in the twenty-four hours. DON'T use a dummy or let baby suck his thumb. DON'T rock baby to sleep . . . ' F. Truby King had no time for the feelings of mothers, or for any thought that their wishes and desires might be considered. 'Were secretion of milk and the feeding of the baby functions of men and not of women, *no man – inside or outside the medical profession – would nurse his baby more often than five times in the twenty four hours*, if he knew that the child would do as well or better with only five feedings. Why should it be otherwise with women? . . . The supposed benefit of frequent feeding has been a great handicap to mother and child.' [15] What he omitted to consider was the possibility that if men produced breast milk, they might have the same instincts which prompt women to put crying babies to the breast. Help, however, was at hand. By the time my younger brother was born, Dr Benjamin Spock was advising mothers: 'Mothers have sometimes been so scared of the schedule that they did not dare feed a hungry baby one minute early. They have even accepted the idea that a baby would be spoiled if he were fed when he was hungry. What an idea! As if puppies are spoiled by being able to nurse when they are hungry . . .' [16]

Nowadays the baby care of primitive peoples is carefully examined, partly in the hope of improving on our own methods of child-rearing. Basically the new interest rests on the Darwinian idea of evolutionary adaptation – that those species survive which have best adapted to their environment. Considering the slow pace of evolutionary change, long since overtaken by 'progress', the human species is probably still adapted to the hunter-gatherer society, or possibly to the later agricultural-settlement society. So far, we are not likely to have adjusted to cities, motor cars, hospitals, and television. In diet, this way of thinking led to the thesis, which has since proved its worth, that many Western diseases could be prevented if we ate more naturally-occurring fibre, less sugar and less fat.

The !Kung – a bushman tribe, that is, primitive hunter-gatherers in South Africa – treat their babies in a very indulgent way. They are fed whenever they cry. They sleep beside their mothers, and are even put to the breast while she dozes. Instead of being left in a cot or cradle while the mother works, a !Kung baby is taken with her in a sling. From the sling the baby can reach its mother's breast, and it can also look at the necklaces and beads hanging round her neck. (These have rather the same function for the !Kung baby as do the objects hung in cots for our babies to look at.) Babies are not weaned until their fourth year. They are encouraged to learn to sit up, to crawl and to walk. Mothers do not just wait for these developmental milestones to occur: they encourage the child to reach them. !Kung mothers are almost permanently supported, encouraged and surrounded by other females: so that they can 'escape' from the demands of their baby, either by temporarily handing it to some other female or by having the interest and stimulation of other adults nearby. Possibly as a result of this, !Kung babies are in some ways more advanced than American babies. [17]

Physiology confirms what !Kung practice suggests – that human babies are evolutionarily adapted towards being fed on demand and carried about. Those mammals who hide their infants in dens, and return to feed them, have a high protein and fat content in their milk. Those whose young accompany them, or are carried by them, and are therefore fed frequently, have milk with low protein and fat content. Human milk, and the milk of our primate relatives, seems adapted to frequent feeding. As we also know that apes and monkeys have evolved a way of life which favours close mother-infant proximity, it is reasonable to hypothesise that this is the kind of life to which human infants are adapted too.[18]

But even if, with the help of ethology, anthropology and a little luck, we happen on the right principles for rearing our children, we can only do a certain amount – after that, time takes over. No matter how loving and articulate the mother, a baby cannot speak at six months. Indeed, at one point some child experts theorised that almost all a child's development depended merely on time, and that its environment had little influence. Now, we think both are important: like the !Kung who encourage their babies to sit up and walk, we can help our babies develop faster. But there may be 'sensitive periods', when a child is ready for the next stage of development. If that is so, then a child needs stimulation at the right time to maximise his potential.

If the right 'sensitive period' is missed, nevertheless most children will catch up later. Experience in later life can change our behaviour, our habits, perhaps even our personalities too. Severely neglected and abused children can be rehabilitated – though it needs special training by those responsible for their welfare. Unfortunately, for ordinary children this special attention is rarely forthcoming. A child who is mildly neglected by his parents may grow up with a low IQ. At school, he is diagnosed as being just below normal. Lessons are accordingly adjusted. Less is expected of him. And in that he has not been physically or mentally severely harmed, he is left with the same mildly neglectful parents. The original harm, effected by the time he was five, is reinforced for a further eleven or twelve years. By the time the boy is eighteen, he has had a quarter of a lifetime of the kind of treatment which helps produce a low IQ. It is unlikely, though not impossible, that any subsequent life experience will reverse the harm. If, however, he had been taken away from his natural parents at the age of five and adopted by attentive high IQ parents, he would have gained several points in IQ. Children with mothers of low intelligence who are adopted, gain a mental level which is equal to the average or even higher. I do not wish to argue that all mildly neglectful parents should lose their children. Only, it is important that people should know the bad effects of bad child care can be either reversed or at least diminished by special attention in later childhood. No child, and no adult either, should be given up as irremediably harmed.

However, the first quarter of a human lifetime is likely to set the pattern for subsequent events. And most children spend all their childhood if not with the same father, at least with the same mother – so that the mother-child relationship of that first sixteen years exerts a powerful influence over the rest of life. In this sense Freud was right. The child is father to the man – though occasionally adult experiences can change the way the individual lives. We have the free will to change our lives, but if a destructive pattern is established in us as children, the change will require great effort. Freud's theories do not seem nearly so impressive in detail, however. The Freudian formulations of the Oedipus complex, the castration anxiety and so forth, may apply to some families (probably Victorian Viennese Jewish ones in particular), but do not seem born out by modern research.[19] Nor do the questions of bottle versus breast, the age of weaning, or the methods of toilet training seem at all important on their own. A flurry of research into these issues produces either inconclusive results, or suggestions that Freud was wrong.[20] His lasting message was to emphasise the early years. The Jesuits had known this before him, but Freud reformulated it and applied it to psychological health, rather than religious belief. Most of the research, however, has shown that children are resilient beings. Day-care nurseries, separations in hospital, working mothers – children can survive all these to be well balanced human beings, as long as they have a loving parent and know they have one.[21] It is the quality of a mother's care that counts, not just the quantity of time spent in her company.

The growth of secure affection starts from the very earliest days after birth. Indeed the post-birth days usually spent in hospital may affect the months ahead. It looks as if a mother should have as much chance as possible to handle her baby, to fondle it, look into its eyes, and care for it herself. This seems to help a secure bond develop. Mothers who do not have this chance, either because the hospital rules do not allow it, or because their babies are taken away for special care, may have more difficulty in developing this secure bond. Among some lower animals such as the goat, cow and sheep, if mother and infant are separated after birth for a few hours, the mother will not care for her young. This extreme form of a special sensitive period does not apply to humans – witness all those loving mothers whose babies were once routinely taken away by hospital staff.

But researchers have discovered there is a difference between mothers who are allowed extra contact with their babies, and those who have contact which is limited by hospital rules. A month later, the extra-contact mothers seemed to show more eye contact and to caress their babies more. [22] Even after a year, there were still differences. The mothers who had had the extra contact with their babies soothed their infants more when they cried, and spent more time helping the doctor examine the baby. At two years, it was still possible in some cases to detect differences. Those who had had the extra time with their babies used more questions in speech with their children, fewer commands and slightly different speech patterns. [23] Not all research projects have had similar findings, and thus the idea that there is a sensitive time just after birth when mother and child should be in close contact remains controversial. [24]

One other, odd, result of separating mothers and babies at birth needs mentioning. It is possible that this kind of separation may affect not so much the bond between mother and infant, but the whole family. One research project in America found that divorces were more common in families where the mother had been separated for three weeks or more from her baby. 'We suggest that separation in the newborn period does have an effect, albeit non-specific, by acting through the family as a stress that creates disequilibrium in the nuclear family structure.' [25] All in all, though evidence remains inconclusive, it looks as though hospitals are not justified in separating mother and child merely for the convenience of hospital routine.

What does mother love do? How does it work? Lately researchers have been trying to break down the mechanisms.

Take, for instance, intelligence. There is, in the first place, a genetic element. Intelligence depends partly upon inheritance, but the environment has an enormous effect too. Just as adopted children usually have a normal IQ even if their natural parents had low IQs, so children will have an IQ which reflects their upbringing. John Bowlby's original report had suggested that intelligence was harmed by the lack of a mother, and subsequent studies showed that children in institutionalised orphanages or crèches quite often showed low IQs.[26] But what they lacked was not so much the loving caresses of a mother, as general attention from anybody – and not necessarily from one individual either. In an institution with plenty of staff and toys available, children will grow up with normal IQs, even where staff turnover is rapid – just as children left with their natural but neglectful mothers will have low IQs.[27] The effect of mild neglect, even from a loving natural mother, can be seen in large families. In large families the older children usually have higher IQs than their later brothers and sisters. Indeed, there is a difference of sixteen months in reading age between the first-born and the fourth or later child.[28] This is presumably because, as her family grows, a mother has less time to give to each individual child – less attention and less time to talk. For language development, as well as IQ, seems to be influenced by the kind of time and effort put in by the people rearing a child. The more a child is talked to, the better he or she will learn to talk.

Other areas of development seem to be linked with the kind of bodily handling a child receives. In their comparative studies of various cultures anthropologists have found that babies who are carried around are more developed than babies of the same age who are left in cots or prams.[29] Monkey infants develop better when they are given a moving furry 'foster' mother, than a stationary one.[10] Tactile contact probably acts in two major ways. It helps the baby define the boundaries of its own body. It also helps arouse him so that the child is responsive to other stimuli. A child who is being jogged or rocked on the knee is in an alert frame of mind to notice what is going on around him; a child drowsing passively in a cot is not. Even quite detached and unloving 'handling' seems to have some effect.[30] It has been tested out in institutions. Babies who are 'handled' to order, develop slightly better 'visual attentiveness' than those who are not.

So, in theory, both intelligence and good physical co-ordination can be produced without love. Impersonal care-takers could be trained to stimulate a child to a timetable – handling a baby, talking and generally arousing the child not out of love but as part of their work. It is good to know this, since some children will probably always be reared in insti-tutions. We do not have to give them up as doomed to lower intelligence and slower development. We can spend money on training and hiring staff who will give the stimulation needed. That said, mother love is usually the motivation which makes for a clever, developed child. A loving mother automatically wants to talk to her child, jog it, rock it, play games, amuse it, cuddle it, touch it and carry it around. Most of all, a loving mother is responsive to her baby's reactions, and this particular trait may be more important than we have previously thought. The mother who responds to her baby's expressions and noises is in fact training it. The baby sees that it can produce this response, that it has power in getting mother to do what it wants. This further encourages other attempts at communi-cation, which in turn affects mental development. The mother who picks up her baby when he or she cries, far from 'spoiling' him, is teaching him that his behaviour affects the outside world. Babies who have a responsive mother are further developed than those who do not.[31] Indeed the sensitivity of a mother's response may be extremely important. 'Where a mother (*habitually* – all mothers do it occasionally) can go in and out of a room preoccupied with other thoughts, and not even acknowledge her baby's existence, or when she pushes herself arbitrarily on him in response to her own needs instead of his signals, the process whereby his behaviour becomes inter-twined with his social environment will surely be seriously handicapped.'[32] A baby with this kind of mother may be better off in a good institution. Sensitive mothers who respond by comforting a crying baby, for instance, do not 'spoil' the child. Rather the reverse. Babies who are picked up when they cry, cry less in later months than those who are not picked up.[33] A sensitive mother, who rightly interprets her child's signals, also seems to produce a more secure child.[34] The phrase used by many reseachers is 'securely attached'. Securely-attached children are – surprisingly perhaps – less affected by separation. They tend to cry less if their mother leaves the room, for instance. They are also more confident with strangers. The theory behind this is that a child who is securely loved has the extra confidence. It is the insecure child who grows up clinging and 'spoiled'. Lots of love lavished upon a baby should produce not a mother's pet, but an outgoing confident child – one who is more friendly towards children of his own age.[35] Here is the unique contribution that mother love has to make.

Children in institutions can be given the right kind of stimulation by trained nurses and caretakers, but, with staff changing around them – and by the age of eight they may have had as many as eighty caretakers – they do not usually get the chance to learn to love just one human being.[36] It may be enough for them to know that their mother loves them, even if she cannot look after them. Children whose mothers keep in touch are on the whole less warped and maladjusted than those whose mothers have definitely rejected them.[37] They feel the rejection. Children are not just little animals requiring feeding and training. They need to feel wanted. 'The child' in an institution 'knows he is different from those children who live with their own parents or whose family at least keep in touch with them, yet he does not, indeed cannot, understand why this should be so.' Those particular researchers concluded, 'It is the element of definite parental rejection which has the most adverse effect.'[38]

John Bowlby has subsequently argued that the human infant is monotropic – that it needs just one secure mother figure to whom it can attach itself. There are grounds for thinking human babies, as well as monkey babies, may be more adaptable than that. Certainly, they need the time to develop a secure bond with somebody – but that somebody does not perhaps have to be an adult. Monkey babies who are reared with one another, but without a mother, grow up more or less able to function in monkey social life.[6] Human children may be able to find that love between brothers and sisters substitutes for mother love. Just after the war, some children who had been in concentration camps were taken to Anna Freud's nursery in Hampstead. From the ages of six to twelve months, these six children had been kept in Tereszin camp. There were no toys and because Tereszin was a transit camp, adults came and went frequently. When the children arrived in England, it became clear that they were extremely closely attached. Unlike normal children, they would not be separated from each other. They shared their food and they shared their toys. 'They were extremely considerate of each other's feelings. They did not grudge each other their possessions . . . on the contrary lending them to each other with pleasure,' reported Anna Freud. [39] Though they were aged between three and four, the children looked at each other in a very loving way. They more or less ignored adults to begin with.

In a rather similar way some children in institutions seem to survive being rejected by their parents, if they have brothers or sisters they can love in their place. Among children in a home who had had no contact with their parents, two were unusually stable. 'Of the two stable children . . . one had a younger brother living in the same home with whom she had a very close and warm relationship. The other child was described by the house mother as warm-hearted and spontaneous: she had always been very popular among children and adults and tended to 'mother' those younger than herself.' [38] There is, one can only conclude, nothing magical about mother love. We have been designed to be loved by our mothers, and to love them in return – this is part of the learning pattern proper to our species. But occasionally we can find substitutes – foster parents, aunts, uncles, grannies, adopted parents, older or younger brothers and sisters. If there is no mother, it may even be enough for a child to mother others. Loving, as well as being loved, is what is vital. As long as the human infant has somebody to love, all is not lost. If there is nobody, then a vicious circle commences. The unloved child cannot love, and will become ultimately unlovable.

3

When Love Goes Wrong

Eight-month-old baby Leonard spent the last week of his life in the same nappy, although the bottom half of his body was burned by the stale urine. Then one evening his thirty-year-old mother beat him to death. The blows were so hard that his stomach was ruptured, his lung collapsed and his heart was dislodged from its proper place.[1] The mother had been getting a lot of help from social workers. Every fortnight a social worker visited her, and every week a health visitor popped in. Four times a week she had a home help. The week before she killed him, she had taken Leonard to the baby clinic. The health visitor there had been so pleased to see her that she had not insisted upon the nappy being changed – in case it put the mother off coming again. Yet in trying to help the mother, the experts had failed to save Leonard.

Within two random months of 1982, there were four cases of cruelty to children reported in the British newspapers. Some of the children were not battered – merely neglected. A ten-month-old girl, Nicola, was left hungry for twenty-four hours while her mother went on a drug trip. Finally the child picked up some brightly coloured tablets which lay strewn on the floor and swallowed them. She died of an overdose strong enough to kill ten adults. It was not till thirty-six hours later that the police could make her drug-stupefied mother understand what had happened.[2] A day later the newspapers reported that police were trying to trace a mother who had just gone off, leaving a three-year-old boy and his two-year-old sister alone in the flat for two days and nights. The children had eaten raw bacon, beetroot and had pathetically tried to make cakes out of flour and water.[3] Occasionally even older children, who are able to run away rather than suffer too much at the hands of their parents, nevertheless fall victim. In New York a father kept his eighteen-year-old daughter tied to a beam in the basement. When fire broke out, she was burned to death. He told police that he was afraid she might become a prostitute.[4]

Such reports turn up in newspapers nearly every week, and it is only those cases which end in death or the law courts that are thought worth reporting. In our society mothers, fathers and step-parents abuse the children in their care with regularity. Such cruelty is usually greeted with horror. We find it difficult to believe that the natural love between parent and child should be warped into cruelty. Just how often children are injured by their parents is not known for sure but, according to British government statistics, in every million children under five years old there are nineteen or so deaths yearly from murder or deliberate injury. That works out about fifty to sixty child deaths in Britain a year – one a week. These figures do not include deaths where there is some element of suspicion but no proof.[5] The National Society for the Prevention of Cruelty to Children suggests, from its experience in cruelty cases, that in 1976 there were at least 65 deaths, 759 children severely injured and a further 4323 'moderately' injured.[6] These figures are probably an underestimate, for they are calculated upon areas where the NSPCC operates special units. These areas, thanks to the NSPCC, may have lower death rates.[7] In a report published in 1984, the charity calculated that about 6388 children were being physically abused in 1982, though the number of deaths and very severe injuries had probably fallen.[8]

At the beginning of the 1980s there was a big rise in the number of neglected children being reported to the charity. In 1980 to 1982 these accounted for twice as many cases as those of physical injury.[9] 'Research indicates,' said the NSPCC's director, Dr Alan Gilmour, 'that child deaths in neglecting families are far above average. Yet neglect as a cause of death will not have hit the headlines. Such deaths will have been recorded as accident or illness.' In America, there are between a quarter of a million to one and a half million battered children yearly. The estimated number who are killed varies from 365 to 700 and upwards yearly. [10]

The odd thing is that these deaths have only been noticed in the last twenty to thirty years. Till then cruelty to children by their parents had often been ignored by the world at large. It was only in the 1940s that child abuse was 'discovered'. Radiologists drew attention to the x-rays of children which showed a whole series of past and present fractures. At first it was suggested that these injuries were the result of 'parental carelessness', 'parental conduct', or even 'indifference, immaturity and irresponsibility of parents'. By the late 1950s researchers were beginning to admit the possibility that the parents had deliberately injured their children. In 1961 Dr Henry Kempe, an eminent American paediatrician, used a deliberately emotive term, 'the battered child syndrome'. A surge of publicity resulted. It is worth pointing out that the term is also a medical one. Child abuse had been discovered not as a crime but as an illness. [11]

How can such men and women beat up children? What kind of brutes are they? A portrait of parents who injure their children is slowly emerging. Many writers on child abuse emphasise that child injuries can be found in all classes. The implication is that all parents are potential abusers. Strictly speaking, this is true. Injured children are found among the aristocracy, the professional middle classes and lower down the social scale. But they are far more often found among classes IV and V both in the USA and in Britain. [12] These are the low-paid unskilled and manual workers. One reason why child cruelty is more common among these families may be because it more often comes to light. The better-paid and better-educated may be cleverer at covering up. It is also more likely that the better-paid in the USA are using private doctors who may not report such cases to the authorities. But this is not the whole story. It is more likely that the well-off families can afford to pay for child care. Children whom their parents find irritating can be given into the care of child minders, nannies, or sent away to boarding schools. Mothers who can pay for it, can have plenty of time off from the relentless crying of a baby. Fathers who dislike young children can keep away from them more easily in a large house. Thus, stress is one reason why parents batter children. People who are overworked, cooped up in close surroundings, unable to get a break and financially worried are more likely to be short on patience. In Britain, many injured children are in families on supplementary benefits.[6] In America, a high proportion of the families are on welfare or public assistance.[12] If there was no poverty there would be fewer children injured.

Yet getting rid of poverty would not exterminate all child abuse. Most poor people do not injured or neglect their children. The NSPCC survey of abusing families in 1976 concluded, 'They were no worse off with regard to their exclusive use of basic amenities' such as bathrooms, phones, etc. compared with other people in their class, 'but were considerably more unsettled in their homes.'[6] Such families seem to move home a great deal – sometimes, perhaps, in order to shake off the authorities which they fear may take away their children. Some of the stress that such families suffer may be the result of their own chaotic lifestyles. Simply giving them more money is not the entire answer.

We need therefore to look more closely at these families. Why are they, rather than their next-door neighbours, beating their children? It is significant that the women are usually young when they first give birth.[13] Of the men concerned, one survey concluded, 'The male presents an almost classic profile of the man in a mid-life crisis. He is in his thirties.'[14] There is a high proportion with a criminal record, particularly for violence.[6] Some of the women have been in trouble with the law also. In general, then, child batterers are people whose previous history suggests an inability to cope.[6]

Their ability to form relationships seems impaired. The mothers are often described as socially isolated, with neither friends nor relatives to help and support them. They do not get on with their own parents, nor did they in childhood. The fathers recollect their own parents as being unreasonable in their discipline. Nearly half the mothers report *having no friends at all*.[15] These women, it seems, are alone though surrounded with other people. It is worth here remembering the !Kung bush folk, whose mothers are constantly in close contact with other women: aunts, sisters and others are always nearby.[16] Being isolated with a young child is not easy. Among working class women, those who are alone with young children and without a job are more vulnerable to psychiatric disturbance, particularly those without a good relationship with their husband.[17] Do women batter their babies because of the stress of being alone with them? Or is it for the same reason that isolated them in the first place – their difficulty in loving?

The families in which injured children are found are somewhat larger than average, often with children who are either unplanned or even unwanted. Contraception is frequently not used.[18] A fairly high proportion of the women, about a third in one survey, are unmarried though some may be living with a man. Some are married but separated. In all, only just over half of the children on the British NSPCC child abuse register in 1976 were living with both their natural parents. In Britain generally, at that time, about 90 per cent of children in comparable social classes lived with both a father and a mother.[6] Thus a high proportion of the families where child abuse occurs have a substitute father or mother. These substitutes are twice as likely as the natural parents to injure a child in their care.[19] It is not easy to walk into a ready-made family and slip into the parental role – as I know to my cost. As a substitute mother, I tried and failed – though, fortunately, I did not batter.

Among the men who batter children, one in three also batter their wives.[14] About a third of the mothers in battering homes report that their marriage is unsatisfactory. The proportion is even higher among the mothers who actually are responsible for the abuse.[18]

Perhaps the most dismaying finding of all is that among these delinquent parents are a high number who report that *their* parents abused them. Problem families seem to link up by marriage with other problem families, and perpetuate the tradition – some researchers have found evidence of children being injured or neglected for three generations, one after the other.[20] Never having seen a loving family, they do not know how to create one. Secondly, their tormented upbringings may have produced psychological problems which they carry into later life.[21] Among the abusing parents are many of low intelligence. This, in its turn, may have been produced by neglect in their own childhoods.[22]

Sometimes, within a family of more than one child, all the

children are hurt by their parents. Sometimes only one is singled out for punishment, while the brothers and sisters go scot-free. The relationship between the victimiser and the victim needs looking at. Why is one child singled out? More than one survey has reported a higher proportion of battered first-born children than would be expected.[6, 23] Is this because the mother is youngest, and most immature, at the time of first giving birth? Or is it that by the time of the second birth the mother has learned how to love and care for her child? We do not know. Yet what is clear is that if we are looking for the 'causes' of child abuse, we need to look at the child as well as the parents. Violence occurs between two individuals.

Some findings are there already. The injured child is more likely to be illegitimate than its brothers and sisters.[6] It may also be the child who is in some other way the odd child out. A high proportion of injured children turn out to be either premature or low-birth-weight babies.[24, 14] Premature babies are taken straight from their mothers and put into nurseries where they can have special care. Till recently parents were often discouraged from visiting, and if they did visit they were not allowed to touch their infants. Depending on whether or not they subscribe to the theory of a 'sensitive period', some researchers therefore suggest that the bond between mother and child was never allowed to form properly. Even if the mother can visit her baby, she may nonetheless feel it is abnormal. Whatever the reason, hospital staff notice that some mothers are unenthusiastic about their premature babies.[25] In such cases, fathers may also fail to make emotional contact. We do not know. And once the child is home, it may be more difficult to rear – fussy, more prone to colic and other troubles. One piece of research has shown that battered babies or their mothers are more likely to have been ill during the first year of the baby's life. This illness may have interrupted the chance to form a loving bond. In battering families, the children who are not injured are likely to have been particularly healthy children.[26] Such hypotheses, though, are still controversial.

Most of the research today centres round the families where children are beaten up – usually young children whose bruises, fractures and skull injuries are so severe that they are noticed by the authorities. But parents can abuse their children in other ways too. There are babies who are classified as 'failing to thrive'. Once it was thought such children failed to put on weight because they were unloved. Now it looks as if the answer is more simple. They are not being properly fed. In our developed rich countries, there are babies who are literally starving. [27] The mother may say she feeds her baby, but she is not bothering. Then there are children who are sexually abused by their parents, children who are left to roam around on their own, or children whose parents have little emotional warmth. Beating up a child is an extreme example of the failure to love. Some parents may not beat their children, they merely fail to love them – or love them inconsistently, or in a warped way. A study of children who were put into council care while their mothers had a baby showed that quite often the mothers did not think of their children's emotional needs. They did not consider that their children might be better off staying with somebody they knew – grandparents, friends or relatives – but thought only of the child's physical needs. They had decided that the nurseries would have good food and good toys. 'Among these mothers the "proper care" of their children was explained in these terms rather than in terms of emotional needs.' [28] Even more marked was the way the fathers did not help. Even those fathers who were unemployed and thus available for child care simply did not volunteer. These minor forms of abuse are perhaps only failures of imagination, but they also leave their mark. Children who have cold, harsh parents are likely to grow up harsh and aggressive. Among boys in particular, this may mean a later life of delinquency and even acts of violence. [29]

It is perhaps no wonder that a fairly high proportion of children have problems which can be detected when they are only three years old. [30] In one London borough seven per cent of young children had moderate to severe behaviour problems, and a further fifteen per cent had mild problems. One in five children, indeed, showed difficulties. This proportion is similar to the proportion of children who have troubles in later childhood or adolescence – suggesting that the problems stem mainly from parents rather than schools.

Much effort has been put into detecting injuries to children; so far, less is being done to help the children grow up normal. Most of them have severe problems in later life. Those with head injuries and those who have been half-starved are likely to show the effects late into adult life. Nor are these victims very adequately 'rescued' by the social services. It is utterly appalling, but the children who are rightly taken away from their own violent parents are often shuttled from one foster home to another.[31] Here is one such case: 'A second child . . . was a twenty-four-month-old boy who had been adopted at nineteen months of age by excellent parents. The boy had been admitted to hospital at one month of age with several bruises about his face and because of failure to thrive, weighing less than his birth weight. From one to nine months of age he had lived in two different foster homes, and at age nine months he was returned to his natural parents. At thirteen months of age he was again admitted to hospital with eighty per cent body burns after having been placed in an excessively hot bath. On discharge from hospital he went to a third foster home and at nineteen months of age he was adopted.'[32] The natural parents had injured this child, but so had the authorities shuttling him from home to home before he was even two years old.

In Britain, the failure rate of fostering is high. Over five years, one half of all fostering arrangements break down and disagreements between social workers and foster parents about what fostering should entail are frequent.[33] Foster parents often want to be full-time parents, a natural aim which seems to me might be in the best interest of the child. Social workers are often keen to retain the links between a child and its natural parents, even though children returned to their parents may do just as badly or even worse than those kept in an institution.[34] Adoptions, where the new parents are allowed to think of themselves as full-timers, are more successful.[33] Even among older abused children, three quarters of the adoptions are successful. On the whole, it looks as if some child-care authorities are slow in putting the children's needs first. Treatment often focuses on the abusing parents and sometimes it is not clear if the child itself is benefiting. Baby Leonard, whose mother was receiving so much care and attention, seems to have gone relatively unnoticed by the social workers.[1] It is as if authorities are so anxious to 'cure' the illness of child abuse, that they forget the child-victim might die meantime.

Of course decisions are hard to take. Social workers may find

that they have almost to snatch away the newly-born of abusing
mothers, to make sure these babies are not battered in their
turn.[35] It is an odd fact that cruelty does not necessarily
diminish a child's love – or an adult's for that matter. Experiments with monkeys have shown that monkey babies will cling
all the longer to an artificial mother who is sending out hurtful
jets of hot air.[36] This reaction confounds onlookers, and may
confuse social workers into thinking that children should not be
separated from their abusing parents. The 'love' of an abused
child for its torturer is part of the same reaction we can see in
other children and adults. The insecure cling more than those
that are secure; some battered wives persist in remaining with
their husbands.

Some aspects of our culture positively encourage child abuse.
Besides the fixed time regime for baby-feeding of F. Truby King
and the forties which still lingers on, there is also a strong
tradition amongst the British unskilled and manual workers of
punishing very young children with slaps or even beatings.[37]
'He that spareth his rod hateth his son, but he that loveth him
chasteneth him betimes' says the Old Testament.[38] Those
parents who physically punish their children can find plenty of
justification, whether from those schools which retain corporal
punishment, or the old traditions of child lore. There is, too, a
tradition of male violence. Almost every TV serial will show not
just the baddies, but also the goodies, thumping, twisting back
arms, kicking or hurting other people: three quarters of the TV
programmes in America contain violence.[39] In general, it seems
that the level of violence in a society will coincide with the level
of parental violence towards children. In American society,
ordinary parental behaviour seems to include a lot of violence.
Three out of a hundred parents admitted to threatening a child
with a gun or knife at some time during their upbringing. One in
five had hit their child with some kind of instrument, and four
out of a hundred admitted to a 'beating up'.[10]

Another tacit encouragement of child abuse may lie in the
practice of separating parents from their children in hospital.
'When I first visited Queen Charlotte's Maternity Hospital forty
years ago,' recalled a doctor, 'all babies delivered by forceps or
Caesarean section, however good their conditions, were cot-
nursed for forty-eight hours and not once picked up, certainly

not by the mother but not even by a nurse.' And hospital routines used to keep mothers away from even perfectly normal babies except for fixed feeding times.[40] If these routines have changed, it is largely because of the research into the mother-infant bond. Evidence has had to be assembled which suggests there might be long-term deleterious effects, as medicine remains uncaring about human emotions unless these can be *proved* to be of importance. The idea that it is wrong to make human beings unnecessarily unhappy simply does not occur. Our society must prove what more loving societies might accept without question.

And there are many more aspects of our society which could well be factors in our rate of child abuse. Increasing social mobility, as we saw in Chapter One, cuts off parents from their roots, separating them from friends and relatives. And our high percentage of marriage break-ups means more step parents and, as we know, an unrelated adult in the family may encourage child abuse, which also flourishes in one-parent families where it's the mother who is missing.[19]

But despite this catalogue of dangerous errors I do not pretend, of course, that our society is the most loveless ever. The Ik people, a small tribe suffering from starvation on the northern border of Uganda, turn their children out of the hut at the age of three.[41] If a child falls into the fire, adults laugh. If it is carried off by a crocodile, the mother is glad there is one less mouth to feed. Among the Mundagamor people in New Guinea, children were not much loved. Mothers nursed them standing up and pushed them away as soon as possible. It was a hostile society – perhaps as a result of this rearing – and people rarely co-operated with one another. 'The Mundagamor's habits of hostility were such that they had begun to eat people of their own language group. There was virtually no tribal solidarity and it was probably a mere accident of history that they capitulated to the mission before they were destroyed by marauding neighbours,' wrote Margaret Mead.[42] Extreme examples, perhaps, but they clearly illustrate the powerful effect of environment on the so-called maternal 'instinct', which can thus be more or less cancelled out.

Nevertheless, 'instinct' is a useful concept in the attempt to understand what goes wrong with love. The baby instinctively turns to a mother figure, tries to 'attach' himself to it. His human imprinting tends to be conditioned by it as the dominant figure in his first few years of life. If there is none to hand, some children will not learn to love at all and may go through life unable to form relationships. If the mother figure is cruel, the child will be able to love it – but in later life its love gets mixed up with cruelty. The child who has been beaten up by its parents, beats its own children in their turn. The instinct is operating in a warped and odd way.

Continuing the analogy, maternal love, like any other instinct, needs the right stimulus if it is to be released. Babies who smile and coo are a release mechanism for love. Watch the next baby smiling at strangers from its pram: see how they will bend down and smile back. Unsmiling crying babies may not produce strong enough releaser signals for a mother to love back.

It is a mistake, therefore, to take human love for granted. The potential to love is there in all of us, but many human beings will have been brought up with that potential unfulfilled. They may be quite unable to love, or they may be people in whom the instinct to love is warped into a kind of cruelty and unkindness. Without help, they will pass this unhappiness down through their own families. For the victims of abusing parents will, in due course, turn out to be the violent or neglectful parents whose actions so shock us when we read of babies dying or children beaten up. The violent father, or the isolated mother with no friends to help her, were once victims too.

4

Friends in Need, Friends Indeed

'I never yet cast a true affection on a woman, but I have loved my friend as I do virtue, my soul, my God . . . There are wonders in true affection; it is a body of enigmas, mysteries, and riddles; wherein two so become one, as they both become two. I love my friend before myself, and yet methinks I do not love him enough. Some few months hence, my multiplied affection will make me believe I have not loved him at all; when I am from him, I am dead till I be with him; when I am with him, I am not satisfied, but would still be nearer him. United souls are not satisfied with embraces but desire to be truly each other; which, being impossible, their desires are infinite, and proceed without a possibility of satisfaction', wrote Sir Thomas Browne in the seventeenth century.[1]

Such high-flown musings about friendship would seem precious in today's essayist. I have never seen the theme touched upon in literary journals, and only occasionally mentioned in magazines or newspapers. Yet Western literature is full of paeans to the joys of friendship, including the classics. Aristotle mused on friendship as an aid to happiness, and decided that 'to love is better than to be loved. For love is an active pleasure and a good thing; whilst merely to be loved creates no activity in the soul.'[2] Montaigne, too, described the love that he and his friend had for one another. 'Our minds have jumped so unitedly together, they have with so fervent an affection considered of each other, and with like affection so discovered and sounded, even to the very bottom of each other's heart and entrails, that I did not only know his, as well as mine own, but I would verily rather have trusted him concerning any matter of mine than myself.'³ Perhaps these passages are mere literary devices. But how is it that today such literary devices are absent? Endless numbers of words are written about our sexual relationships or our marriages, why so little about our nonsexual friendships? Freud, Malinowski, Havelock Ellis, Kinsey, Reich, Masters and Johnson and many others have studied sexual feelings. Why have so few studied the non-sexual bond between adults?

In the past there were friendship archetypes on which to model a relationship – David and Jonathan, Roland and Oliver, Achilles and Patroclus. Other cultures retain a reverence for friendship, and almost formal rules for it. Among the Bangwa of the Cameroon, a friend is as important as a spouse. An Australian anthropologist, Robert Brain, first came across the formal aspect of these friendships when he attended a 'cry-die' or Bangwa funeral. The womenfolk of the dead man were wailing and dancing, and a youngish man was singing a funeral dirge. This man, with torn clothes and tear-stained face, was the dead man's best friend. Brain recorded these dirges, many of them sung by women for their friends, since the Bangwa did not pretend that women were incapable of friendship. These close friendships were expected to be lifelong and fully as strong and enduring as the ties of blood. 'I watched how Bangwa "best friends" behaved, continually verbalising their affection, giving each other gifts, accompanying each other on journeys, being demonstrative almost to the point of "petting" ', he reported. 'It soon became clear that friendship was endowed with a greater intensity of meaning than in our own society . . . Certainly the behaviour of Jonathan and David would be normal and comprehensible to them and the words of Roland and Oliver not at all romantic. Moreover they would not be in the least tempted to presuppose or imagine any homosexual overtones in these classical European friendships since as far as I could make out, and I certainly made enquiries, these practices were unknown between adult men.'⁴

Such close single sex friendships in the Western world, since the advent of Freud, risk being considered homosexual. If sexual activity were taking place between, say, David and

Jonathan, this would not only classify their relationship as primarily homosexual (and only secondarily, if at all, a friendship), but it would also classify them as homosexuals. If a celibate or a heterosexual David and Jonathan were to be found in today's world, their relationship would probably be classified by some as 'latently' homosexual. Once again, even without sexual activity, the primacy would be given to the sexual side. A woman I know left her husband and went to stay in a country cottage near her parents to recover. Her best girlfriend accompanied her. After two or three weeks, her middle-class mother came over to see her for a quiet chat. 'Darling, I do hope you're not becoming a lesbian,' she said. This seventy-year-old lady living in the wilds of the West Country had become so infected with Freud that she felt a close friendship must be sexual.

Of course, there may have been times in history when the reverse was true – when friendship camouflaged the sexual relationship, when outsiders saw the affection and were blind to the sexual. At such times a homosexual David and Jonathan could have lived together and slept together under the guise of affection. Under the guise of? What if such a view – which gives the ascendancy to affection – is closer to the mark than our own?

In Britain's history there have been times when single sex friendships, even very passionate ones, were not classified as sexual. In 1778 Sarah Ponsonby and Eleanor Butler, two upper-class Irish women, 'eloped' together and set up house as a romantic couple. They dressed in men's clothes for their flight, and finally settled in a cottage in Llangollen Vale. Eleanor's journal was full of references to Sarah as 'my tender, my sweet love', 'my beloved', and 'my Heart's darling'. Sometimes the journal mentioned that they had shared a bed, usually during illness.[5] (Sharing a bed in past ages has not necessarily been evidence of the sexual, being sometimes for mere warmth, fellowship or because there were not enough beds to go round. Some American-Indian families sleep together in the same room for fellowship even now.) On the whole, historians conclude that it is unlikely that Sarah and Eleanor were having a lesbian relationship. None of their friends considered this a possibility. They became celebrities and the local papers called them 'the Irish ladies who have settled in so romantic a manner'.

Wordsworth mentioned them in a poem about friendship and Anna Seward wrote about their 'Davidean friendship'. They were admired by the Duke of Wellington, Josiah Wedgwood, Edmund Blake and Sir Walter Scott.

Other romantic friendships between women are known to us – Queen Anne's and Sarah Churchill's, for instance. Less well known is the close relationship between Queen Mary, the preceding monarch, and Frances Apsley. Mary wrote to Frances before her wedding: 'I have sat up this night . . . to tell my dear, dear, dear dearest husband (Frances) . . . that I am more in love with you every time I see you, and love you so well that I cannot express it no way but by saying I am your louse in bosom and would be very glad to be always so near you.'[5] Both Mary and Anne had been brought up at the court of Charles II, where it would be unlikely in the extreme that either could be ignorant of the facts of sexual life in almost all their variety. Yet I do not think we can classify their friendships as lesbian love affairs. Nor can the 'Boston marriages' of later generations when women set up home together, simply be dismissed as covered-up lesbian relationships. Some were sexual; but most were not.

Such friendships between men were rarely thought suspiciously homosexual. Disraeli was able to write in *Coningsby*: 'At school friendship is a passion. It entrances the being; it tears the soul. All the loves of after life can never bring its rapture, or its wretchedness; no bliss so absorbing, no pangs of jealousy or despair so crushing or so keen . . . What tenderness and what devotion; what illimitable confidence, infinite revelation of inmost thought; what ecstatic present and romantic future; what bitter estrangements and what melting reconciliations; what scenes of wild recrimination, agitating explanations, passionate correspondence; what insane sensitiveness, what earthquakes of the heart and whirlwinds of the soul are confined in that simple phrase, a "schoolboy's friendship".'[6] I do not think that any member of today's Parliament would *dare* to write such a passage in a novel.

School friendships, even those that are never sexually expressed, have now been brought firmly into the sexual arena. Havelock Ellis attached an appendix about girls' friendships in his volume on sexual inversion, remarking: 'The relationship is usually of a markedly Platonic character, and generally exists between a boarder on one side and a day pupil on the other. Notwithstanding, however, its apparently non-sexual nature, all the sexual manifestations of college youth circle around it, and in its varying aspects of differing intensity all the gradations of sexual sentiment may be expressed.'[7] This is the famous double bind of popular psychoanalysis. You are intensely loving towards your best friend, but you do not have sex together? Well, then the relationship is *unconsciously* sexual.

In the twentieth century, therefore, we are left only with sexual relationships or those friendships which are not intensely emotional. The intense emotional friendship is axiomatically sexual – whatever the real state of affairs. As a result biographers sometimes find themselves almost unable to explain the intense friendships of the past. 'It is difficult to write of the meeting of Tennyson and Hallam because of the inadequacy of our language to deal with deep friendship', says Robert Bernard Martin, Tennyson's biographer. 'There should be a phrase analogous to "falling in love" to describe the celerity of emotion that brings two persons together almost at first meeting: "falling in friendship" is what happened to Tennyson and Hallam . . . Tennyson's reaction to Hallam was simple: "He was as near perfection as a mortal man can be," he said long after Hallam's death, when his memory was as green as if all the intervening years had dropped away. It would be hard to exaggerate the impact Hallam made on Tennyson; their friendship was to be the most emotionally intense period he ever knew, four years probably equal in psychic importance to the other seventy-nine of his life.'[8] I 'fell in friendship' with a young woman when I was fifteen. The friendship lasted for several years, was on my part intensely emotional, yet never once was I sexually attracted by her.

It is also possible for intimate friendships to flourish between the two sexes — 'platonic friendship' is the usual phrase, showing how we need to specify the non-sexuality of the relationship. 'At forty-three and happily married, I enjoy what I can only describe as "an intimate friendship" with my first girlfriend, Helen, who is forty and also happily married. We met when we were nineteen and sixteen, were close friends for three years and considered ourselves engaged for the last six months of that time. We parted for various reasons in 1960 and resumed contact a few years later when she was married and just before my marriage. Over the past few years we have become warmer and more intimate with each other, and recognise that we are in some sense more ''in love'' with each other than ever in the past. Yet it remains a chaste love (we have never had intercourse in all these twenty-six years), one that does not interfere with but in some ways seems to reinforce our marital loves, one that is pleasurable rather than painful, and one that is undeniably sexual in essence without being so in practice,' confided a correspondent.

'We don't know what to call it or how to regard it, and cannot really talk to others about it – including our spouses – for fear of being misunderstood. Your point about ''platonic friendship'', or at least unconsummated erotic ones, being laughed off as unbelievable, rang very true. Hence we are some-times led to feel furtive about something which, in a better balanced world than we live in, we would be openly proud of.'

Platonic friendships of the past include that of the British Prime Minister, H.H. Asquith, who corresponded at the age of sixty-two with a twenty-seven-year-old woman, Venetia Stanley. He was married, and she was still single. There is nothing to suggest that they became sexual lovers, yet his feelings were undeniably strong. In the year 1914, when the First World War broke out, he wrote to her: 'My darling – I hope you got the little farewell message I wrote near midnight. It was so blank and disheartening to think that I should not be near you again for such an indefinite time. And, tho' yesterday was rather broken up, Saturday was a golden day and I shall never forget (will you?) the hours we spent together under the leaden sky and dripping rain, with the glimpses of heather, and constant change of pine and oak, and (what was worth more than everything outside) the close real deep understanding and love which in these moving times is to me more than anything in the world.' Venetia finally married Edwin Montagu. Asquith's last letter was heartbroken, yet he had assured his wife that his 'fondness for Venetia has never interfered and never could with our relationship'.[9] Today we would label that relationship sexual – though not genital. An earlier generation in France called it an 'amitié amoureuse', a more accurate description. Such friendships were not all that uncommon. Even Prime Minister

William Ewart Gladstone was caught up in one – with Laura Thistlethwayte – though he swore he had never been unfaithful to his wife Catherine. [10]

Today's narrow concept of friendship has lost us much already, including those formal bonds that are obviously asexual: blood brotherhood, and godparenthood. The one has more or less disappeared in our society – only found in children's games; the other is about to – though this is largely because of the decline of baptism from a sacrament to an empty formality. Both these stylised relationships are at odds with modern thought because they suggest the underlying identity of close friendship with kinship, not sex. Blood brothers are two friends who have made themselves honorary kin; godparents are friends brought into the family circle on an equal footing, as co-parents. And, vice versa, in the large families of the past, friends were likely to be brothers and sisters. Today with smaller families we must look outside for our friendships. Other societies have not needed to.

The most famous study of family ties focused on the East End of London, Bethnal Green, in 1951. [11] Sociologists found a society in which half the married women had seen their mothers in the past twenty-four hours, and eight out of ten had seen her within the past week. Sons saw their mothers less often but even so two thirds of the married men had seen their mother in the past week. Each married couple had about thirteen relatives living in Bethnal Green, and quite often a mother's home was the focal point for brothers and sisters to meet. Nearly everybody in the area had grown up together, going to the same schools, working for the same employers, and marrying locally. The sociologists were taken shopping by one lady who in the course of a mere half hour met fourteen people she knew. She kept a record for a week of all the people she met in the street whom she knew, and the total was sixty-three. A slightly similar study of relationships in a Welsh valley, found the same sort of close networks. [12] 'The torrent of information and anecdote which we have now come to expect from our informants concerning kinship relationships is testimony both to the continuing vitality of these relationships in an urban environment and also to one of the most important functions of the network of relationships in which a particular individual is involved – that of providing him with a discoverable social identity in a community context, of "placing" him not as an individual, but as a social person in determinate relationships with others', wrote the sociologist.

The connection between having friends and having family ties is far from clear. Do those people who spend a lot of time with their families have less time to spend with their friends, or vice versa? The sociologists who studied Bethnal Green expected friends to be almost unnecessary, such was the close network of family relations. But 'far from the family excluding ties to outsiders, it acts as an important means of promoting them. When a person has relatives in the borough, as most people do, each of these relatives is a go-between with other people in the district. His brothers' friends are his acquaintances, if not his friends; his grandmother's neighbours so well known as almost to be his own.'[11] Those people who visited family relations most frequently, also visited friends the most, being sociable both in and outside the family – though this seems to vary according to class. Most interestingly for my thesis of friendship these differences suggest that friends and family may substitute for one another to a certain extent. In Britain most surveys have shown that working-class women and men see far more of kinsfolk and less of friends, than their middle-class counterparts. Friends are far more likely to be invited home in middle-class circles. 'Friendships do not just happen, but are both generated and structured by the participants' concluded one researcher of his middle-class informants.[13] Working-class people had friends who tended to be seen outside the home – at work, in the pub, as neighbours, or at some sporting activity. But the exact nature of an individual network of contacts is difficult to measure. Is the working-class woman who drops by her Mum's home once a week more in touch with her mother than the middle-class woman who rings up Mummy every evening? Distance between family members may dictate the frequency of visits, and middle-class kin are likely to be spread out over a wider area.

On the other hand sheer distance may explain away one distinction traditionally made between kin- and other relationships. Sociologists have argued that family ties are not constant. Contact between brothers and sisters decreases during the lifespan, while contact between adult children and their aged parents increases. The ties between adults and their more distant relatives like cousins, also decrease during a lifespan. However, this falling off of contact may have more to do with the high mobility of our society than with the essential nature of family ties. Middle-class couples move away to follow the husband's job, and perhaps in future will move for the wife's job too. They have already moved out of home into a college during their adolescent years. Among lower income groups, married couples get assigned council housing which probably takes them away from their home area. If these distances are taken into account, then the ties between family members seem more constant. We may visit less, as the years pass, but we do not otherwise weaken the contact.[14] In particular, the ties between sisters and brothers seem to endure lifelong.[13] Some sociologists even argue that they become of particular importance in old age. Ageing parents may play an important role in keeping the other family members in contact.

Family ties are not confined to human beings: we meet them in lower animals too. In many species of monkeys, 'aunts' have a particular importance; they may even adopt orphaned babies. Within a group of monkeys, females who are related to one another tend to stick together.[15] Occasionally there are uncle figures too, though on the whole males have more distant ties with their related infants. We do not know as much as we should about the relationships within a monkey troop, and at the moment researchers are concentrating on infant/adult inter-action, the sexual angle and dominance – which mounts or grooms which animal.[16] However some researchers have found that the males form into cliques and it seems likely that there are monkey 'friendships', possibly formed during infancy when mutual play is so important. Rhesus monkeys which are raised with mothers, but without any playmates at all, often have initial difficulty in getting on with others, when they are adult. Some seem unable to adapt to normal monkey social life, ending up loners or outcasts.[17] Others, after some difficulties at the beginning, learn how to cope. But clearly these monkeys do better when they have playmate-friends.

One fascinating finding has come to light about monkey kith and kin relationships. When infant pigtail monkeys were given the chance to play with half-siblings whom they had not formerly met, they preferred their half-brothers and sisters to other unrelated playmates. These half-siblings were related only via the male, and thus could not have been recognisable. Or so researchers thought. The fact that the related monkeys preferred one another suggested that in some way the blood tie had resulted in a 'recognisable' trait, probably a visual one.[18] Was it that they showed some 'likeness' to their relations? As the half-brothers and sisters had never met before, it could not just be a question of familiarity. Perhaps there is truly some biological truth in the old motto 'Blood is thicker than water'.

Among human beings, as with monkeys, it seems as if friendship has to be learned. At the earliest age two babies show very little interest in each other, though both will have strong ties with their mother or mother figure.[19] In fact by nursery-school age children who have a loving and secure relationship with their mother seem to be more 'socially competent' than those whose babyhood has been less secure: friendship is not distinct from the other loving relationships of our life.[20] By the second year, children begin behaving in 'an unmistakeable social way' – smiling, holding out objects and, if angry, hitting or biting. In the first years children seem to think of a friend merely as somebody with whom they spend time. Zick Rubin, one of the few researchers to look into love and friendship, had this frustrating conversation with three-year-old Tony. 'Why is Caleb your friend?' asked Rubin. 'Because I like him,' replied Tony. 'Why do you like him?' questioned the patient researcher. 'Because he's my friend,' said Tony. 'And why is he your friend?' persevered Rubin. By this time Tony was getting mildly disgusted at these pointless questions. He answered, using the words slowly so that this silly adult would finally understand: 'Because ... I ... choosed ... him ... for ... my ... friend.'[19]

At the ages of six to eight, a child thinks of a friend as somebody who does actions that please him. By nine to twelve, they have grasped the idea of reciprocity – that they should do actions that please their friends. But at this point, according to Rubin, they are likely only to think of specific incidents rather than of an enduring relationship of giving and taking.[20] By adolescence, ideas of emotional intimacy have been established. This growth of the capacity for friendship has been described as a change from 'play' to 'talk' to 'trust'.[21] Teenagers, indeed, try very hard to find acceptance among their contemporaries, and will often voice fears of not being liked.[22] I can remember only too well the horror of being the odd one out at school. When all the other girls had best friends, I was left without one – until another girl was added to the dormitory and I at last could pair up too. When yet another girl arrived and was left without a best friend, I do not, to my shame, remember wasting any pity on her. Indeed, if anything, the existence of her as an outsider seemed to make me feel rather more secure.

This teenage craving for friendship, for the approval not of parents but of contemporaries, may have some unconscious perception behind it. Friends or the lack of them seem to mark a person. Those people who have friends in their young adulthood, turn out to be more likely to make a happy and enduring marriage.[23] The ability to love has to be learned from a warm babyhood with a loving mother figure, then practised among contemporaries, and finally brought to marriage. The converse of this is also true: that those who have insecure babyhoods will find friendships more difficult, and probably marriages too – confirmation for one of the Bible's crueller readings: 'Unto every one that hath shall be given . . . but from him that hath not shall be taken away even that which he hath.'[24]

The idea that friends are freely chosen is only partly true. Every examination of friendship suggests that we are friendly with those who are like us. Like attracts like.[25] But if we think back to those pigtail monkeys who preferred the company of hitherto unknown half-sisters and brothers, similarity may also be a feature of family ties. We may – at least partly – love our relations because we have so much in common with them, either in background and upbringing or perhaps also in looks and character. The distinctions we tend to make between family and friends may not be as valid as we think.

Nor is friendship an entirely deliberate choice. We cannot befriend those whom we have never met, and therefore in some ways friends are chosen for us by blind circumstance. A few years ago a sociologist decided to study friendship among forty-four Maryland State police trainees. [26] She asked the men, all of whom had known each other for about six weeks, for the names of their friends among the force. The results were, on the face of it, bizarre in the extreme. Almost half the friendships were between men who were next-door to each other in the alphabetical order of their surnames. Men with a surname starting with C, for instance, tended to be friends with men whose surnames started with either B or D. The secret behind this alphabetical choice lay in the trainees' rooms, which were assigned in alphabetical order. C was friendly either with B or D, not because of their names, but because he roomed next-door to them. Indeed compared with other factors such as similarity of background, religion and hobbies, this propinquity was most important.

A second careful study was made among students who all lived in the same hall on an American campus. [27] This was a tower block with communal rooms at the bottom and eight floors of student dormitories above. Each two floors had their own lounge, so that the dormitories were split into four partly self-contained blocks. Students who lived on the same floor were far more likely to be friends than those who were separated on different floors. Among floormates, like then attracted like, with freshmen tending to be friendly with freshmen, older students with their contemporaries. And friendship tended to reinforce physical closeness – friends tending to ask for neighbouring rooms.

But why do friends and family matter? Common sense and folklore have always insisted that they are important. 'A friend in need is a friend indeed,' runs the old proverb. When we are depressed, or just down at the mouth, most of us turn to our friends for support. [28] When Americans were asked how they dealt with anxiety, most said they talked their worries over with their marriage partner. When they were asked what they did about unhappiness, most said they turned to their friends for comfort. [29] Only a few turned immediately to a professional figure. These answers should not surprise us. More than three hundred years ago Francis Bacon wrote: 'The principle fruit of friendship is the ease and discharge of the fullness and swelling of the heart, which passions of all kinds do cause and induce. We know disease of stoppings and suffocations are the most dangerous in the body, and it is not much otherwise in the mind . . . But no receipt openeth the heart but a true friend: to whom you may impart griefs, joys, fears, hopes, suspicions, counsels, and whatsoever lieth upon the heart to oppress it, in a kind of civil . . . confession.'[30]

Only lately have social scientists begun to explore the value of this traditional wisdom and it is turning out to be surprisingly well founded. One study looked at men who had had a heart attack. They were asked who had helped them on their return home from hospital.[31] Most reported that the immediate family – wives, siblings and parents – had been most helpful. After them came in-laws, and next friends. Even neighbours had helped. The least helpful category seemed to be more distant family members such as cousins. Interestingly enough the scientists were originally going to ask only about practical help, but the men insisted that 'moral support' had been really helpful too. Friends scored high in this, while financial aid was more likely to come from within the family. Money aside, the survey concluded: 'In some instances, perhaps, friends and neighbours may actually function as quasi-kin, with the signs of solidarity and assistance exceeding those for some kin categories.' These findings tie in with the notion that family, friends and neighbours all have slightly different roles in our life. Neighbours are probably those to whom we turn in a short-term emergency, while family are thought of for long-term help or financial aid.[32]

After years of ignoring this informal network, or even of seeing it merely as an obstacle to proper professional help, social scientists are now beginning to see that it may have important benefits. That there is a link between friendlessness and absence of family ties, and mental illness is clear. Those who have close affectionate relationships with others are less likely to show various neurotic symptoms.[33] Proving that lack of affection produces neurosis is more difficult. One has to allow for the fact that some forms of mental illness will, in themselves, drive off friends. However one survey produced some 'soft evidence' for a causal link. Researchers visited some of their population more than once, and 'a number of respondents (sic) began to include our interviewers as significant members of their primary group in whom they could confide. Of those with difficulties or symptoms, some declared that our research interviews had been helpful in themselves.'[34]

The very act of confiding – what Bacon called 'a kind of civil shrift or confession' – seems to be therapeutic for many. Newspaper interviews, TV interviews and radio phone-ins may in this way be fulfilling a very useful function, quite apart from the passing on of information. In support of this idea is the evidence that warmth and empathy are an essential part of effective psychotherapy. Some statistics indicate that people are less likely to be mentally ill if their kin live nearby.[35] Those with a sociobiologist turn of mind argue that human sociability has evolved over millions of years in which we have lived in close communities, that we are evolutionarily adapted to human affection. Isolated from such affection we become mentally ill.

We may also become physically ill. An interesting study looked at people on a family doctor's list in Edinburgh.[36] They were asked about physical symptoms such as headache, back-ache, palpitations, dizziness and breathlessness, and also about mental symptoms such as tiredness, anxiety, depression and irritability. Those with close confidants experienced fewer mental symptoms. Even the number of acquaintances possessed by an individual made a difference. Women with many acquaintances had fewer mental or physical symptoms.

Quite how friendships and affectionate relationships protect against illness is far from clear. Past research has established that physical illnesses often follow some kind of stress like bereavement, unemployment, housing difficulties and so forth. In some way, the body seems made vulnerable by stress. It may be that the loving support of family and friends helps protect us against stress. The most spectacular of all findings came from California, where nearly seven thousand people were studied over nine years.[37] People who lacked 'social and community ties were more likely to die in the follow-up period than those with more extensive contacts.' The researchers tried to take into account age differences, health, economic status, obesity, alcohol intake, and dangerous habits such as smoking. Having a marriage partner protected both men and women from death – something we have noted in an earlier chapter. But contacts with close friends helped too. 'In every age and sex category people who report having few friends and relatives and/or see them infrequently have higher mortality rates than those people who have many friends and relatives and see them frequently.' Another interesting finding was the apparent interchangeability of relationships. 'For instance people who were not married but who had many friends and relatives were found to have mortality rates equal to those who were married but who had fewer contacts with friends and relatives. Similarly it did not seem important whether contacts were among friends or relatives; it was only in the absence of either of these sources of contact that there was a significant increase in the risk of death.'

Yet, despite their importance for us all, friendships cannot be forced. The mere presence of others is not enough. 'Little do men perceive what solitude is and how far it extendeth,' wrote Francis Bacon.[30] 'For a crowd is not company, and faces are but a gallery of pictures and talk but a tinkling cymbal where there is no love.' Just being in the company of others is not enough to cure loneliness. Four out of ten elderly women and men in a Belgian survey said that they felt alone and lonely, even though they were living with others around them in an old people's home. Among the elderly who were individually housed, and therefore physically more often alone, only one in four felt this way. The loneliness in an old people's home can be partly explained by the circumstances of the inmates, who are probably only there at all because they can't get family help. But even when there is a family tie, such people are visited less frequently – perhaps because their relatives think that they are 'well cared for' in a home, forgetting the need for love and affection as well as food and nursing.[38] These old people feel lonely and deserted, even though they are surrounded by others. Clearly their loneliness is nothing to do with the proximity of other human beings: it is the detection of a lack of love. The feeling of being lonely is usually a feeling of not being loved.

Loneliness is a torture for most people. Those who are forced to live without any kind of human contact suffer terribly. Christopher Burney, a member of the wartime Special Operations Executive, was caught by the Nazis in France and imprisoned by himself for more than eighteen months, not knowing whether he would be executed or not. Anxiety and the inadequacies of food and warmth added to his torment. But when suddenly some human contact was available, he found that he was reluctant to make the most of it. One day he was let out for exercise into a small yard about ten metres square. 'Fifteen of us were let out at one time . . . My cell was at the corner of the stairs: no. 238 went before me and no. 240 after me. The former was separated from me by the stairway and meant little to me . . . He was too far away for any trace of his existence to have reached me, and solitude had so far weaned me from the habit of intercourse, even the thin intercourse of speculation, that I could no longer see any relationship with another person, unless it were introduced gradually by a long overture of common trivialities. So no. 238 remained for ever only a human back for me. Even of no. 240, of whom I knew comparatively much, I can remember little except that he was young and grey of face and anxious to talk. He had tried to involve me in the tapping game,' through the cell walls, 'and to bribe me with news (for he was only recently captured) in order to lure me into conversation and perhaps commiseration. But I had no patience for this pastime which was tedious and unreliable and eased none of the real burdens of confinement and I had finally given up the pretence of answering . . . '[39]

In the exercise yard was a babble of conversation. Christopher Burney found that he had no wish to join it. 'I wanted to enjoy the newly discovered things about me and would have preferred to be alone to absorb the sky and grass and air, so that I felt a faint resentment at the noise and a fear that one of my neighbours would waste some of my precious minutes by talking to me, like those people who insist on whispering in concerts.' Finally as the clatter of the doors opening again told him that the brief excursion was over, he picked a small snail off the wall 'to serve as a companion and as a memorial'. His isolation had become so intense that when human company was suddenly offered, he could not take advantage of it. Even after a nearby prisoner had sent him food from parcels, Christopher Burney found it difficult to communicate with him when they finally met face to face for a short time. 'The moment was gone before I could construe my disordered thoughts into a sentence.' If I interpret his account correctly, then it suggests that solitude – like sociability – may be self-reinforcing. This seems to fit the dilemma experienced by those who write to agony aunts and others complaining of loneliness. Because they feel lonely inside, they find it difficult to make friends outside. Being unloved helps make them unable to love, and perhaps even unlovable.

5

Enduring Love or Sexual Excitement?

Past generations have often contrasted the fidelity and loyalty of friendship with the fickleness of sexual love. This contrast has been noticed by both men and women. 'Friendship is a serious affection; the most sublime of all affections because it is founded on principle and cemented by time,' wrote the early feminist Mary Wollstonecraft.[1] 'The very reverse may be said of love. In a great degree love and friendship cannot subsist in the same bosom; even when inspired by different objects they weaken or destroy each other, and for the same object can only be felt in succession. The vain fears and fond jealousies, the winds which fan the flame of love, when judiciously or artfully tempered, are both incompatible with the tender confidence and sincere respect of friendship.' In the Age of Reason, the eighteenth century, many would have united with her in seeing romantic and sexual love as a passing violent passion rather than a sincere respect. Yet in our own age, we try to combine both together in one relationship. We are encouraged to fall in love, then to marry the object of that love. And in marriage, we are told, a full and thrilling sex life can be found to equal any found outside. Indeed, if married sex does not keep up to a high standard, we are encouraged to seek the help of sex therapists to restore its excitement and full functioning. We want to have it all – enduring marriage, sincere respect and an exciting sex life.

'I believe the permanence of monogamous love-unions to be in the line of sexual evolution and to offer the strongest altruistic leaven to the primitive egotism of Nature's mighty urge,' wrote a Dutch gynaecologist, Theodor Van de Velde, in 1928. Like many other people then and now, Dr Van de Velde believed that the sexual urge was the strongest of all human instincts – stronger than hunger and stronger than fear. He was also convinced that it was one of the 'four corner-stones of the temple of love and happiness in marriage'. The result of his thinking was one of the world's best-selling marriage manuals, *Ideal Marriage.*[2] Dr Van de Velde explained: 'Vigorous and harmonious sexual activity constitutes the fourth corner-stone of our temple. It must be solidly and skilfully built, for it has to bear a main portion of the weight of the whole structure. But in many cases it is badly balanced and of poor materials; so can we wonder that the whole edifice collapses, soon? Sex is the foundation of marriage. Yet most people do not know the ABC of sex.' He was convinced that if only man learned to make love skilfully, marriages would stand a better chance of permanence.

In the years following 1928, his book has sold over a million copies and is still selling. Yet – with the occasional dip downwards for a few years – the divorce rate has soared. Others, notably the famous sex therapists Masters and Johnson, have followed in the tracks of Dr Van de Velde, anxious to do their bit for marriage. They have set up special sexual training programmes for men and women, where homework is a series of sex exercises and the aim is a well-oiled properly functioning sexuality. Men are helped to make and keep firm erections, while women are encouraged to produce the necessary orgasms which are a sign that sex is not dysfunctional. If things go wrong it is a sign of 'Human Sexual Inadequacy'.[3]

It is now fairly routine for some marriage-guidance counsellors to maintain that if the sex in a marriage is not up to a certain standard, then the marriage is in trouble. Hospital out-patient departments, family doctors and others now help their patients with their sex lives. Even celibate priests take courses so that they too can advise in this vital area. A great deal of this time and effort results from the widespread idea that making love is literally just that. Just as Dr Van de Velde was convinced that proper lovemaking would lead to more permanent mono-gamous love-unions, so some of today's marriage-guidance counsellors are convinced that if only they can get the sex right, then love will follow.

Yet the exact link between sex and love remains something of a mystery. We are not even sure exactly how and why sex works as it does, and there is a great deal of argument about whether certain behaviours and motivations are innate or learned. Despite this debate, there is now quite a large sex relations 'industry' of counsellors and other paramedical helpers, who do not seem to know the extent of their – and indeed everybody's – ignorance. I was once assured by a very charming sex counsellor that my retrograde views on sex stem from the way my mother had prevented me masturbating when I was a child. I told him that I never masturbated as a child, and that I had only discovered such an activity was possible at the age of nineteen or twenty. He told me that I was mistaken. I had repressed the memory. When I told him that my mother had not even known that female masturbation was a possibility until I enlightened her many years later, he merely assured me that he knew better. It *must* have happened. It was as impossible to argue with him, as it is to argue with Jehovah's Witnesses. His certainty was equal to theirs. The point is not that he held unproven beliefs, but that he believed in all sincerity that his opinions were based on scientific investigations. Those who appeal to the authority of the Bible and an unprovable God will not usually invoke science as well.

On the other hand, we have at least acquired a whole heap of statistics. Some of the best still come from the late Professor Alfred C. Kinsey who, during the 1930s and 1940s, compiled a great deal of information about the sex life of Middle-West Americans. His figures record who did what to whom, and how often. Since Kinsey, other research workers have collected a plethora of statistics from much smaller samples – largely made up of white American psychology students, as the population most available to research workers. Hardly unbiased results.

Two other key figures are Havelock Ellis and Sigmund Freud. Ellis went to a great deal of trouble to collect information, and to disseminate the idea that sex was a proper subject for study. Freud was the theoretician – ideologist, some might say – bent on accounting for man's behaviours.

But despite this accumulation of theory and statistic, we still have a fairly simple concept of sex. Most of us think of it as an appetite which demands satisfaction. Many talk of a 'sex drive', as if there was a kind of inner force welling up inside us, struggling to get out. Kinsey's terminology of 'sexual outlets' suggested that if this drive did not find a vent in sexual intercourse, it would be diverted into alternative channels such as masturbation or nocturnal emissions. If not, he warned, it could be harmful. All in all, the Kinsey model of sexuality was a system rather like some kind of hydraulic engine.

Our ideas about sex as appetite, instinct or 'drive', are not really all that new. Christianity has always acknowledged that the gratification of this urge is enjoyable. But today we are also convinced that its gratification is wholly good. I think the average medieval priest would have granted the pleasure of indulging the sexual instinct, but he would also have warned against its satisfaction outside marriage. Today we tend to think of any restraint on sex as bad.

Sexologists have also re-invented history to create an age of prudery. Ignoring the very open sexuality of the Victorian streets, they have maintained that our ancestors were all dangerously repressed. 'I believe that our culture is gradually convalescing from a sexually debilitating disease: Victorianism. The significant questions are the extent of our recovering to date, and the outlook for an ultimate cure. The essence of the disease is the belief that sex is wicked, loathsome and likely to lead to disaster. This produces a blockage of sexual response to normal erotic stimuli – and possibly also facilitiates an imprinting to perverse erotic stimuli,' writes one sexual-freedom enthusiast.[4] If this view was correct, ours should be an age characterised by 'normal' sex, and perverse erotic stimuli such as sadism and masochism should have withered away in the pure light of satisfied heterosexuality. Like those of the theoreticians who argued in favour of better lovemaking in the marital bed, such Utopian hopes were doomed to disappointment.

Philosophers of sex, like Alex Comfort, the talented writer of that highly popular manual *The Joy of Sex,* have felt that sex has a secret which can transform society.[5] Sex, he argues, forges bonds between people. It is a short cut to intimate relationships. Indeed, sexual relationships may be more intimate than non-sexual ones and may even come to replace the family – or lead to a new kind of family, a brotherhood of orgasm and pleasure.

He hopes that our society 'might find that the relation present in purely recreational or social sex is a uniquely effective tool in breaking down personal separateness – of which the proprietary notion of love is an offshoot – so that, for us as for many primitives, social sex comes to express and cement the equivalent of kinship through a general intimacy and non-defensiveness, reinforced by the very strong reward of realising suppressed needs for variety and acceptance'.[6] It is a high-minded idea. The universal brotherhood of man is to be found in recreational sex. 'Besides reinstating the kinship of men and women, a wider and opener use of sexuality is quite likely to reinstate and reinforce the kinship between men and men, which we studiously avoided erotizing or expressing.'[6]

In the new world of open sexuality, jealousy would wither away. 'Sexuality will become polymorphic, similar in some ways to the diffused sensuality children experience but with the added dimension of sexual communion possible on a variety of levels. No longer will we be obsessed with our anxiety-ridden compulsion to perform genitally at every opportunity. Genital intercourse, both marital and comarital, may be less frequent than now but, integrated in a diffused sensuality, it might well be more valued and enjoyed', wrote Robert and Anna Francoeur in a book titled *Woman in the Year 2 000.*[7]

Other writers are clearer in what they hope for. James Ramey sees a short cut to friendship: 'The current forays into sexual alternatives to monogamy are seen as attempts to build a more complex network of intimate relationships that can absorb some of the impact of the new found complexity of the pair-bond, by short-circuiting the process of developing ancillar relationships in the usual ritual manner. It is believed that this occurs for two reasons: (1) because there is not time to go through a long process of finding a group that needs the roles the couple can fill and (2) because using sexual intimacy as an entry role guarantees the couple that, other things being equal, they can fill that role. Particularly if such ties are to take up the slack of the unavailable kin-neighbor-friendship relational systems, as well as relieve some of the pressure on the newly complex pair-bond interaction, they must begin on a much deeper, more intimate basis than the ties they replace.'[8] Whatever their specific message, these prophets of a brave new world are united in the assumption that having sexual intercourse automatically makes for emotional intimacy and that sex creates love.

Some confusion between sexual and emotional intimacy can be forgiven. Looking at the act in a detached way, an onlooker might assume that intercourse was a kind of bonding mechanism. Certainly it ordinarily uses the body language of love, first developed between mother and infant. Lovers look into each other's eyes a great deal. They caress each other with the same kisses and nuzzles. Indeed normally in our society sexual intercourse only takes place between men and women who feel intimate and friendly. Most couples will have shared some time together, and probably had some conversation before they get into bed. 'While many Americans now use forms of foreplay and coital variations that were shunned by the previous generation, and while they take a somewhat more unfettered enjoyment in their own sensations, by and large they have added to their repertoire only acts that are biologically and pyschologically free from pathology, they have remained highly discriminating in the choice of their sexual partners, and they have continued to regard their sexual acts as having deep emotional significance rather than as merely providing uncomplicated sensuous gratification', reported one of the more recent large-scale surveys of sex.[9]

From this, it has sometimes been concluded that human beings are naturally pair-bonding. Dr Van de Velde felt permanent monogamous unions were a form of evolutionary development. Desmond Morris has taken much the same line of argument. When mankind started to go on hunting parties away from the home base, the sexes had to become more distinct. 'For a virile primate male to go off on a feeding trip and leave his females unprotected from the advances of any other males that might happen to come by was unheard of . . . The answer was the development of a pair-bond. Male and female hunting apes had to fall in love and remain faithful to one another.' Women became sexually available all year round, instead of just in the breeding season. They developed breasts, as a substitute for brightly-coloured genitals. Face to face sex was the natural result, so that sex became personalised. Finally, the female orgasm developed. 'Like all the other improvements in sexuality this will serve to strength the pair-bond and maintain the family unit.'[10] According to this interpretation, human sexuality works towards permanency, monogamy, and happy family life. It is an optimistic view of sex.

There is now a spate of books about the evolution of sex, and clearly there is plenty of room for disagreement. It is difficult to argue pair-bonding is a 'natural' human behaviour, when we know so little about the early natural history of prehistoric man – though there is some evidence that early man carried home his animal prey to feed women and children.[11] But there is also quite a lot of evidence that men and women are different in their approach to sex. I find this a painful admission. If only men were more like women! No doubt men wish just the opposite. Yet treating men and women as if their sexual motivations and behaviour were exactly the same usually results in difficulties for one or other sex.

If we look to our fellow mammals, 'natural' sex certainly does not seem to mean indiscriminate mating. True promiscuity is rare. Experiments with beagles have shown that individual dogs and bitches have their preferences – indeed the results read rather like a soap opera. Blanche, Kate and Peggy – three bitches brought into season with hormones – were kept confined, and the three males – Ken, Eddie and Broadus – were allowed to visit them at will. 'When the scores for the three males are averaged, the order of preference is seen to be Kate — Blanche — Peggy.'[12] In the next test, the three dogs were tied up and the females were free to visit them. 'Peggy clearly avoided Ken, and in this test situation Kate was not strongly attracted to Broadus . . . Eddie tended to be the favoured male as far as Kate and Peggy were concerned, whereas Blanche was relatively impartial treating all three males more or less equally.' In the same way, stud animals often develop preferences. Bulls will sometimes show a distinct preference for cows of a particular colour. [13]

Monkeys and apes show the same choosiness. At first, naturalists studying their behaviour felt that some species were virtually indiscriminate in their mating. 'In multi-male groups mating often appears to be promiscuous: closer study, however, usually shows that this is not the case. Three kinds of constraint are to be found – dominance, and kinship, and affiliative relations.'[14] 'Affiliative relations' refers to 'consort behaviour', that is when a male and female go off together for a time. This relationship may last for only a few hours or, in the case of captive rhesus monkeys, nearly for life. Gibbons live in nuclear families consisting of one male, one female and the infants.

However, ethology is not all that relevant here – human beings do not behave as monogamously as gibbons. Monogamy probably predominates in practice – even in polygamous societies most men only have one wife – but marriage is only part of the picture.[13] It is clear that in monogamous societies a man may quite often have liaisons with women other than his wife. Almost all large human societies have to make arrangements not just for unofficial liaisons but also for fairly impersonal sex. Victorian England had scores of brothels, and prostitutes stood in rows down various streets. Even in the land of sexual freedom, California, prostitutes have by no means gone out of business. This appetite for sex without any kind of emotional bond whatsoever is traditionally a male one. The women involved usually provide their services for economic reasons.

This distinction seems to maintain in the gay world too. Homosexuality produced a thriving sub-culture of bath houses where sexual contact was, if not indiscriminate, then largely without any emotional content. Men would 'make love' with other men whose names they did not know. Bath houses were often run on a system whereby the old, the ugly and sometimes the black were excluded. 'If you did not look beautiful, then they asked for your membership card,' a friend told me. 'There were no membership cards, of course. So you were thus excluded.' In one survey almost half the gay males had had five hundred or more partners. Female homosexuality, in contrast, is often characterised by close, even monogamous friendships between women – the survey found that most gay women had had fewer than ten partners.[15] While there are notable exceptions to those, as to all sexual averages, it is difficult to ignore the implications of these findings, which can hardly be explained away by conditioning. After all, there is no reason why lesbians should want their sex combined with love, just as there is no reason why gay men should be so concerned with relatively impersonal sex – both are operating outside the heterosexual customs of monogamy.

Where does the female orgasm fit into the male pattern of sexuality? All surveys show that some women never have orgasms, and that a proportion have them rarely or only occasionally. There is even a Victorian survey which suggests that Victorian women were orgasmic or non-orgasmic in roughly the same kind of proportion as women are today. [16] The idea that female sexuality must be like male sexuality, with sexual excitement normally culminating in orgasm, is not born out by the facts. Indeed, sexual intercourse may not be suited to female orgasm. [17] Women seem mostly to need clitoral stimulation to reach it. Anthropologist Margaret Mead speculated: 'That whole societies can ignore climax as an aspect of female sexuality must be related to a very much lesser biological basis for such a climax . . . There seems therefore to be a reasonable basis for assuming that the human female's capacity for orgasm is to be viewed much more as a potentiality that may or may not be developed by a given culture, or in the specific life history of an individual than as an inherent part of her full humanity.' [18]

Significantly for those who claim that orgasm is essential for close pair-bonding, women seem well able to form emotional bonds without orgasms. Were orgasms of such vital importance, one would expect men to be best at forming bonds since they have more reliable orgasms. I am myself convinced by the argument that the female orgasm is merely 'a byproduct of mammalian bisexual potential; orgasms may be possible for female mammals because it is adaptive for males.' [19] The bodily machinery is there in some women because if they had been born as men, it would have been needed to produce ejaculation. Like the male's nipples, the female's capacity to orgasm is a relic of the original egg's male potential.

The evolutionary hypothesis maintains that the differences in sexual behaviour between men and women have evolved to promote the survival of their genes. [20] The female can only produce a certain number of offspring in her lifetime, and there is for her no evolutionary advantage in mating with scores of extra males. With the long period of infant dependence, what she needs is not the constant excitement of gang bangs, but reliable help in child rearing. The male, however, can increase the chance of his genes surviving by mating with as many females as possible. It may be well worth his evolutionary while to sneak into the beds of females apparently possessed by other males and leave a cuckoo in the nest. This would suggest that the idea of a 'sex drive' is at least applicable to men. Kinsey had the simple idea that this was an urge which, if it were diverted from the outlet of sexual intercourse, would simply flow into another outlet such as masturbation or wet dreams. But on the the whole this hydraulic model of sexuality is too simple. His own figures show that individuals do not simply switch from one outlet to another.[21] Prisoners who are shut away from women do not immediately show a masturbation rate high enough to fulfill the number of orgasms that their previous 'drive' in freedom would seem to require. The amount of sexual stimulation in the environment will affect their sexual appetite. Indeed there is evidence that men can, if they badly want to, reduce their sexual appetites. The experience of celibate priests and Christian men wishing to lead celibate lives suggests that this becomes easier with practice. 'Total abstinence from orgasm does, I think, produce increased frustration for the first few days if one is not used to it, but when I got to a period of three or four months without orgasms the frustration grew less not more,' reported one young Christian to me.

These objections aside, Kinsey did reveal what seemed to be a very regular pattern of orgasms among his male subjects. Given that sexual stimulation is available, men often show regularity of sexual behaviour over a period of a decade or more. William H. James, the British psychologist who has made a lifetime study of coital frequencies, has examined a variety of diaries kept by people who record their sexual activities. The frequency varies between once or twice a month to once or twice a day, but the regularity over years is remarkable.[22]

The optimistic view of this male appetite is that it will help keep men and women together in a close and loving relationship. The famous American sex therapists William H. Masters and Virginia E. Johnson entitled their second book *The Pleasure Bond,* with reference to this idea.[23] They passionately believed that sex was an important component of the marriage bond, and if it could be 'cured' of any disfunctions, the marriage would be enhanced. Yet the evidence, such as it is, does not bear them out.

Our own experience teaches us that affection and sexual desire can operate quite independently of each other. It is possible to desire somebody to whom one is indifferent, or not to desire somebody for whom one feels strong affection. And studies of young people dating show that having sex seemed to make no difference to their chances of staying together.[24,][25] Thus, using sex to 'land' a man – whether by granting or withholding favours – would seem an ineffective gambit. A study of group marriage was particularly interested to see whether communal sex strengthened bonds. The researchers' hypothesis was that this would be so. But 'we did not find that group sex within the group was reported more often in extant groups than in dissolved ones'.[26]

And whatever it is that cements bonds within conventional marriage, it can hardly be sex as about one in a hundred couples have none at all, and the proportion is higher among older couples.[27] Sexless marriages are usually not the happier ones, it is true. Indeed one would expect that a complete absence of sex might be a sign of ill feeling. 'You don't enjoy sex if you don't get on with someone do you?' a divorced woman said sensibly to the sociologist who was interviewing her.[28] So sexual difficulties may well be a marker for emotional ones. But the idea that putting the sex right will automatically put the emotions right seems ill founded. There are marriages which are extremely unhappy where the sex is up to a very high standard indeed.[29] One major British hospital, which set up a sex therapy clinic along modified Masters and Johnson lines, came to the conclusion that they should spend more time dealing with people's feelings. 'The high frequency of serious marital problems in our couples, and of marital breakdown at follow-up, suggests that the clinic could usefully focus upon marital as well as, or rather than, sex therapy in many instances.'[30]

On the other hand, all other things being equal, most sexual relationships that take place over more than a few hours of time will result in affectionate feelings. If mere proximity is often the cause of friendship, then sex should produce friendly feelings between those who are sharing beds together. Thus the undoubted affection one sees between many couples is probably the result of the time spent together rather than the shared orgasms. It is noticeable that the advice given for a happy marriage usually stresses the importance of shared interests – a point that seems to have been well taken by those interested in communes and group marriages. A study by James Ramey, an American academic, noted that much time was spent in non-sexual activities.[31] 'Study groups tackled a number of potential projects, for example, setting up a free school, converting a brownstone, running encounter groups, discussing the ins and outs of a subchapter-S corporation, setting up a baby-sitting co-op, building a boat, establishing food co-ops, setting up invest-ment pools, buying condominiums and co-ops, building co-ops, discussing non-profit corporation and foundation structure, establishing art and drama groups for the kids, and setting up a home-exchange program.' It is hardly surprising that researchers have found solidarity and emotional intimacy within such marriage alternatives. So much talking will almost inevitably lead to warm relationships, regardless of sex. If sex alone were responsible, then brothels and group sex establishment should be havens of friendship!

For those who hope that sex will bond men and women in monogamy, there is a further great disappointment. In male sexual desire – and perhaps in female too – there is a built-in lack of permanence. It is called the Coolidge Effect, after the story told of the American president and his wife. The Coolid-ges were taken off on separate tours of a government farm. When Mrs Coolidge passed the chicken pens, she asked the man in charge if the rooster copulated more than once daily. 'Dozens of times' she was told. 'Please tell that to the President,' said Mrs Coolidge. When the President got to the chicken pens, he was duly told of the rooster's prowess. 'Same hen every time?' he asked. 'Oh no,' he was told, 'a different one each time.' The President nodded thoughtfully. 'Tell that to Mrs Coolidge,' he said.

The Coolidge Effect is common in many male mammals. The male will cease to copulate, but his sexual desire is roused afresh if a new female is produced. Surveys among humans show that in marriages the amount of sex between a couple declines with time, even allowing for age.[32] The most rapid decline is in the first year of marriage in which the coital rate halves. In the next

twenty years or so, it will halve again. Men, like other
mammals, will be particularly aroused by fresh partners and be
significantly less aroused by a familiar partner, however dearly
loved. Thus male desire is characterised by a tendency which
runs counter to the ideal of close monogamous bonding.

It is not very clear to what extent the Coolidge Effect applies
to women, as the sexual tempo of a relationship will often take
its pace from the male partner. One intriguing finding, however,
came from a London menopause clinic. Only 13.5% of the
women there did *not* have a 'sexual problem' – and of these,
one out of three had new sexual partners, either new husbands
or new lovers.[33] Thus, it could be argued that the best sex
therapy for those who are having problems is simply a new
partner.

One British sex therapist has been brave enough to face this
dilemma, and to write about it honestly. Sexual problems
sometimes melt away with a new person in bed, argues Dr
Martin Cole, who sometimes uses a surrogate sex partner to
show just this. He also believes that some of the couples who
drop out of treatment, may be dropping out in order to save the
relationship.[34] 'Some reflection, however, might have led them
to the conclusion that the very qualities of the relationship
which enabled it to survive were the same qualities which led to
sexual alienation. Trying to change the nature of the relationship, even if it were possible, which is most unlikely, would lead
to its breakdown because they would no longer need each other
– a high price to pay for any possible improvement in sexual
response.'

Thus trying to combine exciting sex and an enduring marriage
may in many cases be doomed to failure. As the relationship
endures, and the affection deepens, the sexual side becomes less
exciting. Some husbands try to counteract this by buying their
wives frilly nighties and peek-a-boo bras – they hope by dressing
up the familiar body in an unfamiliar way to recapture some of
the excitement they have lost. Others become family, rather
than lover, to their wives – we have all come across couples who
call themselves 'Mum' and 'Dad' – and so complete the process
by invoking the ancient taboo of incest.

Utopian sexual liberators of the 1970s hoped that freer sexual
arrangements might take into account this male need for

variety, while keeping the close friendship of more conventional marriages. Yet the communes and group marriages studied were relatively impermanent arrangements. There is on record one thirty-seven-year-old group marriage, so permanence is not impossible. [35] But the sixteen group marriages studied by the Constantines included eleven which dissolved fairly early on, 'three of them before more than nominal contact had been made'. [26] It should be remembered, of course, that group marriages exist in a society which is unsympathetic and sometimes hostile to their very existence. But the very fact that they have not managed to overturn public opinion and catch on in great numbers, suggests to me that in practice they did not work very well, even before AIDS came along.

Another arrangement designed to cater for sexual variety but also to produce emotional bonding was the Californian establishment known as Sandstone. This was a kind of sexual country club, where the living-room resembled a literary salon attended by the great names of the sexual freedom movement, while in the room below was an on-going orgy. [36] Dr Alex Comfort has described Sandstone in his book *More Joy of Sex.* 'The essential point is that in spite of enthusiastic sex on all sides it was wholly unlike a brothel and wholly like a relaxed home, the keynote not being excitement or lasciviousness but innocence, once the freakout produced by strangers in its openness was over.' One doctor described it as 'the finishing school for psychoanalysisys.' Dr. Comfort felt it produced 'the revival of playfulness, childishness and personhood in the group'. There was 'tribal feeling', and people got increased self-esteem. More contentiously, he argued that stereotypes of ugliness, age and fatness were shown to be inappropriate since everybody got a lot of sex. There is no doubt that for Dr Comfort Sandstone seems to have produced what he argued we needed – a combination of sexual variety and warm emotional feelings. [37]

But this new sexual openness seems to have been established within a coterie of wealthy, rather carefully chosen people. James R. Smith and Lynn G. Smith, researchers who are sympathetic to the 'comarital sex' movement, were less impressed with Sandstone. 'It combined the imagery and equipage of the Playboy world with overt group nudity, group

sex, and a lively cocktail party atmosphere.' Brochures adver-
tised 'openness' and 'honesty, sharing and freedom from the
artificial'. Yet there was a fifty per cent discount for single
women, and selection took into account not only the ability to
pay a fairly high membership fee but also the looks and backgrounds of couples. 'Losers were screened out and effectively, if
not directly asked to leave: "beautiful couples" were eagerly
recruited.' Far from being a new kind of warm sexual
behaviour, to the Smiths it looked suspiciously like the old
sexual behaviour only more of it. Women wore chic clothes,
had elaborately careful hair-dos, and expensive jewellery. 'The
men played characteristic sex roles, initiating contacts, encouraging female participation, manipulating female-female
contacts and competing for access to the more desirable
women.'[38] In the Smiths' eyes, stereotypes were confirmed
rather than smashed.

For those in search of sex only, there is nothing wrong in this.
Just as gay bath houses screen out the old or unattractive, so
group sex establishments may well feel that the ugly, the poor,
the old and the physically disabled are not welcome. For there is
no doubt at all that male sexuality is marked by the capacity to
be turned on – and thus presumably off – by visual stimuli.
The same tendency to screen out couples who are ugly, old or of
the wrong race occurs among 'swingers', and wife swappers.
Among the rather conventional swingers of the Middle West,
blacks were excluded from swinging parties, as were unmarried
men and women. 'Age plays an extremely important role in
acceptance or rejection for swinging. Although informants
almost universally verbalize that age is unimportant, in reality
they tend to reject couples who are more than ten years older
than themselves . . . with the emphasis on youth in our culture
today, it was important to appear young and our interviewees
were reluctant to give exact ages,' reported Gilbert Bartell.[39] A
study of swingers in the San Diego area came to the same
conclusions about age. The researcher added: 'The closest
thing to a universalistic factor of acceptance among swingers is
physical attractiveness . . . However an unattractive couple
would not experience universal rejection, for unattractiveness
is much more particularistic in nature – one man's weed being
another man's flower.'[40]

If we put together the various studies of group sex establishments and of group sexual activities, the picture is remarkably like that of sexuality in general: youth and beauty are at a premium, with love having little or no role to play.

There are also strong health disadvantages in sex between relative strangers – disadvantages which were rarely mentioned by those who felt that group sex was an important activity. Even before AIDS it was clear to less optimistic thinkers that the problems of contraception had not been solved. Group sex seems to have relied upon the widespread use of oral contraception, the least messy and most effective of the options. In the 1970s, the dangers of the pill to smokers and older women were not evident, nor were the complications of the IUD. But it was already clear that contraception would never be one hundred per cent effective while fallible human beings were using it. Unwanted pregnancy would remain a risk. Women thus stood to lose more from impersonal sex than did men.

Indeed most women seem to have joined in not because they were keen on getting the sex involved, but as a gesture of faith towards their partner. A study of drop-outs from swinging showed that 'the wife was most likely the one to respond that she could not take it or threatened divorce'. Most surveys have shown, too, that men are the most likely to initiate swinging. 'These findings question some additional beliefs concerning swinging. The first is that swinging emphasizes sexual equality and that swinging greatly benefits the wives . . . Some investigators have argued, however, that women once they "get their feet wet" enjoy swinging more than men. The findings here do not support that view: dropping out was initiated by the wives fifty-four per cent of the time, by the husbands thirty-four per cent, and mutually twelve per cent.' The marriage counsellors who were asked about swinging drop-outs they had counselled, reported that 'wives were forced into swinging as a promise or commitment to the marriage'. Here perhaps is another example of the fundamental sexual incompatibility between men and women. [41]

All in all, the idea that women are 'naturally' sexually insatiable and that this raving sexuality has been suppressed by men, does not seem to have much supporting evidence. [19] It seems far more likely that there is a real incompatibility between the sexual desire and behaviour of men and women. If this is so, we should not expect sex to be a very efficient mechanism of bringing the two together in a happy way. 'Sex is an antisocial force in evolution. Bonds are formed between individuals in spite of sex and not because of it,' wrote Edward O. Wilson. [19]

There remains the difficult question of psychological health and sexual activity. Traditionally, sex counsellors have tended towards the Kinsey view that lack of sexual outlet will produce mental difficulties. Equally traditionally, moralists have argued that monogamous couples are superior in maturity. As an investigation of friendship shows, people do need the love and warmth of others. Those without it may be at greater risk of going mad or dying prematurely. Yet often in our society sex and love go hand in hand. Single people may well have difficulty in finding either love or sex.

Volunteer celibates, however, do not seem to be badly affected in their minds. A large study of Catholic priests in the USA had to conclude that 'there is no way . . . that the priest population can be described as psychologically sick'. [42] The average Catholic priest had much the same psychological make-up as the average American male – neither better nor worse. Of course, the circumstances of celibate priests are exceptional. They have a great many potentially affectionate contacts in their lives – loving parishioners, colleagues – and the satisfaction of helping and loving others. There is besides their love for God, and assurance of His love in return. Thus, the timidity and apathy Kinsey noted in a group of males with low sexual outlets, who were 'afraid of approaching other persons for sexual relations, afraid of condemnation . . . or afraid of self-condemnation', is less likely to have been the direct result of lack of orgasm than that of a fear of human contact – which in turn led to a low number of orgasms. [20] If lack of sex damaged mental health, then there would be a very large number of Catholic priests and nuns in mental hospitals.

And, by inference, swingers should be exceptionally well balanced. Certainly they do not seem to be particularly psychologically unhealthy. [43] There is some evidence, however, that their sexual behaviour may be associated with a lack of love.

Swingers in two surveys reported that their relationships with parents were not as good as they were among the more sexually conventional couples.[43, 44] Swingers also visit relatives and kin less often, though they seem to have adequate numbers of friends.[44] Those in favour of swinging feel that the lack of family ties results in 'social controls' being less firmly established in the swinger, which in turn leads to swinging. I personally wonder whether swingers are perhaps in search of the quasi-kin group that utopian liberators like Dr Alex Comfort feel might be found in group sex. Indeed, some swingers report that there *is* a swinging network which can be activated, for instance, when visiting other cities. Swinging groups may offer the same kind of friendship that is also to be found in non-sexual clubs and organisations, where people with a shared interest come together. Alas, for the ugly, the poor and the old, swinging is a poor prospect for those in search of love – or even for those in search of sex.

Taken all in all, it is difficult to have much confidence in the view that sexual activity and efficiency is the sine qua non for love. For the young, the attractive and the moneyed, it may be that sexual activity will have pay-offs other than merely orgasms. But the affection, kindness and intimacy found in a group sex establishment or at swinging parties are no greater than the love and affection found in women's institutes, men's supporters clubs, church groups, youth clubs, or horticultural societies. Wherever time and interests are shared between people there will be some affection. The addition of sex is merely the addition of sex. It does not produce love of itself and since men and women may well be somewhat incompatible in this area, an emphasis on sex may even reduce the chances of a permanent and abiding love.

Yet the illusion remains that in relationships sex is all-important, and great efforts are made to ensure youngsters know all about it. Sometimes the knowledge is wonderfully and tragically irrelevant. As a nineteen-year-old girl who had attempted suicide explained: 'I fell for this boy Steve, and I was only fifteen when we got engaged, secret engagement, you know, but then he went off with my mate and I felt so rotten. I went to live with Terry who was twenty-seven . . . and then I got pregnant and Stacy was born, and I tried to kill myself then because he said he'd gone off me when I was pregnant, and he thought I was repulsive and ugly . . . I didn't think life would be like that. Nobody told me a thing. I knew about sex, everybody knows about sex. It's people you don't know about. Why is it, I sit and ask myself all the while, people can be so cruel and terrible to each other and even the ones that they love? That's the big mystery. Nobody told me about that.'[45]

Today the sexual liberators and gurus are in retreat in the face of AIDS. Though efforts still are being made to claim that it is a gay illness only, the spread of AIDS in Africa shows how it can thrive among heterosexuals. Casual sex, multiple partners, sex with prostitutes and group sex all carry a greater likelihood of AIDS HIV and subsequent AIDS infection than monogamy. The trend-setting heterosexual group sex establishments have closed down, as have the gay bath houses. Nobody can claim in good conscience that casual and impersonal sex is free from health risks.

But then it never was. The research cited in this chapter was carried out and published well before AIDS was discovered. It was already clear that sex was not a cure-all for mankind's feelings of inner loneliness and alienation. The danger now is that those 1970's years of indiscriminate sexual activity will become a mythical "golden age." While group sex establishments, group marriages and swinging were still in vogue, people could join them and see for themselves if they gained a new kind of emotional intimacy, as well as a lot of sex. Now such establishments and such activities are rarely if ever on offer. The claims of sex gurus cannot be tested. It is an irony that AIDS arrived just in time to get the sexual liberators off the hook.

Well before AIDS it was clear that impersonal sex couldn't deliver some of the promises. It was no substitute for love. It did not usher in a new kind of emotional intimacy. It merely ushered in a new crop of minor sexual diseases and a lot of gonorrhea— even before AIDS. Indeed the high value our society placed on sexual excitement and faultless sexual performance weakened, rather than strengthened, our ability to love one another.

6

Marriage, Divorce and the Disruption of Love

Most of the 'open' marriages, group marriages and communes of the optimistic 1970s have split up years ago. The combination of maximum sexual excitement with loving intimacy proved difficult to sustain in such complex relationships. But things are no easier, it seems, in pairs. For many of the conventional marriages of the same date will have ended too. 'Two developments in the 1960s and 1970s have weakened the force of the permanent union . . . ' wrote Edward Shorter in *The Making of the Modern Family*. 'First the intensification of the couple's erotic life . . . has injected a huge chunk of high explosive into their relationship. Because sexual attachment is notoriously unstable, couples resting atop such a base may easily be blown apart. To the extent that erotic gratification is becoming a major element in the couple's collective existence, the risk of marital dissolution increases . . . Second, women are becoming more independent economically, and can afford to extract themselves from undesired unions . . . With the ability to support themselves came the ability to be free.'[1] Edward Shorter's informed guess about the reasons for today's decline in stable marriage seems to me close to the mark, though no doubt other factors play their part. Whatever the reasons, marriage today is in very poor health indeed – so much so that we are strictly no longer a monogamous society. 'Sequential polygamy' is practised by a growing proportion of women and men.

The raw statistics are appalling. In Britain one in three of the couples marrying in 1982 could expect to be divorced; in the

USA nearly half those marriages will end in divorce.[2] In 1981 the number of American divorces reached an enormous record high of 1,219,000, though in the following two years a small decline set in.[3, 4] There is a further frightening trend. Those who have divorced once frequently divorce again. Thus in 1977 an American man's first marriage lasted an average of 7.5 years, his second for only 4.8 years and his third for only 3.5 years.[5] The divorcing population seems unable to learn by experience, and a population of habitual divorcers seems to have sprung up. Britain and the USA are not the only countries with rising divorce rates. In France the number of divorces doubled between 1970 and 1979.[6] Nor are high divorce rates the monopoly of the affluent West. In Eastern Europe, Africa, Asia and the Middle East marriages are even shorter-lived.[5]

Many people argue that the divorce figures do not really matter. Taking comfort from its long pedigree, they point out that divorce can be traced back to the Hittites in 1200 BC and the Babylonians in 2000 BC.[7] They also argue convincingly that in more recent historical times there has been plenty of unofficial divorce among the poor, whether by customs such as wife sale or by simple desertion. In 1570, in the city of Norwich in Britain, eight per cent of indigent women in their eighties were deserted wives.

Even when lifelong marriage was the rule, the lifetimes were much shorter. Up to one third of the marriages in Stuart England, for instance, were second or later marriages for at least one of the partners.[8] In early nineteenth-century Britain one in three marriages were broken up by death in the first fifteen years – a faster degree of marriage dissolution than the current divorce rate. 'It seems safe to assume that among the bulk of the population the median duration of marriage in Early Modern England was probably somewhere about seventeen to twenty years.'[9] The pattern of consecutive legal polygamy was thus little different from our own – except that death rather than divorce intervened between marriages.

Some may also take comfort in the fact that a rising divorce rate is nothing new. In the USA, for instance, there has been a more or less steady increase since the Civil War. Looked at in the context of the century as a whole, our current sharp increase in divorce does not look so startling. What has made the recent rise so rapid, is that there was, both in the USA and in Britain, a sudden drop in divorce in the 1950s. Thus if current divorce figures are compared with the 1950s, an unnecessarily gloomy picture emerges. [10]

Optimists take the view that the nuclear family and the mono-gamous marriage can look after themselves without any inter-ference by state or do-gooders. [7] Somehow there is a family instinct in the mass of men and women, which means the family will survive whatever the social conditions. As a corrective to hysteria about divorce, this view is useful. But overall, it seems to me, its optimism is not well founded. Should we be content with the idea that marriage is no more stable than it was in primitive peasant England? Is it a good enough defence for sequential polygamy to argue that in conditions of poverty, disease and death it thrives?

Optimists forget the sheer unhappiness of those who divorce. For society, there is the cost of suicides, alcoholism, accidents, violence, the physical and mental illnesses which afflict divorced men, and to a lesser extent divorced women. For the individual, there is an acute sense of failure, shame and guilt. Though it is nearly two decades ago, I can still remember my pain at the time my marriage broke down. I had an acute feeling of failure – a feeling which comes back to life, if I allow myself to dwell on the past. What haunts me still is the anxiety of whether I might have done more to keep the marriage going. Those who want to justify divorce rightly argue that it may be the lesser of two evils. Unhappy marriages which persist for years have their own pains. They may for instance drive women to suicide attempts. [11] They certainly account for much unhappiness.

Good marriages, on the other hand, do marvels for most human beings. As we have seen, living alone is a health hazard to which men are particularly vulnerable. A huge study of ten thousand Israeli men showed that a loving supporting wife could act as protection against her husband developing angina pectoris. [12] And though the joys of sex will not make us mentally healthy, the joys of a loving marriage will – as well as defend us against premature death. [13] 'When I was a bachelor I used to write a lot of poetry,' an old man once told my husband. 'Since I married my wife, I have lived a poem.' There are few poems to long-lasting married love, and few fictional portraits either. The joys of marriage, indeed, are often taken for granted by happy couples, who seem to feel that their mutual and lasting love is something so natural that they need not explain it. Happy the marriage which has no history, runs the old motto. After one unhappy marriage, I have been fortunate enough to find myself in a happy one and I still cannot get over my luck. I think of it, indeed, as a close friendship rather than some permanent romance. It is a kind of shelter against the unhappiness of the world outside, a comfort and a consolation. I would not now change that for all the romantic excitements in the world. Let others have them. 'Oh, the deep deep peace of the marriage bed after the hurly-burly of the *chaise-longue*' sighed the Edwardian actress Mrs Patrick Campbell. It is a kind of betrayal of that happiness to pretend divorce does not matter.

There is another important consideration to be weighed – the happiness of the children concerned. Once it was acknowledged that many couples stayed together 'for the sake of the children'. Nowadays it is no longer fashionable. It is often argued that children are miserable in a marriage which is obviously quarrel-some and unhappy. Divorce will be in their interests too. It will put an end to the tension surrounding them, and perhaps provide a loving step-parent. This is partly true. Children coming from quarrelsome and unloving homes suffer while the marriage continues. During adolescence, the boys are likely to fall foul of the law, the girls of sex – they run a higher risk of illegitimate pregancy.[14] The National Society for the Prevention of Cruelty to Children in Britain have identified what they call 'yo-yo children', who are used as pawns in the violent marriage of their parents. These children are permanently on the move – they are taken away from home by the runaway wife, brought back by her, turned out with her by the husband, placed for a few days with grandparents. They 'can never be sure they will go to sleep at night in the same house in which they awoke in the morning'.[15] For these and other children from very unhappy homes, the divorce of their warring parents can be a relief – if it means an end to the conflict.[16]

But unfortunately, for some it does not. In an American study, one in three children were aware of intense bitterness still persisting between their divorced parents. Divorce can even worsen their situation when the bitterness that follows exceeds the bitterness of the marital conflict; or when they find themselves in the care of a parent who cannot cope, or is mentally ill. 'For forty per cent of the mothers the relationship with the children had deteriorated or remained poor following the divorce.'[17] In a two-parent home, the existence of a bad parent may be compensated for by the care and love of the other. Children who are wholly in the care of an unloving mother, for instance, will be worse off than those who have a father on hand to help them.

All this ignores one other salient point. Children can be happy in homes where the parents are unhappy. 'A surprisingly large percentage of the children considered their homes happy or very happy before they learned that their parents would separate or divorce,' concluded a 1960 study, and later researches have confirmed this.[18] A recent small study of children in Britain showed that though half of them remembered their parents arguing, most of them would have preferred living in the marriage as it was. Only one in ten said they were unhappy while their parents were still living together. Many of the children also remembered their unhappiness and anger at the time of separation. Some felt they had to hide their feelings from their parents. 'I was really upset deep down when I knew my dad was away for good. But I just kept it to myself, I never showed my feelings.' Worst of all was the comment from a boy who said to the researcher, 'You're the first person who's ever bothered to ask me how I felt.'[19] We are fooling ourselves if we try to believe that divorce is not painful for children. My own parents were bitterly unhappy together and on the whole it was better, not just for them but for us children too, that they should part. But we suffered at the time.

A brief period of stress and unhappiness would not matter much, if we could be sure children recover from it without long-term damage. But can we? Many children seem able to cope, if the divorce really does mean an end to conflict, and if they are still in touch with two loving parents. But the American researchers found 'over one-third of the children to be consciously and intensely unhappy and dissatisfied with their life in the postdivorce family . . . Seventeen per cent felt rejected and unloved by the mother and thirty-nine per cent felt rejected and unloved by the father . . . We found thirty-seven per cent of all the children and adolescents to be moderately to severely depressed . . . We were struck as well by the high incidence of intense loneliness . . . ' [17] These are horrifying results, which are frequently ignored by writers on divorce. We want to believe that adults' and children's needs coincide, but perhaps they simply do not? It is a struggle for me to accept this possibility, because of my own conduct. When my first marriage broke up, there were two children in the family. At the time I comforted myself with the reflection that they were living with their natural father, and saw their real mother frequently: a stepmother more or less barely counted. I now wonder if this was wishful thinking.

In the even longer term, there are signs that a broken family may cast a shadow on the children into later life. (I need to pause here and note that life in an obviously unhappy but unbroken marriage probably casts a shadow too, though research on this has not come to hand.) Findings vary somewhat, but it seems there is a slight effect on psychological health later on, particularly for men. The effect is not very great, but it is there nonetheless. [20] The other long-term effect is on their own attitude to marriage. Children of a divorced marriage are more likely to divorce themselves – though exactly why remains controversial. Are they simply more ready to divorce, because they have seen it in practice? Or are they less able to form happy marriages? We do not really know. A complicating factor is that it may not be the divorce, itself, which accounts for this marriage failure in the next generation. Divorce usually means that the children grow up in a one-parent family, which is often pressed for money. Thus, they suffer the disadvantages of a poor economic background and insufficient parental supervision. These, rather than divorce per se, harm the child's chances of a subsequent happy marriage, argue the sociologists. To the non-expert, it must nevertheless seem clear – a broken marriage, whether for emotional or economic reasons, can pass on divorce to another generation. [21, 22]

For society as a whole this is very bad news indeed. If divorce, like child battering, works its way through the generations, then our children's children are going to reap a bitter harvest. The traditional family, with father, non-working mother and children all in one home, is now in the minority in some areas of

London.[23] In 1978 six out of ten divorces involved children under sixteen in Britain. Thirty thousand couples had a child below school age, and some studies have shown that divorce particularly upsets young children who cannot properly understand what is happening to their mother and father.[24, 25] Overall in Britain about one in eight families is headed by a lone parent, and these families, it is agreed, are particularly likely to be living in poverty. For a child born in 1977, the chances of being in a one-parent family at some time before the age of sixteen are now a frightening one in two. In the USA the situation is much the same. One in five children live with only one parent.[26] In 1979 an estimated 1,181,000 children under the age of eighteen were involved in divorces, a figure which has more than doubled in sixteen years and more than tripled in twenty-two years.[27] This is an epidemic of stress to inflict upon our children.

Optimists argue that this frightening rise merely reflects a change in law, not actuality. Marriages have always broken up, but till recently divorce could only be afforded by the middle and upper classes. Legally available divorce simply formalises break-ups which would have taken place anyway. They point to the Republic of Ireland where the number of divorces 'a mensa et thorow', an old and incredibly difficult legal procedure, was just two in 1979. Yet the Irish Divorce Action Group estimate that at least fifty thousand people have broken marriages, either by mutual consent or by the desertion of one partner.[28]

At first some of the rapid increase in divorce in Britain could be accounted for, merely by the legal availability of divorce. Between the two world wars, some ninety thousand men and women tried and failed to get one, because they could not meet the likely legal costs.[29] In the 1960s divorces were registering only half of the total breakdowns of marriage. In the 1970s many of these separated people were legally divorced, once the consent of the deserted partner was no longer necessary.[24] But nowadays this is not the whole story. There are not merely more divorces; there are more marriage breakdowns too.[24, 30]

It seems likely to me, and to many researchers besides Edward Shorter, that one of the reasons for this high rate of marriage breakdown is the changing status of women.[31] As early as 1919 an American author was predicting that 'the fact of women's access to industry must be a prime factor in opening to her the possibility of separation from husband'.[10] The financial independence of a working wife may also make her husband feel he can leave home more easily, knowing that she can support herself. But divorce statistics in Britain show that a far larger proportion of women sue for divorce than do men. At the end of the last war less than half the divorce petitioners were women; now nearly three quarters are female.[32, 33] 'If one wants to understand why the divorce rate is what it is, I think we should pay great attention to the economic status of wives. Many more wives are free to act when their marriage relationships go wrong' is the opinion of Britain's former Lord Justice of Appeal, Sir Roger Ormrod.[34] Women petitioners in the USA also outnumber male petitioners.[32] This might mean that more women than men want to leave their partners. Or it might simply mean that women have the most to gain from going to court, in the way of maintenance and child custody. On the other hand, it has sometimes been suggested that while men walk out of marriages, it is women who go to court to get them formally dissolved. We simply cannot be sure what the ratio of men to women seeking divorce indicates.

What we do know is that marriage seems to offer women far less than it offers men – despite the fact that romantic fiction, which is aimed at women, seems based on the happy-marriage ending. Indeed the high-earning high-status women are far less likely to marry than their sisters, while it is only the lowest-earning lowest-status men who stay single.[35] For even today marriage means that women lose some of their legal rights, are treated in some respects as the lesser of the two partners. 'I may by degrees dwindle into a wife,' said Mistress Millamant in Congreve's *The Way of the World*.[36] Wives are far more likely to suffer from depression than their husbands.[37] Married white women are more likely to be murdered than single women – perhaps because the murderer is likely to be a husband.[13] Altogether, the wife has to make the greater adjustment to her new role.

We might therefore be able to arrest some of the rising divorce figures by simply driving wives back into the home, making them financially dependent upon their husbands, and ensuring that their lives after divorce were so financially penalised that they would think twice about separating. I have heard old-fashioned men and women put this forward as a solution, arguing that the happiness of wives should be sacrificed to the welfare of children. It is also argued that the dependence of wives can be justified by recourse to the Bible, that many dependent wives are happy with their lot and that when the husband is a kind man, then their inferior position does not hurt them. These arguments are remarkably like those that were used to justify slavery in the nineteenth century. But unlike the slaves, women account for more than half the population so that it seems even more unreasonable to insist they should be kept dependent for the sake of society. They, more than men, *are* society. We cannot rescue our children from unhappiness, I believe, at the cost of more than half the adult population.

There are other less controversial reasons for divorce, which can perhaps suggest their own remedies. Money is a factor. High earners have more stable marriages. In both Britain and the USA a very high divorce rate is found in the lowest social class, that of the manual worker.[29, 31] It seems reasonable to suppose that the difficulties of earning a living, managing on a low wage, coping with poor housing and other stresses of relative poverty puts a marriage under strain. We see this same picture emerging among baby batterers too. Yet just handing out more money is not the whole answer.[38] Between 1959 and 1968 in the USA, the percentage of families with a non-white male at the head who were below the 'poverty line' fell from forty-four to nineteen per cent. If shortage of money indirectly 'caused' divorce, then there should also have been a fall in the divorce rate. But there was not. No more does it reflect America's affluence as compared to Europe – their divorce rate is the higher. What seems to put marriages under stress is not an absolute poverty, but a relative poverty. Being at the bottom of the heap, even if the heap is a relatively prosperous one compared to some countries, takes its toll.

Teenage marriages are particularly vulnerable and it is among unskilled workers that the highest proportion takes place. When the wife is under the age of twenty she is more likely to be divorced at the early stages and the later years of marriage.[2] One reason may be that teenagers have simply not grown up, and may mature in divergent directions.[39] Women who marry early, moreover, may be precisely those least likely to make successful marriages at any age. Early-marrying women may be emotionally less well adjusted, have poorer relationships with their families, and are also more likely to be completely financially dependent on their husband. 'If judged by indices from marriage success studies, they were not ready for marriage; by their own criteria for readiness, ninety-five per cent were very ready,' added one study gloomily.[40] Not all research findings agree with this.[41]

'Shotgun' marriages or those with early pregnancies are more likely to fail, as the old tag 'Marry in haste, repent at leisure' has always suggested.[42, 43] Indeed, another conflict between the interests of adults and children appears here. On the whole children seem to add stress rather than happiness to marriage. Marriages decline in happiness over the years, until the children have grown up, at which point they become happier again.[44] Indeed childless marriages seem more likely to be happy than marriages with children.[45]

Finally, some very unhappy marriages are clearly the result of a poor choice of mate in the first place. In my own marriage, the strain was felt very early on – so much so that I wonder whether we married at the end of a relationship rather than at its natural beginning. I am not unusual. In a survey of divorced women and men, the women were twice as likely as the men to believe that their problems were apparent by the end of the first year of marriage. Nearly one in five women believed that their marriages were in trouble *within a month of the wedding ceremony*.[46] Yet a large number nevertheless soldiered on for several years. A survey for a newspaper in 1980 produced one in three divorced men and women who said problems had arisen within the first year of marriage.[47] All in all, we may need help in choosing our mates as much as we need help in making the marriage work.

Nor does sex, alas, offer very much help as a consumer test for mate selection, despite the optimism of sex educators. The divorced are more likely to have had premarital sex than those still married.[46] Even living together, the 'trial marriage' recommended in the first part of this century, does not seem helpful in weeding out unsuitable marriage partners. Divorced or separated women are more likely to have lived with their husbands before marriage than those still married.[48] 'There has been some discussion whether a trial period preceding marriage might increase the durability of that marriage' said the British researchers. 'The statistics presented here show that women who are currently separated or divorced were more likely to have cohabited before their first marriage than currently married or widowed women.' It is not that living together before marriage causes divorce, just that it is useless as a way of forestalling mistakes.

Romantic love is actually a positive disadvantage when it comes to choosing a partner. The image it projects of marriage as a private arrangement between a man and woman to maximise their personal happiness – displacing the older view of it as a functional arrangement for raising a family – gives rise to dangerously high hopes. And any parental attempt to deflate these will only fan the romantic passion. This double bind has been nicknamed 'the Romeo and Juliet effect'.[49] Couples may actually trust each other less, and be more critical, but paradoxically their love increases, so that their 'intense emotional involvement (love and need) . . . is based on external opposition rather than on solid friendship'. For such couples the outlook is poor. When parents have opposed a marriage, it is more likely to end in divorce. This may partly stem from the fact that parents do not help out with finance or emotional support; it may also reflect the fact that the parents rightly foresaw a difficult marriage.[16]

Romantic love is particularly invidious in the attraction it holds for those with poor self-esteem.[50] People who do not think well of themselves are anyway prone to settle for less in others – and led on by romantic love, their choice is likely to be disastrous.[51]

Yet the flood of romance continues, with very little critical opposition. Women are encouraged to read about romantic heroes whose personalities seem wholly unsuited for happy marriage. One tip sheet sent out to would-be authors by a publisher of formula romances describes the ideal hero as 'a successful businessman and/or independently wealthy with some interest to which he devotes his time. He is an enigmatic character, sometimes brutal, sometimes almost tender. He is rugged-looking with features that command attention.'[52] The alternation of moods between brutality and tenderness sounds like a trait guaranteed to produce maximum short-term excitement and minimum long-term married happiness. But such fiction usually pays little attention to marriage after the honeymoon is over. The equivalent heroine in men's fiction, thrillers and adventure stories, is noticeable mainly for her astonishing sexual attraction and immediate sexual response. Neither young men nor young women are likely to get much insight into the nature of love from their staples of cheap fiction, pop songs, television soap operas or the radio. And the most they can expect at school is some sex education. The mundane problems of family life – dealing with money, finding somewhere to live, raising children – are ignored, too, by marriage manuals. No wonder so many of us make a poor choice of marriage partner.

The outlook now is grim. While periodic recession in both the USA and Britain may keep some marriages intact, it is unlikely to contribute much to their happiness, and the growing emphasis on sexual excitement will positively strain it. In the meantime, simply making divorce more difficult will only punish unsuccessful couples and will do nothing to fight marriage breakdowns. Living together will not help either, no matter what some optimists believe. A new generation of young people who have seen their own parents split and divorce, will be coming to marriage even more divorce-prone than the generation before. And simultaneously people are demanding more and more from the institution of marriage. Where once they sought financial security and a home for raising children, they now demand a high degree of love and happiness. These high expectations may in themselves make such things more difficult to achieve.

'I see no determined clear sign that anyone believes that divorce can be stemmed,' said Dr Jack Dominion, an eminent marriage researcher in Britain, talking to a conference in 1983 on 'The Survival of Marriage.' 'In fact the evidence is that we have given up in despair in our attempt to stop divorce, and are concentrating on efforts to diminish its most destructive consequences through conciliation.'[53] Nor is it easy to know what might be done. Perhaps the most useful way to tackle the growing numbers of marriage breakdowns, would be to concentrate on the period *before* marriage. Not so long ago in Britain we lowered the legal age of marriage without parental consent — a change which must have contributed to the rising divorce rate among young people too immature to make a wise choice of partner. Some kind of legal delay imposed on all those who wish to marry might reduce divorce, but would probably be completely unacceptable to society as a whole. Better education for the practicalities of marriage for both boys and girls at school might help too: learning how to budget money, look after children, find somewhere to live, could surely be taught. 'Social skills' – such as dealing with another person's anger, coping with one's own anger, putting feelings into words – could also be taught. But such lessons will probably not be provided. A change from non-directional marriage counselling to positively directing counselling might help too, but that too will be unpopular among the marriage counsellors.[54] We are deeply locked into a very unsatisfactory way of preparing for marriage, dealing with marriage difficulties and coping with divorce: and there is no evidence of any great willingness to change these.

Since we find ourselves trapped in a vicious circle of broken marriages, it is perhaps time we reconsidered the demands we make on it. Having high expectations which cannot be fulfilled is a recipe for unhappiness. If marriage in our society is going to be an unstable relationship culminating in stressful divorce, for a large minority of men and women, they should be encouraged to look elsewhere for happiness. Friends and kinsfolk still remain. There are relationships other than marriage in which we can find love and comfort. These often do not have the same romance, drama and importance, but equally do not threaten the same potential for unhappiness and harm.

7

Friendships Between Man and Beast

In 1936 Princess George of Greece wrote a book about chows. She sent a copy of it to Sigmund Freud, another chow owner and an occasional correspondent of hers. He replied: 'I love it, it is so moving, genuine and true . . . It really explains why one can love an animal like Topsy (the animal in the book) or Jo-fi (Freud's chow) with such extraordinary intensity: affection without ambivalence, the simplicity of all life free from the almost unbearable conflicts of civilisation, the beauty of existence complete in itself; and yet, despite all divergence in the organic development, that feeling of an intimate affinity, of an undisputed solidarity. Often when I am stroking Jo-fi I have caught myself humming a melody, which unmusical as I am, I can't help recognising as the aria from *Don Giovanni*: "A bond of friendship unites us both . . . " '[1]

There have been many friendships between great men and women and their pet animals. Robert Burns kept a pet ewe called Maille, while Charles Kingsley was so soft-hearted that he rescued two wasps from drowning and they took up residence in a crack in his window frame. James Boswell found Samuel Johnson's affection for his cat Hodge rather extreme. 'I never shall forget the indulgence with which he treated Hodge, his cat; for whom he himself used to go out and buy oysters, lest the servants having that trouble should take a dislike to the poor creature . . . I recollect him one day scrambling up Dr Johnson's breast apparently with much satisfaction, while my friend, smiling and half-whistling rubbed down his back, and pulled him by the tail; and when I observed he was a fine cat, saying,

"Why, yes, Sir, but I have had cats whom I liked better than this"; and then, as if perceiving Hodge to be out of countenance, adding, "but he is a very fine cat, a very fine cat indeed." '[2]

The French essayist, Michel de Montaigne, pondered the mystery of the bond between humans and animals. 'When I am playing with my Cat, who knowes whether she have more sport in dallying with me, than I have in gaming with her? We entertaine one another with mutuall apish trickes. If I have my houre to begin or to refuse, so hath she hers . . . That defect which hindreth the communication betweene them and us, why may it not as well be in us, as in them? . . . For, we understand them no more than they us. By the same reason, may they as well esteeme us beasts, as we them . . . We must note the parity that is betweene us. We have some meane understanding of their senses, so have beasts of ours, about the same measure. They flatter and faune upon us, they threat and entreat us, so doe we them . . . '[3]

We have only to look around at the people we know to see just how numerous are these relationships which bridge the chasm between the species. If we talk to dog and cat owners, we must conclude that for them these friendships are important and real. Those of us who had pet animals as children, will probably also remember how the cats and dogs were almost our equals – allies that were definitely not in the grown-ups camp, even if they were not exactly one of us children either. As a nine year-old I used to think that somehow my dog was human – a prince in disguise perhaps. This fantasy explained our relationship, rather than merely adorning it. People who live alone often develop the same trusting friendship with their animals. When their pet dogs or cats die, they go through the stages of mourning – shock, anger, sorrow and only finally acceptance. Cases have been reported where this bereavement has turned into pathological grief.[4]

It is not an explanation simply to dismiss this as sentimentality or to argue that pets are 'only animals'. To do so is to evade the reality of such relationships. If we look carefully and unsentimentally at the way people and their pets live together, their shared activities, their mutual caresses, their eye contact, and their quite enormous amounts of communication by body language, then it is clear that these are mutual friendships. Nor is it such an odd idea that there can be inter-species relationships. We are used to such alliances in the farmyard, where hens bring up ducklings, humans rear orphaned lambs and sometimes bitches adopt kittens. At the University of California they are using dogs as surrogate mothers for rhesus monkeys,[5] and there have been reports of baboons adopting kittens. If we make friends with our domestic animals, then this is in keeping with the veritable network of alliances between the species.

Yet although the idea that people love animals is commonplace, very little investigation has been made into this bond. Most of the research on animals has been concerned with the ways in which they can be used by man. Only in the last couple of decades has ethology developed as a field of study – and it has still to be applied to pets. There is a bias among most ethologists towards the 'natural', the untamed and undomesticated. As a psychiatrist has said: 'The zoophobic bias of ethology was reinforced by the recognition that any cultural context suspends the inexorable play of evolutionary combat. A natural context is one in which animals are competing for survival against other animals. People's pets are domesticated animals living in a context far removed from anything that could be called a state of nature . . . The tendency of amateurs of ethology to idolise the wolf and denigrate the dog as an offshoot of a once noble animal is an example of the power of our feelings about the superiority of beings still "in nature" '[6]

Anthropologists have also largely ignored the human-animal bond in developed societies. Aaron Katcher suggests this is because they, too, are more interested in the 'untamed' – the primitive, the violent and the sexual—whereas 'our life with animals fits much more into the sentimental'. And sociologists have largely ignored domesticated animals, while paying close attention to the parent-child bond, sibling bonds and kinship structures generally. In their studies of family dynamics they have not even asked if there is a family dog or a family cat – odder still, nor have investigations which concentrate on loneliness and isolation. Every now and again a hint surfaces that these family members – pets – should be investigated, but little is done. There is, for instance, a suggestion that battering families are less likely to have pets than better-adjusted families.

This blindness has two main causes, I think. There is an old tradition, enshrined in Christian thought, that man has the right to dominate animals.[7] In the Genesis story of Adam and Eve, God says to the newly-created couple: 'Be fruitful and multiply, and replenish the earth, and subdue it: and have dominion over the fish of the sea, and over the fowl of the air, and over every living thing that moveth upon the earth.'[8] The animals are *for* men – things to be used if possible, cropped, hunted, tamed, destroyed as pests. This idea strongly persists in our society. Another Christian tradition is that animals do not have souls, and that there is thus an enormous gulf between humans and the other species. They do not count. This idea of a gulf was reinforced by René Descartes, father of rational enlightenment. Animals, he declared, are machines incapable of thinking and feeling. The gulf had been redefined. Instead of lacking souls, animals were now lacking in reason.[9]

It is as if the Darwinian revolution had never happened. Indeed what came as a shock to so many, when Darwin published *On the Origin of Species*, was the idea that man was not intrinsically different from the 'lower' animals. It was appalling to think that we might have an ape as an ancestor. We have by now seized on this idea and made it our own – but we haven't properly assimilated it. We point at the animal in man in books like *The Naked Ape*, which purport to explain human behaviour by looking at the other primates. In the same way Kinsey and other sexologists have been happy to argue from their studies of selected ape societies, about the 'natural' sexuality of human beings. It is thoroughly respectable to use Darwin's ideas to put forward the idea that human beings are just animals at heart. But it is not respectable to see the 'human' in animals. It is thought to be anthropomorphic and unscientific. Says Michael Fox, an author and animal expert: 'I do not believe there is much wrong in an owner being somewhat anthropomorphic in his or her regard for the pet, since there is now good scientific evidence to support the contention of many owners that cats and dogs have emotions and sensations comparable to our own – fear, pain, anxiety, jealousy, guilt, joy, depression, anger. The brain centres mediating such states are virtually identical in man and other animals.'[10] Certainly Darwin took this view.

Yet pet animals remain a subject that is rarely found in serious literature. Only in the last ten years or so has research begun to proliferate, and this has mainly been initiated by animal lovers, encouraged by petfood manufacturers. Pets, however, remain a topic that is not chic. For years I wrote about animals, wild and domesticated, for *The Sunday Times*. I made the subject my own because there was nobody else writing about it. In Britain the serious newspapers do not have pets columns: these are confined to the tabloids. The only justification for this is that the highest proportion of pet-owning households are among the C2s rather than the lower DEs or the higher ABs.[11] In the USA there are no figures for the different classes, though the number of households owning cats or dogs is growing.[12] But the difference in numbers is not that great, and many upper-class men and women set an example of animal-loving.

The Queen, herself, had no less than seven pet corgis and two crossbred corgi-dachshunds in 1982. Prince Charles had his own labrador; so did Prince Andrew. Land-owning gentry in Britain are normally seen with at least one dog at their heels. In the USA dogs are often found at the White House. I suspect that a more careful survey would discover that it is the intellectuals and professionals who are responsible for the ABs' low rating in the survey. And these are just the people who have overall control of both media and research.

Historically, human beings have had a long relationship with pets. Dogs were the earliest animals, it is thought, to be domesticated. Fossil remains have been found in the Near East dating from about twelve thousand years ago when human societies were still hunting and gathering groups.[13] Not until man started growing grain was the cat domesticated – or so we think. Positive evidence for their existence comes from an Egyptian tomb in which the bones of seventeen cats were found, complete with little pots for their milk. Tomb paintings show cats under their owners' chairs eating fish, gnawing bones and playing with other animals. Since wild cats are not easily tamed, it is sometimes argued that some genetic change took place to turn a wild species into one which could be domesticated.

The dog was perhaps more naturally fitted for the role. Wolves have been tamed so that they became affectionate towards human beings. And once cats and dogs existed, no other companion animals were needed and therefore no more species were domesticated in this way. So strong is the human need for animal companions that where dogs are absent, we will look for substitutes. In South America various 'wild dog' species were tamed – until the arrival of the domestic dog displaced them. [14]

Human-animal relationships, as Montaigne pointed out, are quite expressive. The body language of both cats and dogs conveys quite clearly their moods to their owners. Darwin remarked on this.

I formerly possessed a large dog, who, like every other dog, was much pleased to go out walking. He showed his pleasure by trotting gravely before me with high steps, head much raised, moderately erected ears, and tail carried aloft but not stiffly. Not far from my house a path branches off to the right, leading to the hot-house, which I used often to visit for a few moments, to look at my experimental plants. This was always a great disappointment to the dog, as he did not know whether I should continue my walk; and the instantaneous and complete change of expression which came over him, as soon as my body swerved in the least towards the path (and I sometimes tried this as an experiment) was laughable. His look of dejection was known to every member of the family, and was called his *hot-house face.* This consisted in the head drooping much, the whole body sinking a little and remaining motionless; the ears and tail falling suddenly down, but the tail was by no means wagged. With the falling of the ears and of his great chaps, the eyes became much changed in appearance, and I fancied that they looked less bright. His aspect was that of piteous, hopeless dejection; and it was, as I have said, laughable as the cause was so slight. [15]

Most of us can read the signals summed up by the Cheshire Cat in *Alice in Wonderland.* 'Well, then, you see a dog growls when it's angry and wags its tail when it's pleased. Now I growl when I'm pleased and wag my tail when I'm angry.' [16] For vocal communication my own cat gives a kind of chirrup which I identify as kitten talk, a cat's version of baby talk. This is quite different from the plaintive mew with which she protests or complains. The local tom cat, who comes to visit, sits outside the back door making persistent and blood-curdling yowls until she goes out to see him. This much of cat language I can understand. They have, besides, a whole repertoire of movements, though dogs' body language is even more expressive. There is paw-giving, a submissive gesture derived from the way puppies paw their mother's teats for more milk. There is nose-nudging, another nursing gesture, and tail-wagging. Dogs also have a good variety of facial expression. Darwin noticed how they grinned with pleasure. It has been said that a dog's expressions are similar to a human's, because the facial muscles are used in much the same way.[17] It may be this similarity of facial expression which makes the dog man's best friend. Certainly expressiveness scored high in a survey of what dog owners like best about their pet.[18] Top of the list, also, came enjoyment of walks, loyalty/affection, welcoming behaviour and attentiveness. The zoologist speculated that attentiveness and welcoming behaviour might be particularly important for the bond between human and dog. 'The functional significance of greeting behaviour in humans has not been studied in any detail, but elaborate and energetic greetings rituals have been evolved in many other animal species and it is popularly believed by ethologists that these displays serve to cement social and sexual bonds.' We know that human beings who love each other indulge in a lot of eye contact. So do dog and cat owners. Indeed I wonder whether eye contact may not be the key to the love between cats and human beings. Cats have particularly flexible pupils, and it has been shown that human beings find widened pupils attractive in women.[19] Do we fall in love with cats because of their strangely moving pupils?

It is clear that there is a reciprocity of behaviour between human beings and animals. They respond to us, and this response is perhaps the most flattering thing about them. Dogs are more dependent on man than cats, and so more vulnerable to neglect. A dog left alone will howl, make itself objectionable by biting things. It may even defecate on its owner's bed. Dogs grieve when they are put in kennels and show signs of depression just as small children in hospital do. When they come home, they may reject their owners. My brother's dog

Wellington would always spend a day or two sulking after he had come out of kennels. Or clinging behaviour may develop. I left my cat to fend for herself for a couple of days (with food and a warm shed). She followed me around mewing for a couple of days after that. Pets can develop behaviour disorders which are similar to human disorders. 'These can range from psychogenic epilepsy, to asthma-like conditions, compulsive eating, sympathy lameness, hypermotility of the intestines with haemorrhagic gastroenteritis, possibly ulcerative colitis, not to mention sibling rivalry, extreme jealousy, aggression and depression and refusal to eat food (anorexia nervosa).'[20]

The relationship between humans and animals can become extremely close. A surprisingly high number of people admit to sleeping with their dogs or cats upon, or even inside, the bed.[6] A Harvard psychiatrist who has studied sleep by taking regular time-lapse photographs through the night has shown that a couple can synchronise their movements even though they are apparently asleep. And so can their cat: there is an amusing sequence of photographs showing Felix the cat asleep on the bed with the couple. The cat cunningly made use of the space allowed by the couple's movements, only leaving the bed when the two people became restless at one stage during their sleep.[21]

Both owner and pet evince a desire to touch and be touched. Charles Darwin noticed this. 'Although the emotion of love, for instance that of a mother for her infant, is the strongest of which the mind is capable, it can hardly be said to have any proper or peculiar means of expression. A strong desire to touch the beloved person is commonly felt; and love is expressed by these means more plainly than by any other . . . We probably owe this desire to inherited habit, in association with the nursing and tending of our children and with the mutual caresses of lovers. With the lower animals we see the same principle derived from contact in association with love. Dogs and cats manifestly take pleasure in rubbing against their masters and mistresses, and in being rubbed or patted by them.'[15] When we caress our pets, we may give them more than pleasure. Touching a dog actually has an effect on its heart rate, slowing it.[22]

The benefits are reciprocal. Petting a dog also affects human blood pressure, bringing it down.[23] Sometimes the mere presence of a loved dog in the room will do this. One experiment involved getting children to read aloud. When their dog was brought into the room, their blood pressure dropped. The mere presence of their pet was calming. Even the sight of tropical fish produces this effect. But with cats and dogs, one of the most important benefits of the relationship must be the giving and receiving of touch. We human beings are allowed to fondle and caress our animals in a way which we cannot do to our fellow human beings. One researcher spent time in the waiting-room of a veterinary surgeon and confirmed that both men and women spent a lot of time in handling their dogs.[6] Whereas even between man and wife, it is often thought bad form to display physical affection in public. President Jimmy Carter was mocked for holding hands with his wife.

This relief of our emotional need of touch can have dramatic physical effects. The most interesting finding of all concerned patients who had been in an intensive care ward for heart trouble.[24] A year later, the pet owners among them were more likely to have survived than those who had no companion animal. Nor was this increased survival rate merely due to the exercise gained by those who walked their dogs. Even patients who had pets other than dogs showed a better survival rate. Other surveys have shown that pet owners, particularly dog owners, have slightly better health than non-pet owners.[25, 26]

For the elderly owning a pet animal may be important simply because it needs regular feeding and attention. This imposes a daily routine upon an owner, and research has shown that a fixed self-imposed routine makes old people healthier. There may be other benefits too. Dorothy Walster of the Scottish Health Education Group reports that in one area where the elderly were all given thermometers to check for hypothermia, one old lady obstinately refused to keep her home warm enough. 'But when she was given a budgerigar, she ensured that the bird lived in a comfortably warm room.'[27]

There are obvious benefits too for the disabled children who are given riding lessons. If you have difficulties in walking, then it is intensely pleasurable to ride.[28] I remember from my childhood days that it was said of three men who hunted with the Heythrop hounds that they 'had two good legs between them'. Strapped to his saddle even the man who had only two stumps was able to ride to hounds, and even jump the stone walls for which the Heythrop country was famous.

The psychological benefits of having a companion animal are obvious enough, one would have thought. But considerable controversy surrounds them. Some researchers suggest that pet owners tend to like people less than do non-owners, or that they will admit to preferring animals to human beings.[29, 30] 'Plus que je vois les homme, plus que je respecte les chiens,' said Madame Roland, eighteenth-century wit, and on the basis of this remark some psychologists would have disapproved of her. Other researchers argue that pet owners show many good psychological traits compared with non-owners.[31] Those who work in animal welfare often also do good works for people too.[32] William Wilberforce, responsible for the abolition of slavery in Britain and for many other humane measures, helped support those who were setting up the Royal Society for the Prevention of Cruelty to Animals.[33] And the RSPCA's secretary, John Colam, went on to set up the National Society for the Prevention of Cruelty to Children. Love of animals need not exclude love of people: often the two go together.[34]

Perhaps there are people who can only experience love and affection through caring for animals. I think there have been moments in my own life when I have been perilously close to this myself. I have at least felt quite useless to human beings, and perhaps writing about animal welfare gave me something to shore up my failing self-esteem. I cannot find much wrong with this. In the struggle to stay sane we must accept whatever help lies to hand. By the same token, we should look in a kindly fashion on little old ladies who lead eccentric lives surrounded by scores of cats, or recluse-like gentlemen who seem to care only for their dogs.

A famous English eccentric was one of these. He had eleven dogs whom he used to place on chairs at the dinner table, where they and he were served by the footmen. If animals are the only source of warmth in a person's life, then every effort should be made to see that he or she is not deprived of this consolation.

A couple of careful surveys suggest that quite often pet animals can form a bridge to human relationships. Some old people living alone were given budgies. Not only did the birds give great pleasure to their owners, but they also seemed to

supply topics of conversation and ways of relating to others. [35]
Similarly, walking the dog can help make friendships. I used to
walk mine every day in a tiny public garden in North London.
Most mornings I walked with the head waiter of a very expensive restaurant. We should never have met except for our dogs.
The friendship was confined to dog-walking, but nevertheless
gave me considerable pleasure. One researcher carefully stalked
owners with their dogs, then asked them to cover the same route
without their pet. Those who were accompanied by their dogs
had more social contact with the other humans in the park. [36]
Like other love relationships, love between human and animal
can flower out into ways of loving others.

And love is what these relationships overwhelmingly convey.
When pet owners are asked why they own their animal,
'companionship' is the most common answer. This implies a
kind of equality. (Dog owners often link companionship with
protection, it must be added.) The time people spend with their
pets is impressive. Two out of five owners spend between two to
three hours in direct communication; twelve per cent spend
more than four hours. [37]

Dogs become part of the family. [38] More than a third of
owners said that 'their dog was a child to them'. They are
valuable members too. When ten families with dogs were
studied by an onlooker, the dog joined in most family activities
and was very attentive. [39] Interestingly enough, a family where
an animal is treated cruelly may also include an abused child. [40]
Most dog owners are passionately fond of their animals.
'People are very uncritical when talking about their dog. They
talk in a very euphemistic way – they say that the dog is very
active, clean, confident, loving, gentle, intelligent, warm,
playful, reliable, friendly, pleasing, genuine, happy, accepting
and trusting. He sounds like God reincarnated as a dog.' [38] Very
eminent men and women admit to being very attached to their
pets. The Oxford historian A.L. Rowse wrote a book about his
cat Peter, and revealed that he would telephone him from All
Souls in Oxford and talk down the phone to the cat in
Cornwall. The then Vice President's wife, Barbara Bush, revealed in 1982 that she was writing a biography of Fred, their
cocker spaniel. 'He's met some interesting people,' she said.

Most of us talk to our pets, and treat them as if they were

personalities, not just animals. Most of us also believe that they are sensitive to our feelings; and many, that they understand a large number of words. If talking things out is good for human beings, then no doubt animals help us get through the stresses of life. The warmth and sympathy which we get from our dogs and cats, has been compared to the manner of a Rogerian therapist, that is, one who believes a warm accepting attitude helps his clients; and their effects, with those of prayer to a warm and loving God who understands all.[6] In this sense, a dog may truly be a best friend – always loving, always sympathetic, always there to comfort or share enjoyment with. Scores of people have *experienced* this, and if the friendship is an illusion, then it is an illusion which helps far more than the detached anti-emotional attitude of those who deny friendships between the species. Others have compared pet animals with social workers – both try to establish communication, 'teach' by example, heal emotional trauma, act as a reliable confidant for the most hair-raising secrets, give people a feeling of being worth something.[41] These parallels, which may seem rather fanciful at first, nevertheless appear to have some validity. Pets are now being used – particularly in America – to help the lonely, the elderly, the mentally ill and the bedridden.

The initial results seem to confirm the healing power of the love between man and beast. In the USA pets have been introduced into nursing homes, mental hospitals, rehabilitation centres, and some of the animal welfare societies have developed schemes whereby rescued animals visit those in need of them.[42] Pet therapy is not designed to replace other forms of therapy, rather to supplement them. With medicine increasingly geared to technological and chemical 'cures', the contribution it has to make is a very real and necessary one.

One trial of pet therapy took place in a geriatric ward, where a psychiatrist had experimented with cat mascots. The cats were kept in the day-room during the day but fed and watered outside the ward at night. When the hospital staff were interviewed, they reported that the cats had helped these sometimes withdrawn patients to be more responsive. 'Mascots were effective in increasing patient responsiveness, giving patients a pleasurable experience, enhancing the treatment milieu and helping keep patients in touch with reality,' it was concluded.[43]

An experiment using dogs in a psychiatric ward had even more noticeable results. Only three out of fifty patients who had 'pet therapy' sessions did not like it. The rest all improved and occasionally the improvement was startling.

Patient Sonny was a nineteen-year-old psychotic who spent most of his time lying in his bed. The staff tried unsuccessfully to get him to move about and interact. Nothing seemed to interest him; he would not participate in occupational therapy, recreational therapy, nor group therapy. In individual therapy he remained withdrawn and uncommunicative. His drug regime did not improve him . . . a token system was introduced but again Sonny showed little response.

Before starting the electro-shock therapy, it was decided to attempt to use a dog as a component of the token reward system. The patient was lying in his bed in his usual mummy position. The psychiatrist sat beside his bed and spoke with him. When the psychiatrist's questions concerned people or Sonny himself, Sonny's response was very slow, the interval being as long as twenty-six seconds. When the question concerned dogs ('Do you like dogs?') or pets in general, the response came more rapidly in one or two seconds. All of Sonny's responses were extremely brief, chiefly 'yes' or 'no' or 'I don't know'. He did not volunteer any statements or questions. He continued to be motionless with a blank expression on his face.

When the psychiatrist brought the dog 'Arwyn', a wirehair fox terrier, to Sonny's bed, Sonny raised himself up on one elbow and gave a big smile in response to the dog's wildly friendly greeting. The dog jumped on Sonny, licking his face and ears. Sonny tumbled the dog about joyously. He volunteered his first question. 'Where can I keep him?' Then to everybody's amazement, he got out of bed and followed the dog when she jumped on the floor.

In the next few days after being introduced to the dog, Sonny became active in working for tokens, though he did not exchange them for rewards. He began to notice the other patients on the ward, saw that some had benefited from electro-shock therapy, began to go to group therapy, and asked that he be given EST. Since he was still operating on a psychotic level, a series of eight ESTs was given to Sonny, and he was later discharged much improved. At the time of his discharge his response to questions occurred in one second, and the duration of his answers was increased to as much as twenty seconds. The introduction of the dog was judged by the psychiatrist to be the turning point in the course of his recovery. [44]

Examples of how animals have helped people are beginning to permeate medical literature. There has even been a suggestion that owning a pet may protect people from suicide. [45] Possibly in the future, doctors and other health professionals will begin to take the relationship between humans and their animal companions more seriously. Pet therapy is not likely to become a panacea. But if it is possible that the love of a good dog may get through to people where human relationships are failing to do so, then surely this should be tried. Animals have a place in our lives. It may be a small place, but for many of us it is a place very close to our hearts.

8

The Healing Power of Love

If the love of animals can help in illness, stress and old age, how much more should human love do for us. One of the oddest experiences of illness is that it can produce a feeling of shame, even guilty embarrassment. A schoolteacher who had suffered a severe stroke told me how during his convalescence he had had to fight not just against his bodily weakness but also against his feelings of depression and failure. He explained, 'A couple of friends used to come round once a week for a drink when I got out of hospital. One week they said to me, "Now it's time you came out to the pub with us." It was dreadful. I used to feel terrible about going out of the house. I didn't want people to see me.' Clearly the whole experience had been a huge assault on his self-esteem.

Illness, even the most straightforwardedly physical like breaking a leg, is not just a question of bodily pain or weakness. The whole being suffers. Anybody who has felt depressed during a bout of influenza knows how the body's minor ills can affect the mind. Tranquillity is almost impossible during toothache. With severer illnesses, the effect can be proportionately greater. From being an active teacher, the deputy head of the local town school, the man I have just quoted became 'a stroke victim'. A victim may be pitied and loved, but he is rarely respected. He felt ashamed of his crippled body, and had been stripped of his status in the community. To become healed again, he needed not just the occupational therapy given by the local hospital but also the will to work hard at various exercises and activities at home. When I met him, he had just won a gardening competition – a success which meant a great deal to him in rebuilding a life that had been shattered.

Human ties had been important to him during his convalescence – his wife had given unstinting support, and his friends had urged him back into the outer world. Just as they are vital in maintaining health, so they are in healing people after illness or injury. The loving husband or wife, friends, and even the affection of the family dog – all these contribute to recovery. Love heals. Indeed to such an extent that it may mask the effects, or non-effects, of drugs. Clinical trials are sometimes deliberately set up so that more than one doctor administers the various treatments. For a good bedside manner – kindness, concern and encouragement – can do wonders. In the 1940s and 1950s, a Dr J.Y. Dent in the USA had great success in curing alcoholics with injections and oral administration of a drug called apomorphine. He felt he had at last discovered a miracle cure. But it didn't work for anybody else, and it is now agreed that his good results were probably due to his empathy and understanding of alcoholic patients. 'Dent without apomorphine would still be much more successful than apomorphine without Dent.' [1]

It would be folly to claim that love is a cure-all. Many loved and loving people have died from illnesses despite all the efforts of their families and friends. In our century we have seen some diseases literally conquered by the discovery of new drugs. Some of the illnesses which decimated whole populations – tuberculosis, cholera, smallpox – have been overcome by antibiotics, better drainage, or innoculation. A patient suffering from pneumonia needs antibiotics not just a good bedside manner. Yet there is now a thin trickle of hard evidence that love can make a difference – particularly in those illnesses where the mind is directly involved. People who deal with the mentally ill are gradually coming round to admitting this. 'While it cannot be claimed that empathy, a caring attitude, objectivity, sensitivity and tact are all that matters in therapy, there is a tendency for therapists with relatively high levels of these qualities to get better results,' said the head of a clinical psychology department in a major London hospital at a conference recently. [2] Every time a member of the establishment goes on record like this, there is a better chance of reform.

The psychology establishment does not like the word 'love'. Indeed, it is an imprecise word that can mean different things in different contexts. Researchers prefer to talk about 'warmth', 'empathy', 'genuineness' or, if they are behavioural psychologists, 'positive reinforcement'. Whatever the terms, these are qualities which we can *sense* fairly easily. We may often feel their absence too, even though the right words are being said. 'I do hope you feel better today, Mrs Jones,' said by a doctor with cold eyes, averted face reading his notes, and defensively folded arms is not convincing. Human beings read gestures, voice tone and eye contact extraordinarily accurately, sometimes without even knowing that is what they are doing. These non-verbal signs are crucial to a relationship. If the person talking is not looking you in the eye, if his voice is cold, the correct 'caring' words are meaningless. One study showed that doctors who showed anger in their tone of voice had less success in persuading alcoholics to go for further treatment. The patients felt they did not care. 'The relationships between an angry tone of voice and lack of effectiveness with alcoholic patients who may be especially sensitised to rejection accords with clinical and anecdotal accounts of doctor-alcoholic encounters', added the researchers. [3]

Sympathy and kindness should by now have become accepted tools of treatment for mental disorders. A series of studies have shown that they make a difference to the recovery of quite widely differing groups – juvenile delinquents, schizophrenics, college 'under achievers' and those having counselling or psychotherapy. [4] Professor Scott Henderson of the University of Tasmania put forward the idea that some disorders are specifically 'care-eliciting' – that is, attempts by the sufferer to get love and attention. In search of the social bonds which human women and men need, some people develop disordered habits. 'By means of a theoretical model derived from ethology, it may now be possible to place under a single rubric a seemingly disparate group of disorders which have one common property: *they tend to occur when an individual perceives himself to be receiving insufficient caring behaviour from others.* These disorders may appropriately be called "the care-eliciting syndromes".' The Professor includes in this category neurotic depression, conversion hysteria, shoplifting, anorexia nervosa, hypochondria and multiple illegitimate pregnancies – together with parasuicide, those unsuccessful suicide bids which folk wisdom says are a 'cry for help'.[5] And perhaps some of these illnesses actually work. They actually do produce caring behaviour from others – or something which will do as a substitute. 'Psychotherapy in the Western World is an institutionalized occasion for symptomatic people to obtain, *inter alia*, a high level of social interaction', remarks the Professor.[6]

Obviously, then, the psychology establishment should be screening for warmth and love in its staff. The problem is, though, that these qualities are difficult to quantify. In one study 'a given therapist who was known by his co-workers to be very warm, friendly, supportive, and understanding sometimes came out with surprisingly low ratings on scales of warmth and accurate empathy when an objective evaluation was made of his tape-recorded sessions with patients.'[7] The opposite was also true. Some therapists who seemed to talk heartlessly in the staff-room, were kind and caring towards their patients. But whatever the problems in detection, and though what little hard evidence we have is occasionally conflicting, it does seem as though warmth and love should be on the medical student's curriculum. While training is no substitute for right feelings, it may at least promote them.

But medical education is quite inadequate. Doctors are trained in illnesses not people. Most of them would agree with this family doctor that a GP's 'primary task is to manage his time. If he allows patients to rabbit on about their conditions, then the doctor will lose control of time and will spend all his time sitting in a surgery listening to irrelevant rubbish.' The tone of his language implies a dislike of patients, and indeed many students are trained in such a way that they graduate with 'views that at least indicated insensitivity towards, and at the worst a positive hatred of people and patients'.[8, 9] An example of their resultant behaviour is given by the experience of a woman I know, who has already had one breast removed because of cancer and was having a routine check-up for the other breast from a consultant. 'Yes,' he said thoughtfully, 'there may be a small lump here.' At this point, a nurse called him out of the room and *he didn't come back*. My friend was left to get dressed and go, not knowing if she had the start of another cancer. Fortunately she is a brave and sensible women. She made an appointment with her GP, and it was finally decided there was no lump. But clearly the consultant who had been examining her, had entirely failed to remember that there was a living breathing frightened human being in front of him, not just a potential breast lump. He had been called away, and had simply forgotten – or perhaps did not even think to remember in the first place – that he had left some fellow being at the mercy of uncertainty and fear.

Medical students are particularly ill at ease with mental patients, suicides and the aged – a large proportion of their future patients. Attempted suicides are particularly likely to be 'punished' by the hospital staff, who feel that hospital beds should be kept for the 'really ill'. Mental patients, too, are sometimes made to suffer. As we know, the outside world of family, friends and neighbours, often feel that mental illness is a mark of disgrace and horror. Unfortunately, patients already crushed by this stigma may well find that entrance to a psychiatric hospital does not lift this burden. It can be an intensely wounding experience.

In Britain, a psychologist, Stuart Sutherland, has left a moving account of his own nervous breakdown and his experiences in hospital. 'There was a further feature of life in hospital to which many inmates found it difficult to adjust. The younger doctors and nurses tended to treat patients as though they were insane, and this could be both infuriating and upsetting. Since all the patients were to some extent mentally ill, it may seem odd to be upset by being treated as such. The point is that none of the patients was totally out of touch with reality, and their illness only affected part of their lives. Many, for example, knew better than the nurses what pills they were supposed to be taking. However, the doctors sometimes wrote up the drug sheets in such a hurry that nurses could easily make mistakes. It could seem very important to be given the right drugs, but when the wrong ones were handed out any attempt to argue with the nurses would be treated as part of the patient's illness and recorded as such in the day book. Because doctors and nurses could always shelter behind the belief that the patients were mad, they were in an impregnable position, and it was easy for patients to feel completely in the power of the hospital authorities. One of the alcoholics had spent several years in prison in Dartmoor; he summed up his feelings: "I'd rather spend a year in Dartmoor than a week here." When I asked why, he said: "At least you can get at the screws there: here there's no one to get at." '[10]

In American psychiatric hospitals conditions are worse. In an ingenious study, eight sane people pretended to be schizophrenic in order to get admitted to psychiatric hospitals. Once there, they behaved perfectly sanely, and indeed openly kept copious notes. But their deception was never discovered. Even when they were let out, their condition was described as 'schizophrenia in remission'. Some of the patients knew they were fake; none of the staff did. While they were there, they saw patients being actually beaten up or verbally abused. But most of the time patients were simply ignored, as if they were not human beings: their questions were rarely answered – hastily, if at all, while the staff member moved off, head averted.[11] The staff also avoided eye contact with patients. 'The encounter frequently took the following bizarre form: (pseudopatient) "Pardon me, Dr X. Could you tell me when I am eligible for grounds privileges?" (physician) "Good morning Dave. How are you today?" (Moves off without waiting for a response).'

With overcrowded hospitals, and a profession which practises impersonal medicine, it is little wonder that so many self-help groups have sprung up. Self-help is less wounding to self-esteem than that doled out by a doctor, or even that received from a non-official helper. A group of people with the same problem gives support to the sufferer, support which cannot normally be either condescending or impersonal. As one study of self-help groups describes it: ' "Support" means giving people a feeling of their own strength and identity by demonstrating that they have the power to cope; a power much shaken, if not destroyed, by the failure of the conventional paradigm to work for them.'[12] The inequality of the conventional relationship between patient and medical authority is not present. Indeed the helped has a chance to become the helper in her turn. 'Knowing that you're being useful to somebody else is the best medicine in the world', a member of the Relatives of the Depressed explained.[12] Quite often the traditional medicine makes the patient feel of little worth – he is the inadequate body to be cured by others. All the power lies with the doctor. The patient is positively encouraged to depend on him. In a self-help group the sufferer is making his own efforts towards health. Of course, some of these groups can do little to change the actual disease itself. The members of a disablement self-help group will stay disabled. But much can be done to help sufferers endure better, cope better and feel better. The disease is eased, if not cured.

However, some such groups exist specifically to treat the disease that has brought their members together. These are longest established in the area of addiction or dependence. Alcoholism, gambling, overeating and drug addiction all have their self-help groups – Alcoholics Anonymous, Gamblers Anonymous, Overeaters Anonymous and Narcotics Anonymous. All four call themselves 'fellowships', and the word is well chosen. All four are run on the same principles, and all four deal with disorders which are thought by the ordinary person to be not only unhealthy but also vicious or immoral. And, indeed, it can be argued that they are all, *even overeating*, to some degree anti-social. The abuse of alcohol and drugs leads to motor car accidents, industrial injuries, absenteeism, crime and other anti-social activities. Gamblers may embezzle money to feed their habit. And overeaters, it could be argued, use up medical resources which could be better spent on involuntary illness. All four addictions also involve self-destruction in some form or another. So, not altogether surprisingly, the outside world is often very unsympathetic. Besides, most people have no difficulty in drinking sensibly, refusing illegal drugs, or only gambling occasionally; they do not understand the hold these things can develop. Overeaters find that others consider them simply greedy. 'How many times we have heard it said, "If only you'd only use a little willpower, you could lose all that weight." '[13]

Addiction is a baffling illness. People often talk in a loose way about addictive drugs, as if the addiction lay solely in the drug itself. Clearly some drugs are more potentially addictive than others. Nicotine is highly addictive, as smokers who have tried to give up smoking and failed know only too well. So is cocaine. Yet the compulsion lies not just in the drug. It is also in the person who becomes an addict. Sigmund Freud discovered the miracle powers of cocaine and prescribed it for his friend Ernst von Fleischl-Marxow, a morphine addict. Poor Fleischl turned into a cocaine addict, took enormous doses and suffered horrifying delirium tremens. But at the same time as he was giving cocaine to Fleischl, Freud was taking it himself. For him it was merely a recreational drug which he seems to have used over a number of years without ever becoming addicted. [14] In a similar way, a large proportion of the population in Western countries uses alcohol as a recreational drug, yet only a relatively small proportion of users become alcoholics. As the saying suggests: 'Alcoholism comes in peoples not bottles.' Studies have shown that even the opiates, like heroin, do not invariably turn users into addicts. Many of the US servicemen who experimented with heroin in Vietnam, stopped using it when they returned home. [15] Food is not an addiction to most of us. Gambling does not even have an obvious connection with our physiology – unlike drugs, alcohol or food, it is not an ingested substance. Yet for some it becomes a compulsion, a habitual activity like drinking or using drugs which can drag the sufferer down to the gutter. Indeed some researchers argue that sex can become an addiction, as can romantic relationships. [16] I think it is true to say that we do not understand addiction, and that the best experts in this field will admit to this.

Occasionally we come across the idea that addictions are in some way caused by a failure to form proper human relationships. 'He turned to drink when his wife died' is a remark one sometimes hears, suggesting 'he' had no one else to turn to. Alcoholism can perhaps be construed as a 'care-eliciting' behaviour. Certainly it often ends in suicide attempts. Overeating, too, has been linked by some researchers with the failure of relationships. 'The abnormal eating behaviour usually starts with the context of the failure of the patient's first major sexual relationship, or following a series of brief but abortive relationships. The patient, wounded, critically examines herself and feels a marked low self-esteem. She feels a failure as a woman and projects this failure on to her body shape', writes one doctor. [17] Indeed most addicts suffer considerable self-hatred. This is hardly surprising since their behaviour, once addicted, is such that it would normally lead to diminished self-esteem. So far there is little convincing evidence about the causes of addiction. But it is clear that most of its victims suffer from increasingly disordered relationships as their addiction progresses. For example, it has been estimated that alcohol is implicated in about fifty per cent of wife-battering cases.[18] As the alcoholic's behaviour becomes more erratic, friendships are lost.[19] Work relationships usually suffer, too.

Drug addiction runs a similar course. 'Addiction insulates us from people, places and things outside our own world of getting, using, and finding ways and means to continue the process. Hostile, resentful, self-centred and self-concerned – we cut off all outside interests as our illness progresses. We live in fear and suspicion of the very people we have to depend on for our needs. This touches every area of our lives and anything not completely familiar becomes alien and dangerous. Our world shrinks and isolation is its goal. This might well be the true nature of our disorder.'[20] Addicts may deliberately avoid their friends. At a Narcotics Anonymous meeting I heard a recovered addict, Roger, relate how he had told his best friend he was going to Australia. 'It wasn't true. I just didn't want to see him. I didn't want to see anyone. I just wanted to stay in my room and fix,' he said.

Among gamblers the same behaviour pattern is found. Gamblers frequently mistreat their families. 'At first I used to give the wife £50 if I won £400,' admitted Len, a gambler in GA. 'Then I wouldn't give her a penny. She would ask me for a couple of pounds for the kids, and I would tell her I hadn't got any money. But I'd have £500 or £600 in my pocket. That all went to the bookmakers. Yet I used to give the girls behind the counter there a tenner every time I won.' A classic view of gambling was once given by William Temple, Archbishop of York, in 1932. 'The attempt (which is inseparable from gambling) to make a profit out of the inevitable loss and possible suffering of others is the antithesis of that love of one's neighbour on which the Lord insisted.'[21] Stories told at Gamblers Anonymous meetings often mention money borrowed and not returned – leading to loss of friends.

Compulsive overeaters also find their relationships distorted, this time in a rather obvious way. Very fat people are figures of fun in our society. They are also, I believe, thought to be of low status. I once found myself watching the editor of an American society magazine being interviewed on TV. 'She can't be editing that magazine,' I said out loud. 'She's too fat.' The remark was unfair, but an indication of how society sees the very fat. With a compulsive overeater, the body can literally get in the way of good relationships. Yet food is what comforts the addict for their absence. 'When I was lonely food was my friend. It soothed and comforted me and filled the hole that was there when I felt unloved, which was most of the time,' explains one overeater.[22] To be a woman and very fat in our society is certainly to be sexually unloved.

Thus addicts – whether of drink, food, drugs or gambling – have a history of disordered relationships, broken social bonds and increasing loneliness as their addiction continues. They have also, of course, acquired bad habits which need changing. Society will continue to offer alcohol, food, betting shops and even drugs in abundance despite the existence of these vulnerable people. Clearly it is impossible to remove an addict from his addiction, except by imprisonment.

Thus it is that addicts tend to relapse. Alcoholics often make a habit of being dried out, whether in expensive health farms and clinics, on the National Health or in prison. Once out, they go back on the bottle. And the huge industry of diet aids and slimming clubs makes it clear that overeaters, too, frequently only slim down to get fat again a few months later. In the course of researching a newspaper article, I tracked down about twenty ex 'slimmers of the year'. About half were a year or less away from their moment of glory. Yet a third had regained all the weight they had lost.

The four anonymous fellowships which deal with these addicts all claim to help them stay sober, clean, non-gambling or abstinent, in a normal world. It is worth pausing here to look at their astonishing growth. To take just one example, Alcoholics Anonymous, which started just before the last World War, now exists in 108 countries. In Britain there were an estimated 1600 groups at a count in 1982.[23] In the same year in the USA there were 26,608 AA groups with an estimated 500,000 members.[24]

All four fellowships are distinctly unusual. Perhaps the oddest point of their behaviour is the way they return financial

contributions from outsiders. If the grateful wife or husband of
a sober alcoholic, say, bequeaths money to AA, it is refused.
There is even a limit on the amount that a member can give,
either during life or after death. There are no public appeals
for money, no requests for grants, and no fund-raising activities. It is deliberate policy not to become rich, in case too much
money diverts the fellowships from their proper function. Apart
from a few eminent outsiders on the governing board, membership is limited to those who have the addiction.

Controversy is avoided. 'GA has no opinion of outside
issues; hence the GA name ought never to be drawn into public
controversy.'[25] This means that the fellowships do not campaign – whether for changes in the law, more treatment centres,
or more research. Today when most self-help groups are active
in their own interests, this attitude is confusing. Before I
investigated further, I used to expect Alcoholics Anonymous to
talk to newspapers about what should be done. It was odd to be
told that it had no views on outside issues. Another curiosity is
the almost total lack of hierarchy within the fellowships. Each
of their constituent groups whether of NA, AA, OA or GA, is
self-supporting and self-governing. It can run its affairs as it
chooses. In theory an OA group could spend its funds on cream
cakes, and there is nothing to stop a GA group blueing the lot
on a bet. This rarely if ever happens.

Their oddities aside, what immediately impresses the outsider
is the warmth of the friendship and fellowship offered by these
people. Psychologist James J. Lynch, author of *The Broken
Heart*, a book about loneliness, said in an interview: 'When
people with particular problems band together with a common
goal, they can be very helpful. I am very impressed with such
groups as Alcoholics Anonymous, Reach to Recovery, and
Parents without Partners. They are compassionate self-help
groups that aren't out to make money for themselves.'[26] In an
interview with *Playboy* magazine, Kurt Vonnegut Jnr was asked
if there was a religion he considered superior to any other.
'Alcoholics Anonymous,' he replied rather startlingly.
'Alcoholics Anonymous gives you an extended family that's
very close to a blood brotherhood, because everyone has
endured the same catastrophe. And one of the enchanting
things of Alcoholics Anonymous is that many people join who

aren't drunks, who pretend to be drunks because the social and spiritual benefits are so large.' On the whole, most serious alcoholism clinics and hospital departments in the USA, and to a lesser extent in Britain, try to co-operate with AA. Some even model their whole treatment on AA principles. The Betty Ford Center, which has treated Elizabeth Taylor, Tony Curtis, Peter Lawford, Robert Mitchum, and many other film stars, is based on the Alcoholics Anonymous recovery programme. Few people would deny that AA has had a great deal of success in changing drinking alcoholics into sober men and women. In due course, the same recognition will probably come to Narcotics Anonymous and Overeaters Anonymous.

The common basis of their characteristic warmth is the simple fact that all four 'Anonymous' fellowships operate in groups. They offer help and support from fellow sufferers. They exist as an artificial friendship network. This may not be the reason *why* they work, but it is certainly *how* they work – or at least one of their guiding principles. Unlike the self-help groups which campaign to change society, they aim more modestly to change the individual. 'Because the whole self-help process of Alcoholics Anonymous is not a matter of solving problems: it is a matter of changing people' concluded one study.[27] If the addict is to survive unscathed in a world full of temptation, he or she must be changed. None of the four fellowships runs clinics, hospitals or counselling centres – just meetings, held in rented rooms often in church halls or community centres. If there are doctors, clergymen and lawyers present, it is because they too are addicts. At the heart of it is just the group, not behavioural treatment methods, not expert advice, just fellow people. 'The AA program teaches the alcoholic to redirect a great deal of his affection away from himself toward God, toward the fellowship of other alcoholics and to the unredeemed alcoholic who needs his help', is one view of how it works.[28]

I have been to meetings of all four fellowships, and it seems to me that a great deal more touching goes on than is normal at ordinary social occasions. Not only do women hug and occasionally kiss people – so do men. Men quite often shake hands – perhaps 'clasp hands' would be a better phrase. For it is not the handshake of formal greeting. Sometimes I have seen a man put his hand on another's shoulder for a second, or merely reach out during conversation to make a physical contact. This kind of body expression is not usual in Britain. In the USA some AA meetings end with everybody holding hands as they recite a prayer. The conversation also varies from what is normal on social occasions. The query 'How are you?' is answered literally. 'I'm all right. I think I'm worried about one or two things. I'm worried about cakes when I'm on holiday' was the answer one overeater got. This was followed by the questioner admitting to the same anxieties, then offering a few words of advice. She appeared to *listen*. Obviously the original query 'How are you?' was not a question which expected the automatic response 'Fine, how are you?'

The new entrant receives a lot of attention. All four fellow-ships have a saying: 'The newcomer is the most important person in the room.' I have seen one at a GA meeting being taken aside by two or three members and talked to earnestly before the formal meeting began. In AA I have seen a clearly drunken man being carefully given half-filled cups of tea throughout the meeting by a middle-class lady, who was also trying gently to restrain him from talking too much. A researcher in the early days of AA reported: 'I came away from this participant-observation experience much impressed by the warmth and deeply felt human concern that had been expressed in the meeting. Contrary to popular misconceptions, the compassion was displayed in an unsentimental manner and the support was offered in a context of realism.'[29] Another researcher who went to an AA meeting without telling the members who he was, concluded: 'Interesting to examine these events in the light of their belief that I was seen as a newcomer. After an initial pause, there was a rush to see me and get me involved. The first member seemed to get forced out by the second, and the third was waiting to work a flanker by carrying me off to a new group.'[27]

It would be folly to suppose that all the meetings are invariably warm and supportive. Sometimes the ideal and the actual practice do not concur.[30] Clearly groups made up of, say, alcoholics and drug addicts and including some who are still on their particular drug, must sometimes be disruptive and chaotic. But all four fellowships try to make the newcomer welcome, sometimes appointing special persons as 'greeters' to make sure all new faces are welcomed, usually inviting the first-timer to coffee afterwards. Indeed, this process is vitally important. Those who become regular AA members are the ones who have been drawn into not just the formal meeting, but the informal 'chit-chat' before and after.[31]

The exact organisation of each individual meeting varies, but the heart of it is usually the same – the common problem. One or more people tell the story of their addiction, how they came to the fellowship and how they recovered. Sometimes a speaker will start off with the phrase 'and now for some indentification . . . ' Though people have seen parallels with Methodist class meetings, the speaker is not so much unburdening himself – indulging in the luxury of confession – as establishing common ground with the newcomer.[29] I have sat next to one at an Overeaters Anonymous meeting and seen her absolutely lost in the story. She was alternately laughing and muttering 'That's me' or 'I've done that'. She gave little noises of pleasurable recognition. Her identification with the speaker was giving her something – I would guess this was the feeling that she was not alone, not the only fat person who overate compulsively.

This identification is vital. Just offering love is rarely enough. Countless heartbroken parents and partners have tried to love addicts clean or alcoholics sober. But they cannot lead by example. The high success rate of these four organisations is firmly based not on shared strength, but shared weakness – a common disgrace. 'We have discovered that if people in this program love us, it is not for our strength but for our weaknesses and our willingness to share that with others', says the *Overeaters Anonymous* book.[22] A bond which relies on another's strength and goodness might fail, if they failed. Shared weakness and disgrace is a surer foundation. And it is a shared disgrace in most cases. In the USA laid-back Californians may join for the friendship,[12] but for the most part AA is still 'a last hope organisation' according to a thorough recent study in Britain.[27]

The fellowships themselves recognise the vital importance of this community of experience. Great emphasis is placed on the idea that only those with the common problem can 'truly understand' each other. 'We feel our approach to the problem of

addiction is completely realistic,' says a Narcotics Anonymous
leaflet, 'for the therapeutic value of one addict helping another
is without parallel. We feel that our way is practical, for one
addict can best understand and help another addict.'[32] It is
significant, too, that AA dates its foundation from the visit Bill
Wilson made to his co-founder, Dr Bob Smith, in 1935. Bill
Wilson, a stockbroker, had sobered up earlier and stayed sober
with the help of the Oxford Group, a religious movement now
known as Moral Rearmament. But AA split from the Oxford
Group and does not date its beginnings from Bill Wilson's
sobriety, but firmly from the moment when he sobered up Dr
Bob Smith. One alcoholic talking to another has been called
AA's 'core idea'.[33]

All four fellowships emphasise the shared problem by their
custom of introducing remarks with 'My name is —— and I am
– an alcoholic, an addict, a compulsive gambler or compulsive
overeater . . . ' Of course this functions partly as a self-
reminder, but its repetition also ensures that the newcomer
realises from the start that those speaking are not do-gooding
outsiders. As the repetition continues, it also produces a change
of meaning in the words. The man who gets up and says 'My
name is Len and I am a compulsive gambler' is, in fact, *a man
who no longer gambles.* The sting of disgrace has gone. 'To be
able to say "and I'm an alcoholic" without embarrassment,
and perhaps sometimes it seems even with a certain inflection of
pride, is the badge of an AA member' it has been said.[34] The
longer-standing member is helping others by thus classifying
himself; he is also turning a label of disgrace into a badge of
success.

Helping fellow-addicts is actually built into the recovery
programme as the twelfth and final step: 'Having had a spiritual
awakening as the result of these steps, we tried to carry this
message to other alcoholics and to practise these principles in all
our affairs.'[35] Usually this involves long-standing members
going out to visit would-be newcomers either at home or in
hospital, and taking them to their first meeting. Sometimes this
is all that it involves. But some newcomers tell of the way they
were 'twelve-stepped' by frequent lifts to meetings, many phone
calls, and weeks of undoubted effort and care lavished on them.

The raison d'être of this is not so much that the sufferer

benefits, as that the helper does. 'You can't keep it without giving it away' is a common saying in the fellowships. The aim of helping others is to maintain one's own abstinence. Transactional analysts claim that this is the key to the fellowships' success – the victim exchanges roles for that of the rescuer. Indeed Eric Berne, author of *Games People Play*, has even claimed that an AA group might collapse if it had sobered up all the drunks in town. [36] It is significant, probably, that a much earlier body called the Washingtonian Movement had similar success in sobering up a hundred thousand alcoholics by the same method. [33] One very important effect of helping others is to increase the self-esteem of the helper. He or she can feel that the disgrace they went through in drinking days is now utilised to help another. The meaning of the disgrace changes, as did the classification 'alcoholic' or 'addict' earlier in the programme. Members are given a chance to love themselves better, by offering love to others.

And indeed there are close bonds between members, united as they are by the sense of sharing the same plight, of having escaped the same dangers. 'We AAs are like the passengers of a great liner the moment after rescue from shipwreck, when camaraderie, joyousness and democracy pervade the vessel from steerage to captain's table', wrote Bill Wilson. [35] Each fellowship has developed a jargon of its own – binding members together, just as language binds other groups. And there are also unofficial activities ranging from two people getting together to go to the theatre, to full-scale parties. Narcotics Anonymous had a party to celebrate its third year of existence in England. Gamblers Anonymous run 'Pin Nights' when successfully abstinent members are awarded symbolic pins. Alcoholics Anonymous has Christmas Day meetings and a New Year's Eve party in London. Local groups organise discos, parties, picnics, river boat trips. Some researchers have maintained that these get-togethers are enormously important in keeping people within the group. 'Being an AA member does not just mean being involved in formal AA activities. It is a matter of forming relationships and friendships with other AA members which in turn leads to informal activity outside AA meetings . . . Three quarters of the members in the survey said they had made a lot of new friends in AA.' [27]

Such friendships are built into the system. The newcomer to Gamblers Anonymous is 'given a telephone list and you're told that here are some twenty members of your group and you soon get to know their names and you can phone any one of these people during the day or night.'[12] The other three fellowships also swop phone numbers with newcomers. Bonds are further reinforced by the tradition of anonymity. In public members do not say that they belong to the fellowships, and they undertake not to reveal the identity of other members. This 'helps members to emphasise what is shared, their alcohol problem, and to play down the things that separate them – last names, origins, occupations and the assumption that help or support is related to outside standards or position.'[12] Nor are the friendships merely surface ones. AA, NA and OA have a system of 'sponsorship', whereby a relatively long-standing member will help a newcomer. The sponsor is a mentor to the newcomer – a relationship which may involve considerable time and effort from the sponsor. In OA some newcomers phone their sponsor every single day to discuss with them the 'food plan' for the next twenty-four hours.[37] Within this relationship may also occur what Bacon called the 'civil shrift or confession' of friendship. For the newcomer is encouraged to make 'a searching and fearless moral inventory' which is then spoken out loud to 'another human being', often the sponsor, who will in turn reveal similar secrets about his or her own background.[38] With this intimate disclosure, the relationship usually becomes one of intimate friendship.

All four fellowships aim not merely at giving the new member a substitute network of new friends, but also at helping him put right his existing relationships. This is done by making a list of 'all persons we had harmed' and of making amends to them.[38] Interpretation varies, but members talk of repaying money owed, trying to restore family ties, apologising for bad behaviour. Making amends is 'the beginning of the end of our isolation from our fellows' according to AA literature.[38] A 1981 survey of OA members showed that they considered they had shown improvement in 'family life', among other areas.[39] Of course when an addict stops his self-destructive behaviour, the strain on relationships eases. But the four fellowships all recommend active attempts to repair the damage.

Psychotherapists urge putting relationships right too; so do most therapists. The point about the fellowships is that they lead not just by advice but by example. And they can tolerate the deviant and disruptive newcomer better than many psychotherapists. AA 'provides emergency attention whenever it is called upon to do so. Being a large group it can meet these needs in a way that would be impossible for individual psychiatrists. Whereas a person seeking psychiatric help would make an appointment to see a psychiatrist, the candidate for AA is seen immediately on demand. He will receive just as prompt a response the twelfth time he asks for help as he did the first time.'[40] Allowing for individual failure, this is so. Failures to stay off the addiction are known as 'slips', a trivial little phrase designed to take away the sting of it.

There is one other major difference between the fellowships and the conventional medical services. Psychiatrists and social workers will help as long as they are paid to, or required to by their job, or as long as they think they are needed. The four fellowships offer – like true friendship does – the possibility of lifelong commitment. 'It seems to me that an important difference between AA and most other forms of group therapy is that the participants expect to belong to the group for life,' wrote a social worker who had come into contact with AA. Unlike most conventional helpers, he considered this an advantage. 'I think AA has stumbled on the same dynamic which Christian dogmas try to enshrine but usually fail to transmit. A group committed to each other on the basis of shared need, to help themselves through helping others, can become the arena for intensely creative interaction.'[41]

Certainly most of the members of all four fellowships that I have met have not been afraid of talking about love. Sometimes this talk may seem rather Californian in tone, as in the T-shirt worn by a NA member which said 'Hugs not Drugs'. But usually the mention of love is backed up by stories of kindnesses and care given. In the book *Overeaters Anonymous* a member explains: 'I lost my feeling that I had no friends, for I gained a nationwide fellowship of "instant" friends, and many close special friends as well as a sponsor who knows me inside and out and loves me anyway!'[22] 'The AA programme is just a question of following the commandment "Love one another" ' one AA member told me, while another remarked: 'I found an almost compelling love in the fellowship. It was difficult to ignore it.'

Certainly if imitation is the sincerest form of flattery, then the fellowships are much flattered. In Britain there is now a Depressives Anonymous, Emotions Anonymous and Parents Anonymous. Not all are run on quite the same principles. In the USA I have heard of Incest Survivors Anonymous, Credit Cards Anonymous (for compulsive credit card users), Pills Anonymous, and Sex Offenders Anonymous. There has even been a mention of an Analysands Anonymous open to 'anyone who has been in analysis for twelve years or more and who needs a power greater than their own or that of their analyst to terminate the analysis'. [12]

The mention of a 'Higher Power', often spelled complete with Godly capital letters, points to another mystifying paradox of these four fellowships. All insist that the dependence they exist to treat is an illness, not a moral fault. Yet they use the language of religion, speak of a 'Higher Power' and of 'God' in the twelve-step programme. Though there are atheists and agnostics among their ranks, most members will say that they believe in some kind of god. This is usually followed by the remark: 'This isn't anything to do with religion. This isn't a religious programme. It is a spiritual one.' It is an emphasis which ordinary outsiders find bewildering.

For in some ways the fellowships work rather like a religion. Those who have studied AA have often drawn parallels between its methods and those of organised religion. An early study of AA was entitled 'Conversion as a Psychological Phenomenon'. [42] Looking at the lives of all the members, there is a distinct sense of 'before and after'. They will dwell on their bad behaviour during their addicted days in something of the same way a Salvation Army convert used to dwell on his sins before conversion. Then follows a description of what seems rather like being born again, the advent of a new life. Indeed, the GA British magazine is called 'New Life'. And clearly for some of the members, it *is* an almost entirely new life. Drunks who have been on meths in the gutter, now become sober members of society with rents, rates and taxes to pay and often with responsible jobs. Gamblers who have been quite unable to keep money in their pockets, are now able to run their financial affairs just like anybody else. Drug addicts who have plumbed the depths of squalor in their addiction to heroin, become clean young men and women full of the joys of life. Their very lives are proof of some kind of conversion from sickness to health, and usually also from despair to happiness.

9

From the Love of God to the Love of Others

Some doctors and medical staff are mystified by or even occasionally hostile to Alcoholics Anonymous and its three counterparts for gambling, drugs and overeating. The hostility arises not just because these organisations displace professional with self-help, but because they unashamedly talk about God. Indeed, their members quite often maintain that their maladies were not just physical and mental illnesses, but also spiritual ones. They are encouraged to believe and trust in a God or at least a 'Higher Power' – and many would maintain that this belief and trust have been central to their recovery in the long term. This spiritual content often embarrasses doctors, nurses and social workers. Even the religious sometimes feel that it has no part in a health programme, while others see it as an embarrassing addition to what would otherwise be a thoroughly straightforward and worthwhile organisation. In Britain at least one organisation has been set up specifically to imitate much of Alcoholics Anonymous, but leaving out all the embarrassing nonsense of God and a spiritual programme.

But what if the religious side of these organisations has something to do with their success? What if the religious side plays a part in the healing process, in the inner change required of these ex-alcoholics and addicts, or in the spirit of fellowship within their organisation? Our own age has chosen to treat religion as if it were simply a personal taste, like wearing navy blue for preference – something that an individual may believe in, but which should remain resolutely part of his private life. Anybody who holds so strongly to his religion that it seeps out either into his daily life or his conversation is often thought embarrassing. Nor is this a response confined to our own century. Religious 'enthusiasm' was equally disliked in Britain in the eighteenth century, even though Christianity's tenets were more widely held.

The modern fallacy is that religion is worthless – just because its beliefs cannot be proved. I have been guilty of this sloppy thinking. I have believed that the only information worth having is information which has been proved by scientific investigation. At some points in my life I have refused to consider ideas – let alone accept them as useful – on the grounds that they could not be proved. Yet much common sense and collective wisdom in mankind has not been proved – yet. My rejection was not a thought-out one; it was an emotional one. I had a strong belief that my brain was an entirely logical organ, and that the way I lived my life required only hard facts to be considered. I now regard this belief of mine as silly, as odd, as downright perverse as any minority religious cult. It now seems to me far more likely that the human brain has an innate capacity for belief, and that it needs this capacity in order to function at all. Indeed, logic has its roots in the way that the human brain can trust in various beliefs and concepts. J.Z. Young has written: 'The development and construction of the whole human brain model depends upon this capacity to accept or have faith in certain fundamental methods of operating. It is a fascinating paradox that believing produces both the essential foundations of logic and all the many schemes, extravagant, metaphysical, and even irrational, by which men explain their universe.'[1] If the capacity to believe is as essential to man as language, then we need to ask ourselves whether we are justified in sneering at religion. And does the reductionist view of man and the universe have as much to offer mankind as other more generous – including religious – beliefs do?

I think not. The reductionist concept of a meaningless universe – the senselessness of all moral statements, human beings who are merely super-intelligent naked apes – usually goes hand in hand with claims that religion causes misery. Psychotherapists often blame it for unhappiness and guilt. Some go so far as to suggest that all guilt is bad, forgetting perhaps how unpleasant a community would be one of guilt-free psychopaths. Sex educators likewise argue that religion causes 'sexual dysfunctions', and that human happiness depends to a fairly large extent on the absolutely unrestrained satisfaction of whatever sexual appetites an individual possesses. The Marxist, arguably himself a fervent believer in his own religion, condemns other faiths as the opium of the people. Everywhere there are passing references to the primitiveness of religion, to the ills it causes, to its inability to co-exist with the scientific method.

In the West Christianity has not surprisingly declined and continues to decline. The falling number of those who go to church and chapel is well charted. But, it is worth pausing here to consider the past. A secular majority is nothing new in the U.K. In 1821 Sheffield's Anglican churches had 4000 seats, of which only 300 were free and thus available to the working classes. Sheffield's population was then about 65,000. Even if every seat was taken, only about 6% of Sheffield's population could have attended church on Sundays. Some nineteen years later, it was estimated that 75 to 90% of the urban working class did not go to church. At the end of the century, a census of 2000 factory workers found that only five had ever been to a church – these being three Catholics, one Non-conformist and one Anglican. Clearly, in Britain at least, church-going has been a minority pursuit in the past, as well as in the present.[2]

When people do not go to church, they are not necessarily atheists. I am still amazed at the proliferation of fringe cults, even among educated men and women. 'Once upon a time, when I was the features editor of a London evening newspaper,' recalls Mary Kenny, 'a terrible event took place. Panic telephone calls early in the day from members of the public told us that we had omitted from that day's newspaper the astrological column, the reading of the stars which told people of their daily fate . . . It was a dreadful oversight.'[3] In almost every large party I have been to, it has been possible to find at least one person who believes in palmistry, or astrology, or reflexology or some such method of reading the future. Oriental cults also abound. Bewildered and rather embarrassed Indians are now getting used to seeing American upper-middle-class boys and girls who have taken up the Krishna Consciousness Movement. 'From time to time, English language newspapers in

Bengal publish mildly patronising accounts of the latest development in what is mainly American-supported enterprise.'[2] God is not dead, though he may take some unfamiliar forms today.

There also remains in Britain today what two sociologists have called 'common religion'. This 'common religion' is probably quite widely spread in the west of Europe and the USA too. In a very small survey, sociologists found a large number of people who did not go to church but who nevertheless counted themselves religious. 'I don't go to church . . . I pray every night, I have to. It's funny, isn't it?' The sociologists felt that they had demonstrated 'that a large grey area which we have termed common religion, exists as an important part of the religious orientation of ordinary people'.[4] It is premature to declare the death of Christianity on the basis of falling numbers in church.

Religious beliefs have a tendency to creep back into people's lives, even when the authorities are against their existence. The Buryat Mongols in the Soviet Union believe that members of the Paris Commune of 1871 – heroes in the Soviet Union – were changed into otters and live in a nearby lake. If sacrifices are made to them, they will help with the fishing. A Buryat Shaman explained: 'The October Socialist Revolution, Soviet power, the building of Communism, etc . . . all this is the will of the gods. The Communists are their emissaries on earth. Lenin, Sverdlov, Kalinin are also deities which hold meetings in the sky and decide about matters which are important to living people.'[5]

Marxism has claimed that religions other than its own ideology will wither away in a socialist society. This has not happened even in the more sophisticated areas of the Soviet Union. The Russian Orthodox Church claimed 30,000,000 regular churchgoers in 1961. This is less than half its membership before the revolution, but still a staggeringly high figure. Ten years later, the Baptists claimed more than 500,000, the Pentecostalists, Jehovah's Witnesses and the Mennonites about 40,000 each, and the Adventists 25,000 to 30,000. These believers exist despite decades of active government opposition to religion. Soviet sociologists have had to fall back on some very un-Marxist explanations to account for it. One is the suggestion that people enjoy the emotional impact of religious ritual. Another, that religion, even in the Soviet Union, is a way of solving personal problems. 'As it stands, this psychologist approach implies the completely non-Marxist hypothesis that religion is a universal phenomenon existing in any society regardless of its social system.'[6]

For once, I find myself in agreement with these Marxist sociologists. If religious belief (which might well include belief in the coming kingdom of Marx) is an innate human tendency, then perhaps human societies need to cultivate it. Certainly, the received wisdom used to be that a man with a belief in nothing other than his own strength and intelligence is a fool. To perceive the universe as ordered is preferable to nihilism. 'Either the world is a mere hotchpotch of random cohesions and dispersions, or else it is a unity of order and providence. If the former, why wish to survive in such a purposeless and chaotic confusion; why care about anything, save the manner of the ultimate return to dust; why trouble my head at all; since, do what I will, dispersion must overtake me sooner or later? But if the contrary be true, then I do reverence, I stand firmly, and I put my trust in the directing Power.'[7] Religion is a great source of meaning, and is perhaps needed as such by many. The men and women who never go to church and yet hold to some 'common religion', often speak of this. They are convinced that religious belief makes life bearable. 'I've often felt that if I didn't have any faith to believe in I'd be lost, be really depressed,' said one.[4]

It is from the concentration camps that we have some of the starkest testimony to the power of belief to help men in their direst need. If there has ever been a hell on earth more horrifying even than the hells imagined by the religious, then the concentration camps of Hitler's Germany must qualify. The survivors tell us that spiritual faith – not necessarily attached to a particular cult – helped them live through their unimaginable torment. 'In spite of all the enforced physical and mental primitiveness of the life in a concentration camp, it was possible for spiritual life to deepen,' wrote Viktor E. Frankl who was in Auschwitz. 'Sensitive people who were used to a rich intellectual life may have suffered much pain (they were often of a delicate constitution) but the damage to their inner selves was less. They were able to retreat from their terrible surroundings to a life of inner riches and spiritual freedom. Only in this way can one explain the apparent paradox that some prisoners of a less hardy make-up often seemed to survive camp life better than did those of a robust nature.'[8]

An inner spiritual life sometimes gave meaning to an otherwise senseless fate. A Zionist survivor of the camps, a doctor, had thought about emigrating to Palestine in 1940 but he had decided the life would be too hard. 'I was often haunted by the reflection that it was all my own fault. I reasoned to myself: "If you had not preferred the illusional safety of a physician's existence in the Netherlands, but had suited your actions to your words, you would not have had to go through all this." Thus I could not deny a measure of justice to my fate, *and this made my sufferings less difficult to bear*', he wrote in a book about concentration camp life.[9] (They are my italics.) Deserved torment may, to some at least, be more easily borne than undeserved torment. If the bearing of suffering is what is required, a certain measure of guilt may indeed help endurance.

Man's extremity is God's opportunity: there are times when an unbeliever needs to seek whatever spiritual succour may be available. Christopher Burney, kept in solitary confinement for many months by the Germans, found some help in the religion of his childhood. He recalled the words of the prodigal son. 'I will arise and go to my Father and will say unto him, Father, I have sinned before Heaven and in Thy sight; and am no more worthy to be called Thy son.' These words gave him hope and he began to wonder if God might be a source of help. 'There was certainly no other possible source, though it seemed that the "worth trying" frame of mind would be unlikely to produce results.' In his extreme need, there was no conventional Christian conversion, no sudden access of certainty, but there was some comfort. He could perceive that he was merely 'a small part of one creation'. In this moment of humility he found some calm. 'Having in this way relinquished my illusion of being the pivot and focus of all things, I found that the imminence of death was less oppressive than before. Perhaps this was partly because I had no further decision to make in the matter.'[10]

Not all found faith in the concentration camps; some lost it,

unable to worship a God who permitted such cruelty. Sometimes religious belief led away from survival to martyrdom.
Conditions were so extreme that an act of altruism, sharing a
slice of bread, could lead to death. Some inmates of the camps
were there because of their religion. The Jehovah's Witnesses
were offered release, if they abandoned their doctrine and
joined the army. Almost all refused. 'Many of those who did
not survive, outside as well as inside the camps, perished
because of the unconquerable will to maintain their standards of
values at any price. It was this will that forced them into actions
for which – they knew well – they had to pay with their lives.'[11]
Father Maximilian Kolbe, a Catholic priest, volunteered for
death by starvation in Auschwitz. Three prisoners had escaped,
and ten of the inmates were chosen for death in reprisal. One of
these, Franciszek Gajowniczek, cried out: 'Oh my poor wife, my
poor children, I shall never see them again.' Father Kolbe asked
to take his place, and with nine others was shut up in an under-
ground bunker to be starved to death. Two weeks later, when he
was the only one still living, he was finally killed by an injection
of carbolic acid in the arm.[12]

    When we read about actions like this, we see that a religious
belief, strongly held, can change the course of human life.
Individuals may become extraordinarily brave. They may
sacrifice themselves, undergoing torment, for their faith. Like
other Protestants, I was brought up in the knowledge of some
of the martyrs for our faith in Britain. Bishop Latimer was
burned at the stake in Oxford with Bishop Ridley, and as the
flames were lit, he said: 'Be of good comfort, Master· Ridley,
and play the man. We shall this day light such a candle by God's
grace in England, as, I trust, shall never be put out.' John
Bunyan, the Non-conformist author of *Pilgrim's Progress*,
spent twelve years in a Bedford prison because he would not
promise to cease preaching. 'In which condition,' he wrote, 'I
have continued with much content thorow Grace, but have met
with many turnings and goings upon my heart both from the
Lord, Satan, and my own corruptions; by all which (glory be to
Jesus Christ) I have received among many things, much conviction, instruction, and understanding, of which at large I shall
not here discourse; only to give you a hint or two, a word that
may stir up the Godly to bless God, and to pray for me; and

also to take encouragement, should the case be their own, *Not to fear what men can do to them.*'[13] Catholics, in their turn, remember the many priests persecuted in Britain, whose writings and trials also testify to outstanding courage. 'If I were a man that did not think of God Almighty, or conscience, or heaven or hell, I might have saved my life; for I was offered it by divers people here, if I would but confess my own guilt and accuse others,' said Oliver Plunkett to the Chief Justice who was trying him on a trumped-up charge in the seventeenth century. 'But I had rather die ten thousand deaths, than wrongfully to take away one farthing of any man's goods, one day of his liberty, or one minute of his life.'[14]

The secret of this extra strength to endure is not, I think, anything to do with a particular theology or the particular meaning it gives to life. It seems to me more likely that what produces this courage is the believer's attachment – his love of God, if you like, or at least love for his faith. My authority for equating belief with love is J.Z. Young: 'The essential feature of all a man's beliefs is that he believes in them, they are the props and stays of his brain programme. The very word belief implies love and trust. The German version of it is *glauben*, and both words come from the Aryan root *lubh*, to "hold dear", in fact to love. We love our beliefs.' St Augustine had something of the same idea when he wrote: 'Thou has created us for Thyself, and our heart cannot be quieted till it may find repose in Thee.' And Blaise Pascal's words – 'The heart has its reasons which reason knows nothing of' – confirm religious faith is no question of intellectual conviction. From the small mammals and birds who will face enemies on behalf of their young, we know that maternal love creates extraordinary courage. This maternal courage also exists in us. It is a cliché that love of country leads people to lay down their lives in war. Friendship, too, can produce sacrifice. Is it so odd that the love of God, or the adherence to a religious or political ideal, should have a similar effect?

To love others, it is not necessary to be loved in return. Many young children have a special soft toy or 'security blanket' to which they cling in the absence of their mother. Clutching this inanimate object is not a sign of maladjustment. On the contrary disturbed children tend to use such objects less.[15] 'It seems clear that, whether in human infants or monkey infants, whenever the "natural" object of attachment behaviour is unavailable the behaviour can become directed towards some substitute object. Even though it is inanimate, such an object frequently appears capable of filling the role of an important though subsiduary attachment-"figure". Like a principal attachment-figure, the inanimate substitute is sought especially when a child is tired, ill, or distressed.'[16] The point is, I think, that these objects *work*. Loving creates security. We need to love, rather than be loved. I still keep my childhood teddy bear; so does the redoubtable Margaret Thatcher. I still experience something of that fierce childhood emotion when I look at the incredibly tattered face of that loved bit of stuffing and fur. That is, the fact that a creed per se is incapable of response, loving or otherwise, and that God – any God – lacks a tangible presence, does not invalidate the connection I've traced between religious faith and love. It is also worth remembering in this connection that children will cling to mothers who batter them; monkey babies clutch even more fiercely to the substitute mother figure which is blasting them with painfully hot air.[17] We can love the unloving. Indeed, the fear set up by an unloving God may make us cling the more to our faith.

Another similarity between the two lies in the way both are formed: each can be acquired entirely through familiarity. Just as love grows between two people who are thrown into proximity, so can it grow between an individual and a creed. Belief can be gained by the sheer persistence of habit – as Pascal pointed out. When I was searching for a religious belief, I had to decide to set aside questions of theology and, instead, look for the belief that would be best for me and the others round me. I needed, desperately needed, some help and comfort in my attempt to lead a good life. Christianity seemed to promise that support. But if I had waited to be convinced by the weight of historical argument or by the logic of theological dogma, I should be godless still, and without the meaning I need in my life. If it seems an odd argument for Christianity, this pressing need of mine for God, no matter. Some Christians will understand. Somebody told me the other day how he had found his way to God. 'I wanted to believe in God, and then started to pray. I found that I had to pray, then start to believe in God.' It was much the same for me. The beginning of belief was attaching myself to a religion I did not believe.

Finally, but perhaps most important of all, the most obvious of the qualities common to both love and belief is their power to comfort. The Marxist, for example, contemplates the idea of historical inevitability when his cause here and now is suffering. And, as a woman follower of Islam explained, 'If I can't go to mosque, that's something different. I don't have to go to mosque to pray to God – but I can sit inside the house and pray. But whatever happens if the worst came to the worst, my faith cannot be snatched from me. That's a part of my body, that's something attached to my heart, that only dies when I die.' [18]

There is, of course, a quite different side to most religions – the magical, which represents the various techniques of prayer or sacrifice as ways of controlling the material world. We tend to think it is only found in primitive societies, but it exists quite happily in our own in the form of superstition. Any one who walks round a ladder or throws spilled salt over the left shoulder is sharing in this magical way of thinking – as is the worshipper who makes such specific requests as John Ward, the MP for Weymouth: 'Oh Lord, Thou knowest that I have lately purchased an estate in fee simple in Essex. I beseech Thee to preserve the two counties of Middlesex and Essex from fire and earthquakes: and as I have also a mortgage in Hertfordshire, I beg of Thee also to have an eye of compassion on that county, and for the rest of the counties, Thou may deal with them as Thou art pleased. Oh Lord, enable the bank to answer all their bills and make all my debtors good men, give a prosperous voyage and safe return to the *Mermaid* sloop, because I have not insured it, and because Thou hast said, "The days of the wicked are but short", I trust in Thee that Thou wilt not forget Thy promise, as I have an estate in reversion, which will be mine on the death of that profligate young man, Sir J. L—g. Keep my friends from sinking, preserve me from thieves and housebreakers, and make all my servants so honest and faithful that they may always attend to my interest and never cheat me out of my property night or day.' [19]

From this, it is not far to the prayer of more primitive countries. An anthropologist has listed the reasons why offerings were made at four village temples in West Bengal over six months. They were: for the cure of disease, for good health; for the birth of a child; for prosperity in trade; for employment; for good crops; for gaining property; for curing cattle disease; for educational progress; for success in a lawsuit; for domestic harmony; for victory in a football match; for success in local amateur dramatics; for a good marriage. I have to admit here that I know people in our so-called sophisticated society who do use prayer in this way – praying for the next bus to come quickly, or for their God to find them a parking meter. Obviously this has little to do with attachment to God. It is merely a shopping-list technique for altering the world in a way which suits the supplicant. And as magical thinking becomes discredited, it often dies away. In West Bengal there is now smallpox vaccination. As a result, the local goddess has fewer offerings.[2]

This kind of prayer has been investigated, and found wanting by the scientific method. As long ago as 1872 Francis Galton looked at the way the royal family in Britain was frequently interceded for in the prayerbook services of the time. Yet they did not seem to live any longer than people in trade or commerce who were hardly prayed for at all. From this he deduced that prayer did not work. In 1965 a similar investigation was set up – in the form of a double blind clinical trial, in which some people were prayed for while others were not – and came to the same conclusion as Galton's.[20]

I have however met individuals who feel otherwise, including non-believers. 'In 1949 I was taken very ill in Tokyo,' a retired diplomat, who is an agnostic, told me.

The doctors admitted me in some haste to the Seibo Hospital, run by Catholic Japanese nuns under an Irish matron. I knew that I had jaundice but not that I had the dreaded leptospirosis. For the only time in my life it seemed to me likely that I should die; and I was frightened. The doctors gave me antediluvian treatment (but I have subsequently heard of someone else so treated who recovered against the odds). Throughout my illness, Japanese nuns, clearly detailed for this duty, prayed in my room for my recovery. There was nothing demonstrative about it. They just came in, smiled, knelt, and, when they had finished, got up and left. It all reminded me of 'Little Gidding':

> '. . . you are not here to make report
> You are here to kneel where prayer has been valid.'

I found it immensely encouraging, but it made me very uncomfortable. 'How smart a lash that speech doth give my conscience', but all the smarter since there was no audible speech, and no propaganda. They were just getting on with their job. Later I learned that leptospirosis is often fatal and that my fear of death had been by no means exaggerated.

Prayer – however ineffective in the realms of this world – has not died out. Many people who belong to no formal religion nevertheless pray, if only occasionally. In a large survey of Americans published in 1960, sixteen per cent prayed as a way of handling their daily worries. One in three prayed when faced with a crisis in their lives.[21] In most faiths prayer is there to benefit he who prays, and the crude concept of a shopping list sent to an almighty power is rarely accepted among sophisticated believers. As Marcus Aurelius wrote: 'The gods either have power or they have not. If they have not, why pray to them? If they have, then instead of praying to be granted or spared such-and-such a thing, why not rather pray to be delivered from dreading it, or lusting for it, or grieving over it? Clearly, if they can help a man at all, they can help him in this way.'[6] Indeed, much prayer consists of asking for acceptance – 'Thy will be done on earth, as it is in heaven.' – rather than for change in material circumstances. And most people who pray regularly will agree that its importance lies in the effect it has on their inner selves. 'Prayer has become such an important part of my life now, that I simply couldn't do without it: it is the answer to stress, the anodyne to frustration, the antidote to anger, and the pool of self-knowledge that enables me to have the energy to go on being the natural extrovert that I am. When I feel I can't cope, I simply say: "Please, dear Lord, you cope for me; if it is to be accomplished let it be accomplished; if it is not, help me to face that serenely." '[3] There is also a kind of prayer that is an experience rather than anything said or thought in words.

Quakers practise silent prayer while waiting on God, or some inner impulse to speak. To take part in one of their meetings is to gain an extraordinary insight into the unquietness of one's heart. Taking the mind and heart to God without words is difficult indeed. But mystics are sometimes seized with emotional states of mind when words are not needed. 'What surprised me most is that I had great difficulty in saying my spoken prayers which I had been in the custom of saying. As soon as I opened my mouth to pronounce them the (divine) love seized me so strongly that I remained absorbed in profound silence and in a peace which I cannot express,' wrote Mme Guyon. [22] It is at such moments that Christianity comes closest to those Indian religions which try to achieve union with – rather than speaking to – the eternal deity. That people have these moments of deep spiritual meaning in their lives cannot be denied. They can seem as real as any outward event. Sometimes atheists report them. Their exact significance, or religious importance, is more than I can understand.

There has been, as far as I know, no investigation into the effect Christian prayer might have on those who practise it. There is some evidence, however, on the effects of meditation – it is more amenable to clinical testing because it can be practised without a belief in a God. It is, besides, immune from the medical prejudice against our national religion. Researchers have tried teaching patients with high blood pressure the techniques of Transcendental Meditation – as taught by the Beatles' Guru. In the first three months the patients, except for one individual, showed a drop in blood pressure. But this benefit disappeared when four were left to meditate on their own, without help. [23] A British doctor has added relaxation techniques and some yoga with better results on her patients' blood pressure. [24]

Traditionally, religion has been seen as a source of consolation for the distressed. 'When thy passions are most vehement, then seeke for succour in Heaven, flie under the wings of Christ', advised T. Wright in 1601 in *The Passions of the Minde*. [25] But nowadays the professionals no longer seem to believe that religion might be helpful. The nearest there is to an accepted religious technique for consolation is that form of treatment known as rational-emotive therapy, which concurs with the Stoic idea that man's freedom consists in choosing his emotional reactions rather than letting outside circumstances dictate them. [26]

Though undervalued by the medical establishment, few would disagree that religion does offer a real consolation for the distressed – and one not easily matched in secular life. In Britain there is a befriending organisation known as the Samaritans, which offers help to those thinking of suicide. One of the danger signs of acute suicide risk, used to assess the urgency of a telephone call, is 'lack of a philosophy of life, such as a comforting type of religious faith'. [27] In other words, the devout are less likely to kill themselves. This may be simply because, among others, Christianity and Islam prohibit suicide as self-murder. But some experts have taken the view that religion guards against suicide not because of this prohibition, but because it integrates the individual into a social group. [28] Those who have lost their religious faith, on the other hand, feel guilty and may be more prone to suicide – just as those who have lost a loved one by death, or by the break up of a relationship, seem prone either to suicide or to deliberate self-harm such as overdosing. It seems to me that the protective effect of religion can be seen in terms of an attachment to that religion. When the attachment is broken, it results in depression, like the unhappiness produced by a broken marriage or widowhood.

Suicide apart, religion is a source of help to many. The relatives of those who have committed suicide often ask for religious counselling. [29] The same American survey which showed that one in three pray at times of crisis, showed that large numbers turned to clergymen and ministers for help. [21] The survey organisers asked how effective they found it, as compared with that forthcoming from psychiatrists. Psychiatrists were expected to show up well, but this was not so. People found them the least effective. Clergyman and ordinary doctors were rated more helpful than psychiatrists. 'In most cases clergymen were appreciated for their ability to offer comfort or, more vaguely, for their capacity to give advice. Both of these benefits were ascribed to clergymen proportionately more often than to either physicians or psychiatrists. These results, taken together, substantiate the assumption that clergymen serve as emotional supporters.' This seems to me very significant indeed. Clergymen offer love rather than solutions to problems. And it is love that most human beings find so helpful in times of trouble. Alas, it is love that conventional psychiatry and medical science in general tend to forget in their preoccupation with either objectivity or the new pharmaceutical nostrums. Clergymen do not offer emotional support just because they are nice kindly men. They offer it because to do so is an essential part of the practice of their faith.

What they also have to offer, as do all religious leaders, is some kind of explanation for human suffering. Buddhism is a religion shaped by it. The Buddha perceived the so-called Noble Truths, that 'birth is suffering; ageing is suffering; sickness is suffering; death is suffering; sorrow and lamentation, pain, grief, and despair are suffering; association with the unpleasant is suffering; dissociation from the pleasant is suffering; not to get what one wants is suffering – in brief, the five aggregates of attachment are suffering.'[30] The Middle Way, the Buddhist programme for living, is aimed at diminishing and eventually extinguishing this suffering in oneself.

Though not all religions focus so sharply on the anguish of the human condition, most try to explain it, find a use for it. In some parts of the Old Testament, there is the assertion that human suffering is God's punishment for wickedness – and before we cry out against this, we should remember the Dutch doctor who found in the concentration camp that he bore his sufferings more easily because in some sense he felt they were deserved. In the book of Job, however, the idea that human suffering is always God's punishment is found wanting. The solution to the mystery of why God should have let his faithful servant suffer is simply this: that mankind cannot understand the ways of God, and should not expect to. In other parts of the Old Testament, there is the suggestion that suffering is part and parcel of God's interest in mankind – 'For whom the Lord loveth, he reproveth, even as a father the son in whom he delighteth.'[31] In later Judaism, as in Christianity and Islam, the idea of the Last Judgement is brought in to redeem the suffering here on earth: those who have suffered will be rewarded, and the evil who had an easy time of it, will get their reward in hell. Something slightly similar occurs in Marxism, where revolutionaries may have to endure now that future generations may be free. There is also the idea that come the revolution, the humble will be exalted and the rich shall be sent empty away.

Suffering may also be seen as some kind of test sent by God, or at the least an opportunity to practise virtue. The Koran says: 'We alternate these vicissitudes among mankind so that Allah may know the true believers and choose martyrs from among you (He does not love the evil-doers); and that He may test the faithful and annihilate the infidels. Did you suppose that you would enter Paradise before Allah has proved the men who fought for Him and endured with fortitude?'[32] In the epistle of St James in the New Testament, suffering is seen as a blessing. 'Behold we count them happy which endure. Ye have heard of the patience of Job, and have seen the end of the Lord; that the Lord is very pitiful and of tender mercy.'[33] The exact explanation of human suffering varies – some explanations are more satisfying than others. But I do not think it is the quality of the dialectic in religious faiths that gives comfort. It is the assertion that, whatever the reason, suffering is not senseless. In his extremity man seeks for something that might tell him his pain is not meaningless. Sometimes religion only asserts that we cannot know what its meaning is. But it asserts at the same time that God can. For those who suffer, this assertion of man's inability to know the reason is itself comforting.

Besides the private solace derived from communion with God or creed, the practice of religion also seems to enhance human relationships. It is normal for intellectuals to sneer at the social side of church life – the church fetes, whist drives, bingo in the church hall, and coffee mornings in aid of the church tower fund. There are youth clubs, wives' groups, amateur dramatics, jumble sales galore, and usually some kind of parish magazine. 'The annual parish church fete is one of the most important features of life in rural Norfolk and over forty per cent of the region's population attend it.'[34] Studies of church membership over and over again report on the central importance of such social activities. 'At Wesley, for example, the outstanding event of the year was not any of the Christian festivals but the Christmas Market for which old members who had moved away often made a special effort to return . . .Bethel did not have an annual bazaar (and felt themselves a little superior to

Wesley because of this) but when in 1966 they mounted a Spring Fayre, the enthusiasm surpassed even the zeal of their fellow Methodists up the road. The minister at that time can recall no other occasion during his five-year stay at Oakcroft when so many members and adherents at Bethel were so energetically involved in a church event.'[35]

This may be poor religion, but we cannot afford to mock it. In a large investigation into the pattern of deaths in Alameda County, California, church or temple membership seemed to have a protective effect. Admittedly the decisive factor was social ties of any kind, but that religion should promote these is a significant part of its contribution to society. It has also been found that 'People who attend church regularly report less distress than those who go to church infrequently, a finding that is perhaps related to both the religious commitment involved . . . and its reflection of social integration in the community.'[36] Those who sneer at the fervour of church bazaars are sneering at something which may well be keeping church members healthy and happy.

In more intimate relationships, religion can play a part too. Just as it often pronounces on suicide, so it deters and sometimes forbids divorce. Thus we should expect the religiously devout to stay together even if their marriage is an unhappy one. However, their ranks do not seem to be made up of the unhappy but still married. Rather the reverse: 'That small part of the population who call themselves agnostic or atheist or have no preference among the various religions are on the average most critical of their marriages: they are also the most likely to have been divorced from an earlier marriage.' (Indeed agnostics and atheists are generally less likely to describe themselves as happy and satisfied with life.)[37] And bizarrely enough for those who have been led on by Masters and Johnson and their followers to think it anti-sex, religion seems to enhance sex within marriage.[38]

The reason why religion enhances social relationships may well lie in the fact that most creeds specifically promote kindness between people. 'Love thy neighbour' is not an exclusively Christian message. It can be found in the Old Testament – in Leviticus: 'Thou shalt not take vengeance, nor bear any grudge against the children of thy people, but thou shalt love thy neighbour as thyself: I am the Lord.'[39] Buddhists cherish compassion. 'According to Buddhism for a man to be perfect there are two qualities that he should develop equally: compassion (karuna) on one side, and wisdom (panna) on the other. Here compassion represents love, charity, kindness, tolerance and such noble qualities on the emotional side or qualities of the heart, while wisdom would stand for the intellectual side or the qualities of the mind.'[40] Among the sayings of Mohammed are, 'Do you love your Creator? Love your fellow creatures first' and, 'Thou wilt see the faithful in their having mercy for one another, and their kindness towards one another like the body: when one member of it ails, the entire body ails, one part calling out the other with sleeplessness and fever.'[41] In St John's Gospel Christ is reported to have said: 'A new commandment I give unto you, That ye love one another; as I have loved you, that ye also love one another.'[42]

This brotherly love is quite often confined to those who follow the same path, belong to the same tribe, or hold the right theological tenets. Yet some religions have gone beyond this. The idea that the concept of 'neighbour' embraces not just fellow believers but the whole of mankind, was already a commonplace among Hellenistic Jews of the diaspora at the time of Jesus.[43] The most elevated vision of Christian love, as found in those gospels probably predating St John's, comprehends even the outcasts of society. In the story of Jesus nearly all versions show him being kind, courteous and sometimes going out of his way to be helpful to those whom society rejected – not just the sick and the mad, but also the soldiers of an occupying power, the heretic Samaritans, the woman who had been married five times, the woman taken in adultery, tax gatherers and public sinners. This ideal of brotherly love is the highest possible. 'Ye have heard that it hath been said, Thou shalt love thy neighbour and hate thine enemy' Jesus is reputed to have said in the Sermon on the Mount, 'But I say unto you, Love your enemies, bless them that curse you, do good to them that hate you, and pray for them which despitefully use you and persecute you.'[44] If Christianity can be said to be the imitation of Christ, then Christian love should extend to the sad, the mad, and the frankly evil. Alas, this is not always so, even in the New Testament. In the epistles of St John, it

looks as if love is to be confined to Christians, rather than given
to any and everybody. He warns against heretics saying: 'If
there come any unto you, and bring not this doctrine, receive
him not into your house, neither bid him God speed: For he that
biddeth him God speed is partaker of his evil deeds.'[45]

Few Christians practise this love, and few of those that follow
Islam or the Middle Way or Judaism live up to the ideals of
their faith. Some fall short without even knowing it – congratu-
lating themselves on their virtue, unaware of their sinfulness in
the light of God's glory. Some respectable churchgoers are so
short on self-criticism, and perhaps imagination, that they are
quite willing to say: 'But I simply have never sinned, vicar.'
There are hypocrites who say the right things, but do not live
their faith. There are also men and women who deny all religion
and even sneer at ethics, yet practise them – a much more
likeable form of hypocrisy. Those outsiders who look at the
hard hearts of church members and from this conclude religion
is a sham should remember that most religions specifically
condemn religious observance which is not accompanied by
ethical conduct in daily life. 'Woe to those who pray but are
heedless in their prayer,' says the Koran, 'who make a show of
piety and give no alms to the destitute.'[46] 'If therefore thou are
offering thy gift at the altar, and there rememberest that thy
brother hath ought against thee, leave there thy gift before the
altar, and go thy way, first be reconciled to thy brother, and
then come and offer thy gift,' says Jesus in the Sermon on the
Mount.[47]

Nor are good works alone sufficient, if they are not accompanied by sympathy and tender feelings. The religious man
whose time is taken up working for the mass of mankind, but
cannot show warmth and sympathy for individuals, fails the
spirit of his faith. 'A kind word with forgiveness is better than
charity followed by insult', says the Koran.[48] In the New Testament, the disciples objected when a woman came up to them
during a meal and poured expensive ointment over the head of
Jesus. They argued that it would have been better to sell the
ointment and give the money to the poor. Jesus defended her
gesture. I have always interpreted this to mean that the feeling
gesture – even a foolish one – is worth more than the coldly
calculated but more prudent action. As St Paul wrote: 'And if I

bestow all my goods to feed the poor, and if I give my body to be burned, but have no love, it profiteth me nothing.'[49]

If religion is an attachment, then its nature must be love. And as we have seen in examining friendship, love is self-generating. Because we love one thing, or one person, we are more likely to be able to love others as well. The power of attachment is not a finite property, that may be used up and must be hoarded just for one relationship. So, setting aside the fact most religions preach love, we should expect them to promote it in their disciples. Being attached to God turns the personality away from self-centredness, in the same way that friendship turns the self towards others. How much more so when the God worshipped is experienced as loving. St Thomas à Kempis wrote in 1486 of the 'familiar friendship of Jesus'. 'The love of creatures is deceivable and failing, but the love of Jesus is faithful and always abiding. He that cleaveth to any creature must of necessity fail, as doth the creature; but he that cleaveth abidingly to Jesus shall be made stable in Him for ever. Love Him, therefore, and hold Him thy friend; for when all others forsake thee, He will not forsake thee, nor suffer thee finally to perish.'[50]

From this, it is hard to take my mind to another truth – that religion has caused wars, tortures, and many petty human unkindnesses. Good Catholics stoked the fires that burned Latimer and Ridley. Good Protestants watched Oliver Plunkett being hung, drawn and quartered. Jonathan Swift who made his living out of a religion he may have believed but did not seem to feel, remarked: 'We have just enough religion to make us hate, but not enough to make us love one another.' No book about love can fail to explore a disconcerting truth – that love, itself, may be abused.

10

The Abuse of Love

It is easy, sometimes fatally easy, to be sentimental about love. 'It's love, it's love that makes the world go round' cries the Good Fairy in pantomimes, while poets make verses on the theme of Love Conquers All. There is also built into the human mind the idea that while love may not in actual fact always conquer, it always justifies. 'But I love her,' says the married man with four young children, as he leaves home for his new young mistress. 'But I loved him,' says the girl secretary who has passed government secrets to a spy. Love is the cry of those who murder unfaithful wives and ask a jury to pardon them. Love is the excuse for suicide pacts, sometimes even for the murder of small children. In 1983 a British father killed his two children, rather than take them back to his estranged wife. Love is also the justification of those women and men who try to depend upon another, compensating for an impoverished self-esteem by exaggerating the qualities of their partner. Love is fast becoming base currency, so indiscriminate and constant are our appeals to it. It is the word mouthed by every social worker, by every teacher, by those bureaucrats whose unpleasant job it is to try to help the inadequates of our society. It is the cry which sells shoddy goods, silly women's magazines, books about sexual technique, pictures of naked women. Finally, of course, there is hypocrisy *tout court*. Love is spouted from every church pulpit just a few minutes before the congregation, myself included, go home for coffee and a malicious gossip about the other church-goers.

It is easy to ignore this potentially dark side of the human instinct to love, the instinct which warps love into something wholly other. For we need love, all of us, so desperately that we are very vulnerable to its imitations, whether they be found in an advertising campaign for a perfume or a self-made Messiah aiming at a multi-million dollar income rather than crucifixion. All of us are prey to those who would exploit our need for love. That is our shame. But what is worse still is that all of us are quite capable of exploiting and abusing love in our turn – even as justification for the most unloving behaviour. As Blaise Pascal said: 'We never do evil so fully and cheerfully, as when we do it out of conscience.'[1] For guilt obliges us to delude ourselves when we want to do evil, and once provided with a good excuse, we feel free to let rip our worst instincts. A mundane example is the way we persuade ourselves that unwarranted, even malicious interference in another's affairs is 'for their own good'. We do it because we love them, of course. On a grander scale, we will murder thousands out of love – love of country or perhaps love of our religion – and never feel a moment's twinge of conscience.

Men and women can love an evil cause, or an evil religion. In the nineteenth century the British in India were shocked to discover a religion which dictated hereditary gangs of men should travel the roads, making friends with innocent travellers, then slaughtering them. The British called this religion 'Thuggee'. Yet the murders were not proof of the individual worshipper's evil mind or sadistic intent. They were sacrifices to the goddess Kali. Her worshippers were, on the whole, family men who were neither brutal nor cruel ordinarily. Yet, out of conscience and love for Kali, they were willing to murder. 'We all feel pity sometimes,' explained Feringeea, one of the thug leaders, 'but the *goor* (sugar) of the *tuponee* (sacrifice to Kali) changes our nature.'[2] Another explained that the murders were not counted as crimes since they were done for the sake of Bhowanee, another name of the Goddess Kali. 'If a man murders anyone without reference to Bhowanee, he will be haunted by ghosts. But we who kill under the patronage of Bhowanee are not troubled in the least.' The tone of his explanation recalled the way a young British anarchist told me about some anarchist executions in the Spanish Civil War. 'They used to take the landowners up on a hill to watch the sunrise before they shot them,' he said admiringly. Because he was attached to the anarchist cause, these murders seemed admirable.

Human beings are bad judges when love clouds the issue. We are all liable to excuse bad behaviour if we think it is for a good cause. Even Kali is still worshipped – though by animal, not human, sacrifice. 'It's believed that if you do not offer in worship by the sacrifice of an animal, then she takes somebody from the family. Believe me or not, it has happened in two families. It has happened in my family: I lost a sister, and everybody told my father he should give up worshipping Goddess Kali, and he didn't. He said, "No, if Kali likes that, I wouldn't stop" ', explained an Indian woman living in Britain.[3] And we cannot dismiss the worship of Kali as the exception. There are many other examples of how religious attachment can lead to cruelty. In the name of Allah the Compassionate, Iranian Muslim extremists are currently persecuting and executing those of the Bahai faith. In South America, Indians are being corrupted in the name of Christianity.[4] Modern religions are just as potentially evil. In Jonestown, Guyana, in November 1978, the Reverend Jim Jones of the People's Temple commanded his followers to commit suicide. More than nine hundred women, men and children did so. Fathers and mothers handed poison to their children. Other loves lead to murder too. In Britain animal lovers have set off bombs with the aim of stopping laboratory experiments on animals. John Hinckley shot President Ronald Reagan, because he loved a film star, a girl he had never met. And in the West most murders are domestic – depending on the society, a third to two thirds are between relatives.[5]

Sometimes people talk as if we are nowadays wiser than past generations. It seems unlikely. Certainly we are just as vulnerable to religious fervour as ever we were. Christianity may be retreating, but in its place have mushroomed a series of cults which are often morally much less admirable. There are the Moonies, the Maharaj Ji's Divine Light Mission, Bhagwan Shree Rajneesh's Orange People, the International Society of Krishna Consciousness, Ron Lafayette Hubbard's Scientology, and hundreds of smaller cults. Between them they claim millions of devoted followers.[6] 'It is a sobering thought that in

1974 six and a half thousand predominantly white, middle-class people paid forty dollars each for the privilege of attending a seminar set up by the EST group in San Francisco's Civil Auditorium', writes Shiva Naipaul.[7] 'The theme: Making Relationships Work. Six and a half thousand people listening raptly to the words of a former encyclopaedia salesman . . . six and a half thousand of the most affluent and privileged humans in the world willing to be taught how to live.'

The leaders of these movements are often rich, while the followers are painfully poor. The young devotees may have high standards, and live in an idealistic way. The young Moonies, for instance, labour night and day for their leader, a portly Korean who lives in style. His followers live in communes, celibate until marriage, having all things in common and excited by common ideals. They have literally given up everything, even their personal clothing, for their god. These young idealists may seem rather like the early Christians: willing to go to any lengths to serve their Heavenly Father, the podgy Mr Moon.

Their recruitment methods exploit mankind's need for love. Moonies specialise in picking up youngsters at airports, stations or other places where they are away from home. They pick them out by their knapsacks and suitcases.[8] The newcomer is assigned a Moonie companion who never lets him out of his sight. Christopher Edwards, a 'recovered' Moonie who has left the cult, recalls following a newcomer into the lavatory rather than risk leaving him alone for a few minutes.[9] This constant surveillance is accompanied by what the Moonies call 'love bombing'. The fresh recruit is given a great deal of intense eye contact and many smiles. A girl recalled what she felt at this stage. 'We went into the room next door where tea and coffee were being served and all the time people were coming up to me, smiling, looking deep into my eyes, and saying things like "Hi, I'm Jake. Lovely to have you with us" . . . I had come from a close-knit loving family. I'd had plenty of good friends at college. But I had never experienced warmth like this before. It was quite overwhelming.'[10] Once they are fully committed to the Moonie movement, the devotees are kept working so hard, so short of sleep, and impose so many ordeals on themselves that they scarcely have time to think or a mind to think with.

The new Moonie is also quarantined from his former friends

and family. Parents of Moonie recruits 'found it extremely difficult to maintain communication with young converts because the latter's views had become highly ideological . . . and members were constantly on the move with their whereabouts frequently unknown even to the leaders of the decentralized Unification Movement' reported a sociological investigation of the Moonie Church.[8] Significantly the Reverend Moon and his wife are described as the 'True Parents', in contrast to mere 'physical parents'. Indeed, Moonie converts are discouraged from seeing their parents alone. As a former Moonie explained: 'I sometimes felt homesick and longed for the warmth and comfort of my family. But Moon's teachings about such things were very clear. Parents in the Fallen World had never brought up their children the way they were supposed to; and so they had become the greatest barrier of all to spiritual salvation.'[10] Another Moonie recalled the moment when a friend, Alex, knew his mother was dying of cancer. 'Alex looked worried. I thought it might have been another letter from his physical parents. His physical mother is dying of cancer and the letters upset him. We both wish they'd stop writing. Alex could never leave his mission to go home to be with her. His parents just don't understand how insignificant physical death is. She will know once she gets to the Spirit World.'[11] It is perhaps significant that when Moonies were allowed to operate on their own, instead of in close-knit communes, the drop-out rate from the movement was high.[8]

The Unification Church of the Moonies is not the only body to cut off its converts from the outside world. In South America, the Protestant New Tribes Mission used similar tactics to persuade Indians into their sect. 'Indians' explained an anthropologist, 'like to do everything together. They share everything, particularly their food. They're very close to each other. The missionaries understood this so they worked out that the best way to punish those who didn't want to be converted was by isolation. As soon as they had a strong following in a village they would order the converts to have nothing more to do with those who held out. No one, not even their own parents, was allowed to talk to them, and they were obliged to eat apart from the rest. It was the worst punishment an Indian could imagine, and often it worked.'[4]

Sometimes, when only one parent joins a cult, there is great suffering over the children of the marriage. In a celebrated case in America, Joey, a twelve-year-old boy, was taken by his mother, a member of the Hare Krishna movement, and 'disappeared' into the cult. There seemed no way in which the cult was voluntarily going to allow the father to see his child. Only after a prolonged struggle did the father obtain the right to see his child. [12] Similar tugs of love occurred when the People's Temple finally left the United States for Guyana. It set up a community some way away from the local towns, cut off from the outside world. The Reverend Jim Jones encouraged whole families to belong to his church, but where a relation left the church then ties had to be severed. A group called the Concerned Relatives was formed, which alleged that the Reverend Jim Jones was unduly influencing church members. [7]

Another feature common to many cults is the deliberate creation of guilt. Some of the South American Indian tribes being proselytised by the New Tribes Mission, seem to have no words for sin, punishment or guilt. In order to supply the omission, the New Tribes Mission has produced literature which claims that Jesus Christ was killed by the Indians. [4] In pursuit of converts, they were quite willing to rewrite the Bible's story of Jesus's crucifixion in Palestine some 2000 years ago. Moonies spend a lot of time undergoing self-imposed punishment ordeals to assuage a guilt whipped up to artificially high levels by the community – a way of emotionally hobbling recruits.

Further, the Unification Church does not rely on isolation from family ties to retain its members. It induces a state of near-paranoia about the outside world. Moonies are kept in a state of constant alarm about evil spirits, which they believe are surrounding them everywhere. They are told stories about the atrocities committed by parents who kidnap their children out of the movement. 'In theory I was free to leave the Moonies at any given moment. I could have simply walked away. I would have been love bombed by my companions; but no one would have made any physical attempt to stop me. However I would have been stepping back into a Satanic world, abandoning all hope of salvation; and these are the bars which keep the Moonies in a prison of their own making.' [10]

The People's Temple employed similar tactics. Its newspaper was full of appalling stories about the United States. At Temple services there were special psycho-dramas, in which Ku Klux Klan lynchings were a popular theme. 'Deep racial terror was mercilessly exposed and exploited in the People's Temple', writes Shiva Naipaul. 'Jones stripped bare his following and left them naked and defenceless. He did not liberate: he assaulted and traumatised those who believed in him. One can sense at a certain level his raging hatred for the blacks whose God he claimed to be; a hatred, so deep-seated, so tormenting, that, in its fury, it turned itself inside out and called itself Love.' The Nazis never reached that final stage of self-delusion. Their hatred of the Jews was open. But the accompanying wild paranoia, in which the Jewish "race" was blamed for all kinds of ills, was of the same genus as that spread by Jones.

How can we distinguish between good and bad love? Which religions abuse it, and which make their appeal in simple sincerity? Still more confusing, among those who undeniably believe what they preach, which nonetheless misconceive love and so lead their followers astray? Where do we draw the line? Why is the Moonie love bombing wrong, while the similar techniques of certain Christian cults are right? Why was it wrong that the Rev. Jones and his followers committed suicide in Guyana, yet the mass-suicide led by the Jewish rebel Eleazer at Masada, when besieged by the Romans, is usually presented as one of the great moments of history? And what shall we make of that supremely uncomfortable saying of Jesus Christ: 'Think not that I am come to send peace on earth; I came not to send peace, but a sword. For I am come to set a man at variance against his father, and the daughter against her mother, and the daughter-in-law against her mother-in-law. And a man's foes shall be they of his own household. He that loveth father or mother more than me is not worthy of me'?[13] Why is it right to give up everything for Christ, but wrong to do the same for Mr Moon? After all, while Christ's teachings seem to many to be faithful to the spirit of love, and Moon's not, His name is no guarantee that all those sects which call on it follow Him.

Many Christian churches discipline their members by the

withdrawal of love. I have heard a member of the congregation, not named but probably known to regular attenders, denounced from a Protestant pulpit as being unfit for membership in the congregation. This came from a minister whose life seemed otherwise to be the practice of love. I can only think he felt such a denunciation his duty. In 1984 even the Church of England, usually noted for its laxity and tolerance, declared from the pulpit that a man and a woman would not be allowed Holy Communion because they had committed adultery – a move which, due to its public nature, seems equivalent to me to withdrawing love. And in Collinsville, Oklahoma, the elders of the Church of Christ wrote this letter to a divorced woman who was having an affair with a divorced man. 'If by the close of worship Sunday morning, you have not indicated a penitent heart by a public acknowledgement of your sin of fornication, a statement will be read aloud to the congregation, so you might hear them and repent. If you choose not to heed these exhortations, a statement will be read by the elders to exclude you from the Fellowship of the Body of Christ and notify sister congregations, which means not to associate with you. Our purpose in exercising this discipline is to save your soul.'[14] It is difficult to find anything in the life of Jesus Christ which is at all similar to these public denunciations. He forgave the woman taken in adultery without demanding her repentance first. Those rebukes he gave in public were usually to the righteous, not to sinners. Yet clearly all these Christian churches felt their behaviour was justified. 'Saving a soul' came before the practice of brotherly love – though it seems extremely unlikely that any souls will be saved in this way.

There is another way in which the Christian establishment abuses love: by treating it as if one kind of love was incompatible with another. The believer is therefore faced with an unnecessary dilemma. Karen Armstrong is a former nun who has written movingly about her experience. Unlike the Moonie recruits, she was neither deceived nor put under undue pressure to join her convent. Yet, once inside, she was encouraged to cut herself off from all the human sources of love – family and friends. Letters from her parents were first read by her superior, and as a novice she was only allowed to write once a month in return. Nuns and novices were not allowed to eat with their relatives on the very rare occasions when visits were allowed –

a ban which was extremely hurtful to the relatives. One novice left the convent because her mother said she was severely ill. As a novice nun – just like Alex in the Moonie commune – she was expected to stay away from her natural parents, even in this crisis. Karen asked one of her superiors if Adèle would be allowed to return to the convent, should her mother not be severely ill after all. 'Of course she could, Sister. But then she'd have to decide whether she was going to stick it out this time. After all, if this can happen once it can happen again. And a commitment to the religious life must be for ever, whatever the difficulties,' replied Mother Albert. [15]

The theory behind this behaviour is that only by destroying all human ties can a person concentrate on loving God. The Christian behest to love God and your neighbour was reformulated as a choice between the two. 'The emptier your heart is of all other loves, the more He can fill it with His love', Karen Armstrong was told. And because of this, nuns who felt friendship for each other would positively avoid each other. A kind of cool serenity was substituted for human warmth.

Furthermore, the novices were trained in total obedience – 'Ignatian obedience which aims to break down the will and judgement of the religious so that he unquestioningly accepts the will of God as it is presented to him *through his superior.* [my italics] . . . It is not enough for a nun simply to perform her superior's command. She must empty her mind of her own judgement and tell herself that this – *whatever it is* – is the best thing she could possibly be doing.' Pointless commands were given to ensure that judgement was never made. Common sense had to be given up. The individual conscience was surrendered entirely. To train herself into this complete surrender, Karen Armstrong was ordered to scrub steps which she had washed the day before, with a nail brush. She was made to practise sewing on a sewing machine with no needle.

Together with all this, there was a considerable amount of what seems to the outsider to have been simple unkindness and lack of charity in the behaviour of some of her superiors – all for the good of her soul, they would have said, no doubt. Unkindness between people in a closed community must be inevitable at times; but in this convent it had the justification that it was for the novice's own good. In one other way her natural judgement was overridden. In her theological studies she was encouraged to follow the correct theological path, even when she and her teacher knew that the arguments put forward were inadequate. Intellectual dishonesty was thus institutionalised. Clearly we Christians cannot shake our heads disapprovingly at the wilder religious cults, without first dealing with the beam in our own eye.

Despite my doubts, I can trace some dividing lines between these various abuses of love by various religions. The Catholic convent encourages the newcomer not to commit herself till she has had time to think things over. With a Catholic education behind her, she should have considerable knowledge of the religion she is going to give herself up to. There is also a period of trial during which she can freely walk out, without any particular difficulty or emotional pressure. Yet with the Moonies and some of the other cults, deception is built into the recruitment system. Newcomers are encouraged to visit a Moonie centre and stay there before they are told anything about Mr Moon. Once committed, they are encouraged to deceive others, and to collect money by telling half-truths or lies – 'heavenly deception'. Moon has said: 'Telling a lie becomes a sin if you tell it to take advantage of a person, but if you tell a lie to do a good thing for him that is not a sin. Even God tells a lie very often.'[8] Thus fund-raising Moonies will pretend they are collecting for a Christian cause. Likewise Hare Krishna followers claim they are collecting for 'missionary work', giving the impression that the mission might be Christian.[12]

Significantly, one of the fund-raising leaflets handed out by yet another cult, the Children of God, has the title 'Love is News'. 'Changing the world through love', it claims, promising 'a new world of love'. The text sounds conventionally Christian with pictures of missionary work and so forth. But there is no name given on the leaflet, so that anybody sending money would have no knowledge of what he or she might be contributing to. And the Children of God are far from conventional Christians. With their charismatic and authoritarian leader David Berg, known as 'Mo', they emphasise shared sex, and women members are encouraged to gain recruits by 'Flirty Fishing', i.e. sexual allurement.[16] One of their booklets, 'My

Little Fish', suggests children can be sexually used by adults, as well as being encouraged in sexual play with each other.[17] This is very far from conventional Christianity, yet there is nothing to warn the innocent passerby who is given one of these leaflets. This kind of deception seems to me quite clearly an abuse of people's desire for love.

The devotees of some cults are more obviously exploited. The Reverend Moon and the members high in the Unification Church live in luxury, according to the reports of former converts. Individual Moonies are short of sleep, overworked, and sometimes fed only on scraps donated by shopkeepers. The leaders live in very different style. Moon's bedroom in one of his many houses has a white carpet, silken gold coverlets on the bed, and special silver chopsticks were bought for his table. The contrast with his overworked slaves in the kitchen, who would take naps wherever they were working, is remarkable. Common sense suggests that a religious leader who imposes on others ordeals that he will not share is abusing their devotion. The followers' own common sense should help them smell a rat – but it does not. Indeed it is possible that the trials and tribulations of the followers simply increase their devotion, just as children cling to battering parents.

This blind devotion can lead to tragedy, if the leader is immoral, violent or even mad. The son of the Rev. Jim Jones claims that his father had become quite insane by the time he ordered the mass suicide. 'My father was nuts . . . he was a drug addict,' said Stephan Gandhi Jones, who escaped suicide because he was not in Jonestown on the fatal day.[18] Jim Jones was taking so many barbiturates, amphetamines and tranquillisers that his speech was slurred and he was unable to leave the house. Stephan and his mother realised that he was a sick man, who needed help. They discussed what they could do about it. 'Mom,' said Stephan, 'we're talking about a man who thinks he's God. You don't tell God "You're not going out of the house. You're not taking any more drugs." You don't tell God he needs help. It won't work.' It didn't work, and as a result of Jim Jones's drug addiction, 911 women, men and children had to die.

The idea of giving oneself up to a higher cause is an enticing one. I have always known that I was vulnerable to this possibility and for much of my life have therefore been on guard against it. Finally, it has seemed better – for a variety of reasons – to follow a religion of my own. But many people feel that they are exempt from such an appeal. They argue that *they* would never let obedience overrule their conscience, that their common sense and stability would triumph over any undue influence others might seek to exert over them. They feel secure that they would not shrink from disobeying. Alas, they are probably wrong. Human beings are obedient by nature, it has been argued.[19] We are vulnerable to the appeal of the charismatic figure, or merely the person whose status is far above our own — so vulnerable that most of us will behave cruelly if ordered.

This natural obedience was highlighted by a carefully contrived experiment, in which volunteers were ordered to inflict electric shocks upon a person in order to make him learn a lesson. Without bullying or threatening being needed, most people were willing to inflict extraordinarily powerful shocks. Though they could see the person first objecting, then screaming, then finally falling into silence, the volunteers still went on administering shocks. There was absolutely nothing which suggested that these individuals were sadistic brutes. Most were normal people who were clearly not enjoying the task. Yet they obeyed. Some even justified their obedience by blaming the victim for not learning well enough.[20] And these volunteers were not doing it out of love – merely obedience to the experimenter in charge. No wonder, when people feel they are obeying an object of adoration, they are capable of acts which would otherwise horrify them.

Many of the recruits to extreme religious cults are reasonable, well-balanced youngsters; only some are already emotionally disturbed. But after conversion, individuals seem drastically altered in personality – and not to the good. 'Mood disturbances, sometimes with striking changes in effect, were not uncommon, as was totally uncharacteristic sociopathic and delinquent behaviour. Proud, able individuals were reduced to peonage and garbage eating not unlike simple schizophrenics of the past. On the other hand many borderline individuals appeared, at least for a while, to improve strikingly, dropping suddenly all the most blatant self-destructive habits and forms of behaviour. The extreme "highs" and mystical experiences

with hallucinations that were sometimes reported suggested
temporal lobe epilepsy, while wild alterations of weight,
appetites, energy levels and sexual functions pointed to the basic
regulating mechanism of the body centred in the mid-brain',
reported a psychiatrist at the Harvard Medical School.
'Somehow, I believe, a draconian experiment on the entire
regulating system of the human being was occurring before my
eyes – one which no ethical scientist would consider under-
taking today. Psychosis was being imposed, socioneuroendo-
crine relationships demonstrated; the gap between the mind and
body was being bridged.'[21] Others who treat people who have
left cults report that they often have difficulty in dropping
habits of total obedience. Ordinary remarks of friends or
acquaintances are taken as commands. It is as if they have lost
their ability to judge or evaluate what is being said.[22]

If we are trying to decide whether a specific religion abuses
man's need for love, and his willingness to obey those higher
than himself, perhaps we should look at its results. Do the
followers practise what they preach? Does their love for their
God flow outwards into love for others, or does it confine itself
to the small in-group of worshippers? One good example of
high ideals which somehow did not seem to translate into
practice, is the hippie movement. Hippies talked about love
and peace, about contempt for money, about living a life free
from the artificial constraints of the existing societies. In the
'Summer of Love' in 1967 in the Haight-Ashbury area of San
Francisco, there sometimes seemed a genuine outbreak of love.
Outsiders were moved by the attempt to break down the differences between white and black, between rich and poor, the
attempt to be not to do – thus the term 'be-in'. There were free
grocery stores, where you could just turn up and take goods
without paying.[23] But the experiment did not last. Haight-
Ashbury became a drug ghetto. The hippies either turned back
into the 'straight' society they so despised, or they fell victim to
drug abuse and all the ills it brings in its train.

Only three years later, the peace and love had turned into
terror and hate. 'Many of the young people who hang out on
Haight Street are not only overtly or potentially psychotic, but
also physically ravaged by one another as well', reported the
director of a medical clinic in the area. 'Some seem to spend

their lives in plaster casts. Others frequently exhibit suppurating abrasions, knife and razor slashes, damaged genitalia and other types of traumatic injuries – injuries all caused by violence. Even more visible is the violence they do to themselves.'[24]

And the drug-induced 'religious' experiences hippies bruited about seem to have had little to do with real spiritual enlightenment – were just easy turn-ons. An anthropologist who wanted to study hippies took up residence among them. He happened to be an Indian, and just because of the colour of his skin many hippies would come up to him and ask him to be their guru or spiritual teacher. He concluded that 'despite the conversational forms of the hippie community which very often contain apparently sophisticated and complex notions from Buddhism and Hinduism, this generally signifies no more than an acquaintance with the jargon'.[25] The words were right, but there was little practice, only preaching. It is not simple credibility that is at stake – can we believe in a religion whose adherents fail to practise what they preach – it is also that religious experiences are surely irrelevant unless validated in daily life. As the Quakers believe, the important thing is to live Christianity, not to talk about it or to hold the right theological beliefs.

But perhaps the most important criterion of all in this difficult matter of judging a creed, is the quality of the love it preaches. For religion's strongest raison d'être, alongside its gift of meaning to an otherwise apparently random universe, is perhaps the love it promotes between fellow men. I think it is worth asking if the love for others preached by the creed in question is conditional. Is it conditional on the other person being converted, reformed or in some way changed? If so, this is a poor kind of love – a love which is being used, perhaps even abused, to gain something. No matter if the conversion or reformation is thought to be in the best interests of the person concerned. To refer back to St Paul's definition, 'Charity . . . seeketh not her own', and the fact remains that a promise of 'I will love you if only you will change' is not a free offer of love. It is the same kind of pressure as is used in an extreme form by the Moonies. Only if a religious organisation offers love with no recruitment strings attached, can it claim to be showing true brotherly love.

The dangers inherent in a religion which only practises a

qualified form of brotherly love are great. For it contains no built-in inhibitions against the human tendency to revile the outsider. And one of the ways of justifying harm to others, is to denigrate the victim – to suggest that he has put himself beyond the pale. One has only to think of Nazi propaganda against the Jews: the propaganda was necessary to justify the mass slaughter. But it would be wrong to think it a gambit exclusive to Nazism. Other political movements and ideologies have resorted to it. Christopher Burney, who found himself in Buchenwald, relates how the imprisoned Communists became the privileged group in the camp. They not only disposed of their rivals, the common criminals who had previously run the camp, but also those they considered their political enemies. Among their victims was the French tyre manufacturer, Michelin, who had been sent to Buchenwald for resistance activities. 'Michelin was a man over sixty and would have been automatically exempt from transport by the SS for that reason, but he was a capitalist and therefore condemned as an enemy of mankind,' wrote Burney.[26] The Communists, after several thwarted attempts, managed to slip him into a death transport to another camp.

The point is that when a class or race is not considered to hold full human rights, then violence is very easily justified. Most religious persecution justifies itself in this way: the victims are regarded as having disqualified themselves from the right to be treated as human beings by their hostility to God. There is in addition a terrifying tendency for us to despise the victim, because he is a victim. Some of the volunteers who were giving painful electric shocks in obedience to their experimenter's demands, justified their behaviour by blaming their victim for not learning fast enough. We tend to assume that somehow those being punished must have brought it on themselves and are therefore somehow beyond the scope of our compassion – outsiders. Any religion or political ideology which claims outsiders are somehow not deserving of love, will have a ready-made excuse to indulge in cruelty, even violence towards others.

The abuse of love is not confined to certain religions. The salesman, for instance, who talks his way into the home and tries to sell encyclopaedias under the guise of friendship is exploiting the human desire to be loved. It is not for nothing that some firms specialise in door-to-door sales, or in getting housewives to set up selling parties in their homes. Friendship will probably make the guests buy something. And good salesmen and women use many of the techniques and body language of love because they are seen to work. A textbook entitled *How to Master the Art of Selling*, by a man who is known as the 'Marketplace Messiah', analyses the steps involved in making a contact. The first is to 'Smile almost to the point of grinning', the second to 'Look into their eyes'. He adds 'A nice warm smile is almost always a necessary first step to a sale.'[27] Such techniques become an abuse of love, it seems to me, when the sale is deceptive, or lands people with goods they do not want.

The most common abuse of love is one that our society conspires to enjoy. Most of us share in this conspiracy. For we place a high value upon romantic love – that instant sexual excitement which gives an impression of love at first sight. Indeed, so highly is this particular folly valued, that it is what first springs to mind when the word 'love' is mentioned. It is prized beyond the longstanding love of partners, the comfort of friendship, prized far far above the truly lasting love of families. For romantic love, men and women will happily break up families, damage their children emotionally, and betray their friends. Perhaps this is not surprising since sexual desire is so powerful. It has always existed no doubt. But there is one difference between romantic love today and in the past: now most people think it a justification, not just an explanation, for bad behaviour.

This folly is one that I have shared myself; but today I find it difficult to see anything of value in romantic love. True, if things go well, it will commute into the kind of love that lasts a lifetime. But if things do not work out, then it can do irreparable harm. Should we, after all, value what is a compulsion rather like the effect of imprinting which impels a gosling to follow its mother? It is pleasurable and exciting, I grant you. I have felt so eaten up with romantic love, that I have had to vomit each time I met the beloved. I was literally lovesick. Yet romantic love carries no guarantee that it will end happily, and indeed literature is full of romantic tragedies. Such tragedies are sentimentally pleasing. But if I were a child that had lost its father and its settled home because of a parent's romantic love, I should not enjoy the sensation. Nor would I like being the cuckolded wife or husband.

The telltale signs of romantic love are its ardour and its blindness. The beloved is often granted virtues that he or she does not possess, and the accompanying faults are simply ignored. 'Since no person can, in the long run, live up to the expectations of her (or his) idolatrous worshipper, disappointment is bound to occur', writes Erich Fromm.[28] Romantic love is often most violent in adolescence, when some individual is loved from afar. I remember that for two years from the age of fifteen, I used to daydream about a boy whom I had literally only met once. I could have had no idea what he was really like, but I loved him nonetheless. Sometimes a romantic love is so ardent, so unrealistic and so selfish, that even the wishes of its object are not taken into account. The lover will positively persecute his beloved with his attentions under the guise of love. This is idolatrous love, of the same kind felt by devotees for their somewhat ridiculous gurus and Gods-on-earth.

Blind love of a spouse can lead to similar excesses. When Arthur Koestler, the naturalised English writer, committed suicide he was aged seventy-seven and severely affected by Parkinson's disease and leukaemia. His body was found in an armchair with a glass of brandy still in his hand. Not far away, lying on the sofa, was his wife Cynthia who had taken a huge dose of barbiturates like him. But Cynthia was only fifty-five and in perfect health. Nevertheless she wrote: 'I cannot live without Arthur despite certain inner resources.' She also left behind an unfinished autobiography, written jointly with Koestler, which made it clear that she had given up her life entirely to him, to the point of having two abortions. 'Though I knew nothing of the abortions myself until I read of them in these pages, Arthur had once told me that he had decided at an early age not to risk bringing up any children', wrote a friend in the introduction to the autobiography.[29] 'Of course there is an element of sadness in all this, just as there is in the way she (Cynthia) surrendered her life to his on an all-inclusive scale. But sadness was not the impression she gave . . . she was happy in her total devotion as wife-secretary-cook-housekeeper-companion and happy, above all, in Arthur's total reliance upon her.'

Cynthia Koestler was fortunate that her idol required merely two abortions. The girls who lived with Charlie Manson were happy too in their self-chosen bondage. But Charlie Manson required more than Arthur Koestler of his women. 'They seemed to radiate inner contentment,' said Vincent Bugliosi, the prosecuting lawyer at their trial for murder. 'I'd seen others like this – true believers, religious fanatics – yet I was shocked and impressed. Nothing seemed to faze them. They smiled almost continuously, no matter what was said. For them all the questions had been answered. There was no need to search any more, because they had found the truth. And their truth was "Charlie is love".'[30] There is obviously no real comparison between the great writer and Manson, who had spent hours and hours inducting his womenfolk with paranoid fantasies of the coming 'Helter Skelter'.[31] In exchange for his love, the girls had had to be ready to give their obedience. And so, obediently, they went out and murdered the pregnant Sharon Tate and several other victims. For love, they tortured, knifed and slaughtered, writing graffiti on the wall in the blood of their victims.

What are we to make of that love, which clings to a marriage partner right or wrong? Is it always morally acceptable? Teresa Stangl was a loving wife to her husband, an Austrian policeman when she married him. But then Franz Stangl got on in life. First he was put in charge of the General Foundation for Institutional Care in Berlin, where thousands of patients were gassed on Hitler's orders. Next he was promoted to commandant of an extermination camp, and finally to commandant of Treblinka, the largest of the death camps round Warsaw. Somewhere between 900,000 to 1,200,000 people died in Treblinka. Yet all this time Teresa Stangl stood by her man, loving him and caring for him when he came back after a hard day's work.

Years later she admitted: 'I have thought very hard . . . I am answering . . . because I think I owe it to you, to others, to myself: I believe that if I had ever confronted Paul (her name for Stangl) with the alternatives: Treblinka or me: he would – yes, he would in the final analysis, have chosen me.'[30] But she never did confront him. I do not wish to argue from this that women are responsible for keeping their menfolk on the right path. They are not keeper of the marriage's conscience. But they should keep their own conscience. To act as helpmeet to a man so vilely incriminated in evil as was Franz Stangl, cannot be justified in the name of love.

It is also a sad fact that men and women can be intimately linked together by a love which has turned to hate. Tradition justifies violence within marriage. 'A woman, a dog and a walnut tree, the more you beat them the better they be' runs the old rhyme. Occasionally a wife kills her husband, but the ordinary run-of-the-mill beatings, mutilations and killings, are perpetrated by men. Women are victims. This physical abuse is widespread. In one mid-Western American town, just under a fifth of would-be divorcers reported violence in their marriage. 'The most commonly reported form of violence was that the husband was physically abusive of his wife.' Sometimes this violence reaches a horrifying level. 'It is still true that for a woman to be brutally or systematically assaulted she must usually enter our most sacred institution, the family. It is within marriage that a woman is most likely to be slapped, and shoved about, severely assaulted, killed or raped', reports a well-argued study of violence against wives. [32] The figures show that while marriage reduces the chance of a man being murdered, it increases a woman's; her murderer is likely to be her husband. [33]

It is a terrible shock to be beaten up by the man you love, as I know to my own cost. When the man I was living with turned on me, my overwhelming reaction was not fear but surprise and fury. I fought back, until I found myself lying on the floor having my head punched. Then, for the first time, I realised I was going to lose the fight, and that I might well be severely injured unless I acted in a conciliatory fashion. The following day brought the apology: 'I thought women liked being hit.' Oddest of all was the fact that this was a man who seemed gentle to outsiders, the last man – I had thought – to batter a woman.

From that moment on, our relationship started dying – in me was a great contempt for him, a contempt which has, over the years, changed to pity – and I knew that I could not stay with him for very much longer. Yet there are women who stay for several beatings. Some stay because they do not know how to go: the outside world is not very sympathetic to the beaten wife.

But others seem almost to enjoy the violence. Is it because they are bent on self-destruction, that they hate themselves so deeply that violence upon them seems like their just desserts? I have come close to self-hatred that deep. Or is it that they enjoy the drama of violence? 'The typical violence-prone woman would arrive in the middle of the night with only some of her children, for she had left a hostage or two at home,' reported Erin Pizzey, founder of the movement to give a refuge to battered wives in Britain. 'Usually after getting immediate money to cover her need for cigarettes, she would recount with great relish the appalling violence . . . that she had experienced . . . The next request would be that she should be accompanied by a member of staff to "get her clothes from back home". This usually means a further confrontation with her partner, with the cards stacked in her favour.'[34] Sometimes she would make sure that her husband knew where she was. In either case, the violence-prone woman would seem to provoke further violent confrontations. She had become, it seemed, an addict of violence.

Even love's power to heal can be perverted. A horrifying proportion of psychotherapists and unqualified sex therapists sleep with their clients – the attractive clients, that is. Encounter groups which offer mental health, sometimes deliver mental illness to their members. About one in ten people who attend such groups are positively harmed by the experience – yet the so-called therapists who preside have no idea of this.[35]

These casualties occur mostly with a particular style of leader – 'intrusive, confrontive, challenging, while at the same time demonstrating high positive caring: . . . the most charismatic of the leaders . . . authoritarian . . . They asserted firm control . . . seemed ready, willing and able to guide participants forward on the road to enlightenment.' The quieter, calmer and more gentle leaders on the whole do far less harm. But the most frightening part of the study which produced these findings was its statement that 'those individuals who came believing in miracles, were more likely to reap pain'. An effect similar to that produced by extreme religious cults in which 'individuals who are psychologically vulnerable and who overinvest their hopes in the magic of salvation through encounter groups are particularly vulnerable when they interact with leaders who believe that they can offer deliverance.'

There is no easy deliverance from ourselves – not by dictatorial religious cults, nor by beloved husbands, nor by sensational encounter-group cures. When love seems to demand the relinquishment of our own consciences in exchange for 'freedom' of total obedience, we must be most cautious. We need to approach offers of love with clear, even suspicious, minds. We need to investigate before committing ourselves, for after commitment our judgement may well be flawed. It seems to me, then, that we cannot treat love like a kind of cushion – something to which we abandon ourselves without effort and without reservation. We need to practise reason, clear careful reasoning, at the same time as we need to practise love. Love by itself, without care and without thought, is not enough. Nor does love conquer and justify all. As Oscar Wilde said, 'A thing is not necessarily right because a man dies for it.' The attachment a cult promises might be a good end, but it cannot justify foul means – deception, brainwashing, the deliberate creation of paranoia. In the same way the brotherly love of such cults cannot justify their product – authoritarian rule by one leader, even extending to mind control. Besides, cults do not merely require that their members be ready to die for them: sometimes they may seem to require that their members should mistreat others. If the result of any attachment or love I feel is to make me cheat, lie, beat somebody up, or behave cruelly, then there is something rotten in my love. It is frightening to see how human love can be abused and can, indeed, abuse others: but it is no reason for giving up on love. We should have more feeling in our society but not at the expense of reason and right judgement.

11

Learning to Love

We need love. Literally. Over the million of years that our species has developed, the need for love has been bred into us. As our monkey and ape cousins need loving mothers and the bonds either of small family groups or of big troops so, like them, we need others around us. We need motherly care to stimulate our intelligence. Without friendly people, either in families or in close friendships, we become unhappy, and some of us die. For without love the human individual cannot live in a happy and healthy way. It is as important to our bodily and mental health as vitamins, good food, exercise and healthy living conditions. In the West our societies have put a lot of effort and organisation into ensuring better conditions for all – good drains, clean drinking water, health care, guaranteed social security payments, special payments to mothers for children, schools, old people's homes, hospitals. An enormous structure of state organisation has been created to make sure that the basic bodily needs of human beings are supplied – but we do not recognise love amongst them.

Of course we pay lip service to it. We talk of the 'caring' professions, as if doling out pills, getting wheelchairs for old ladies, or teaching children were the same as offering love. Many individuals do offer warmth and tenderness along with bodily care, medicine and education. But on the whole the principles by which the whole elaborate structure of state care is run, ignore our need for tenderness and love. Take, for instance, education. A great deal of money and energy is put into state education – to procure new buildings, swimming pools, smaller classes, new teaching methods. Yet research has shown that this is so much wasted effort. The buildings, the size of the school, or the differences of administration within it, make little or no difference at all to the way pupils turn out.

What makes a difference is something far more elusive, something that I would call 'institutional warmth'. Research has shown that it is the atmosphere of a school, not its outward shell of buildings or organisation, which tells on pupils. It shows itself in general morale – with teachers willing to give extra time and care to the children, emphasising encouragement and praise rather than the correct apportioning of blame, entrusting pupils with responsibilities and finally simply, with the staff setting a good example. Head teachers who allow their staff to arrive late, behave discourteously, fail to give the children extra time and care, will have bad schools. Their pupils will be more likely to end up in trouble with the law, or with poor qualifications. [1] Yet there are, as far as I know, no arrangements for ensuring a good atmosphere. Hardly surprisingly, I realise – how do you legislate for something so difficult to evaluate? But it should at least be a recognised goal.

We pay lip service to love in other ways, in particular in connection with old people. We provide geriatric hospitals and old people's homes when they can no longer care for themselves. The food in them is good. The standard of physical care is good too. But in unthinking ways we diminish their sources of love. Quite often, the price of entry into an old people's home is the slaughter of their cat or dog. Nor are there any pets kept communally in such homes. Pets would be unhygienic, it is thought. Many council flats and houses ban cats and dogs altogether. [2] The price of good housing is the absence of our favourite companion animals. Yet there is no need for such a ban: only for regulations which stop certain irresponsible individuals from keeping pets. We know that companionship from animals is an important part of many people's lives. We know it. We may even acknowledge it. But in practice, it is ignored.

By now it is abundantly clear that love and kindness are helpful when people are ill. It is therefore unprofessional behaviour when doctor or nurses behave curtly, roughly, and unfeelingly towards their patients. Yet some doctors persist in doing so. In Britain, a doctor can be struck off the medical register for making love to a willing patient; yet that same doctor can abuse his patient's need for kindness daily without the slightest chance of any rebuke. In mental hospitals, where research has actually proved that warmth and concern help patients recover, patients are still often treated as if they were mentally subnormal rather than just mentally ill. And till the 1970s the conditions in some of Britain's mental-subnormality hospitals were a disgrace – rows of beds, no lockers for patients, communal clothes, and no organised activities.

Often, it is not the fault of the individual doctor or nurse that patients are treated roughly. Hospitals in Britain are organised in such a way that outpatients rarely see the same doctor more than once. GPs are encouraged to cut down on time spent with patients in the interests of efficiency – their efficiency, not the patient's. And there is always the retreat into 'professionalism' to justify these practices. 'In day centres and day hospitals, inspection of everyday living practices indicates silent messages about the superiority of the professional culture. Separate quiet-rooms for staff to rest, separate lunch arrangements for staff, separate (and usually better) toilets for staff, the non-reciprocal use of Christian names of patients and clients by the staff, all are messages about superior and inferior cultures', it has been pointed out. [3]

Some changes are at last under way. Mothers are now allowed to cuddle their newborn babies, and to keep them by their side even if it does make the ward look untidy. In 1984 British doctors for the first time were being encouraged to record whether their patients were divorced, bereaved, or in the throes of a broken engagement. Some acknowledgement is now being made of the toll taken by the disruption of love. [4] The medical profession is also beginning to realise that doctors can be taught some of the skills of love – listening, being sensitive to and respecting the patient's feelings. [5] Medical students, unfortunately, are still being turned out of the schools thinking a doctor should never admit he is wrong, or that a doctor should always convey superiority to the patient. We could make it compulsory for all medical students, nurses, social workers and 'professional carers' to do courses in empathy and love. The ways of teaching kindness are now well established. We *can* teach the mechanics of love, but too often we don't. Those in authority persist in believing, against the evidence, that such skills cannot be taught.

I wondered if I should devote this last chapter to a survey of this kind of learning. Reluctantly, I decided not to. The inertia in human behaviour, the clinging to a false superiority of 'professional detachment', the way our whole society and its institutions are organised, make real change unlikely. I do not think in this book or in any other way, I can do anything to change our society. Nor can I change the behaviour of other people.

But I *can* change myself. I know that this is anathema to all those who believe man is the product of society, and that society is inexorably shaped by the forces of economic organisation, or the logic of history. Yet, I believe individuals can do something to shape their lives. They may not be able to alter events, but they can choose how they will react to them. Such freedoms, small though they are, are possessed by all of us. Of course, changing one's own behaviour is also unpopular with those who believe society should change first. 'Let others change, then we will change' is their angry cry. As I do not believe that others will change, or that society will change, I cannot share either their despair about themselves or their optimism about others. I must tell myself 'Let it begin with me.'

But even small changes in small people like myself may not be entirely wasted. If I can learn to love, I shall benefit from my ability, and perhaps occasionally others may too. For love is learned by example. This is not just a pious platitude; it is a literal truth, as I have shown. We learn to love at our parents' knees, and without their example we risk lovelessness through-out life. So if I can practise more love in my own life, I will contribute – infinitesimally, it is true – to a warmer society.

'Love your neighbour as yourself' is the message of most religions, though their definition of 'neighbour' varies. For some of us obeying that commandment would mean that we loved our neighbours very little, since we have so little self-esteem. Loving others and loving ourselves are inextricably bound together. We cannot do one without the other. 'Love for others and love for ourselves are not alternatives. Neither are hate for others and hate for ourselves alternatives. On the contrary, an attitude of love for themselves will be found in those who are at least capable of loving others' wrote Erich Fromm in 1939. [6] 'Hatred against oneself is inseparable from hatred against others, even if on the surface the opposite seems to be the case.' We cannot love others unless we love ourselves.

This particular insight has displaced the received wisdom of most religions – which adjure their followers to love others and try to forget self. Modern therapy encourages people to love themselves that their self-esteem may eventually flow out as love for others. In this particular formulation of the principle, another influential thinker was Harry Stack Sullivan, who laid down the rule, 'As you love yourself so shall you love others. Strange but true with no exceptions.' [7] In a world without God, this new emphasis seemed far more logical. What, after all, was the point of loving others? Loving oneself had greater appeal. Starting with that, one might go on to love others.

This link between self-love and loving others seems a real one – a fact of the human condition. Those who speak slightingly of others, who are hostile or suspicious of people around them, also have a very low opinion of themselves. [8] The forging of this link seems to start at birth, with children being closely affected by how far their parents love themselves. The men and women who batter their children, do not love themselves. 'Low self-esteem and a poorly integrated sense of self are common' says one survey of battering parents. [9] Nor is this self-hatred merely the result of their behaviour to their children. Even before the mother has lifted a hand to her child, before she has given birth to it, she lacks love for herself. [10] And this lack of self-love is not just found in the families where children are abused. In more average families the link exists too. Mothers who do not have what one researcher calls 'self-acceptance' are likely to have less acceptance of their child than mothers who do. [11] They would like their children to be different from what they are. The behaviour of parents transmits itself to the children, who judge themselves in terms of how much love they receive. Among battered children, very few think well of themselves. [12] They grow up without much self-esteem, and may in their turn be liable to beat their own children.

One of the mysteries of self-love is that it is not a reflection of worldly status or achievements. It is possible to be poor, have a lowly job, little education, be ugly and yet to esteem oneself. Those who have this gift of inner love for themselves 'do not differ greatly from the rest of the population in their economic status and very little of their positive self-evaluation can be explained this way'.[13] It is therefore also possible to be rich, good-looking, successful, well educated and high in status and yet tormented by feelings of unworthiness. The burden of self remains, and cannot be lifted simply by success in the eyes of the world. The child who learns low self-esteem from his parents is unlikely to be able to improve on it in later life – however much acclaim he may eventually receive.

Anyhow, whatever the genesis of self-love, it would indeed seem that without it we cannot love others. Though whether or not in the history of the individual it predates the ability to love others is more difficult to determine. Certainly, that is what both Erich Fromm and Harry Stack Sullivan believed, and thus they felt that the first necessity was to love ourselves. By testing schoolchildren over several years, researchers have found that those who were low in self-esteem went on to have difficulty with other relationships. This seemed to be more important than the reverse effect, which is that bad relationships will help produce low self-esteem.[14] But clearly, the two are intertwined. Those that are disliked by others will have low feelings about themselves. There is unlikely to be a clear-cut cause – self-love – and a clear-cut consequence – love of others. The two intermingle.

What, though, of the person unable to love himself. How does he then begin to love others? This, according to Erich Fromm, is the quandary of the selfish – which would seem to fly in the face of common sense. Certainly, selfish people are people who do not love others. All of us know self-centred and selfish people who simply go through life grabbing what they can. Their own needs and desires are put before those of other people. The truly self-centred person may literally be blind to the feelings of others, hurting them without knowing or caring about it. Another may take a pleasure in doing others down, hurting deliberately because they enjoy the power that the ability to hurt others confers. But how can one say that these selfish people do not love themselves, that they are full of self-hatred? The way they look after their own interests suggests just the opposite. 'Selfishness' explained Erich Fromm 'is one kind of greediness . . . close observation shows that while the selfish person is always anxiously concerned with himself, he is never satisfied, is always restless, always driven by the fear of not getting enough, of missing something, of being deprived of something . . . The selfishness is rooted in this very lack of fondness for oneself. The person who is not fond of himself, who does not approve of himself, is in a constant anxiety concerning his own self . . . He must be concerned about himself, greedy to get everything for himself, since basically his own self lacks security and satisfaction.'[16]

I myself have been trapped in self-hatred. During that time, when I felt most appalled by myself, I was asked over lunch how I saw my own life. It was just an idle query. 'I suppose it's just a question of doing things I like, just kind of grabbing one pleasure after another,' I found myself saying. My own words surprised and worried me. It seemed no way to live. At that time, though, I was torn between self-hatred and arrogance. I cultivated an extraordinary and baseless idea that I was a particularly special, gifted, attractive and even genius-filled person. I felt I was far more talented than the colleagues with whom I worked. This rather mad arrogance sometimes made me feel as if I was a kind of living brain, a gigantic intellect attached to a body but with no heart for feelings. How could this arrogance be self-hatred? How could the arrogance and the self-hatred co-exist? Looking back on it, I believe it was a kind of self-imposed infatuation. I hated the real me so severely, that I had to invent a fantasy-self, that misunderstood genius. In the same way that immature lovers fall in love with invented images of a beloved, rather than the real woman, so I loved an invented self. I should say that during that time I knew I was on the edge of a nervous breakdown. I had feelings of paranoia, and I could feel a kind of insanity hanging over me. I was more than a little mad already.

The traditional way in our culture to relieve such self-hatred is to get some kind of professional help. Whether it is psychoanalysis, transactional analysis, cognitive therapy, group therapy, or even something rather odder like acupuncture, we unhesitatingly consign those who feel on the edge of insanity to the professionals. From professionals they will get time and attention – the chance to talk about subjects unsuitable in ordinary social intercourse. They can confide their secrets to the therapist, things which they might not dare tell anybody else, particularly if they feel distrustful and suspicious of others. We know, moreover, that if the therapist is warm and caring, then the patient is more likely to get well. The therapy of Carl Rogers explicitly offers not just professional expertise but a loving relationship. 'It appears possible that one of the characteristics of deep or significant therapy is that the client discovers that it is not devastating to admit fully into his own experience the positive feeling which another, the therapist, holds towards him. Perhaps one of the reasons why this is so difficult is that essentially it involves the feeling that "I am worthy of being liked".'[15] By loving the client, the therapist hopes to help him start to feel lovable.

The therapist's love can be bought, either simply by paying his fees or where free medical aid is concerned by presenting oneself as a person who is medically ill. In the same way, people can get love from self-help groups like Alcoholics Anonymous or Overeaters Anonymous if they are willing to wear the label 'alcoholic' or 'overeater'. But what of the people who are not willing to wear the label of illness, those who cannot afford the fees, or simply do not know they are emotionally ill? What can they do? In ordinary life, love cannot be bought or forced. People try, of course. Young men take women out to posh dinners, or give them presents, in the hope that they will be loved in return. Others throw parties, the kind where nobody knows the host very well because these are not established friends, but people whom the host hopes will become so. I know one individual who throws parties at which only ten per cent of last year's guest list is present.

I have met people whose need for love is clearly desperate. They have tried to corner me prematurely into a friendship I do not want; or they have been super-sensitive to slights, behaving rather like jilted lovers if I missed the slightest jot or tittle of friendship. And quite frankly this behaviour, and the very need itself, is extremely unattractive. Who wants a friend who is always on the look-out for some imagined slight or who picks up any momentary failure of friendship and turns it into a great betrayal? Who wants a lover who pushes the beloved into a whole series of obligations, before she is ready for it? Who wants a jealous friend or a mistrustful lover, checking out one's every movement? Most people do not? Their behaviour repels the very love they need so badly. It is those who seem to have love enough already, to be secure enough not to force a relationship, who are attractive.

The lonely and unloved are often advised to go out and *make* friends. I have been insensitive enough to advise this, and have heard the response, either in bitter or in despairing tones, 'I have tried to do this, but I don't seem to get anywhere.' The lonely either go all out in an obsessive and unattractive search for human companionship, or they simply withdraw all the more from society. 'One of the basic feelings that accompanies human loneliness is shame . . . Unlike some cancer patients, alcoholics, drug addicts or obese individuals, lonely people often aggravate their condition by suffering alone. Rather than publicly meeting with others similarly afflicted, the lonely tend to shun each other. Seeing other people suffering from the same problem embarrasses the lonely all the more, making them feel all the more ashamed,' says James Lynch, author of *The Broken Heart*.[16] Besides, those who are short of friends are often very fussy about whom they will admit to friendship. Their expectations of others are high and their disappointments frequent. The vicious circle is hard to break.

I do not think either that we can change self-hatred into self-love simply by a change of circumstances, more money, a job, a new husband or some kind of acknowledged success. Sometimes such a change acts as a catalyst which sets off inner change; more often it does not, having only a temporary palliative effect. I once felt that if only I had had a book published, I should feel worthwhile. But afterwards, I only felt better temporarily. Somehow once I had achieved my desire, it no longer counted. Besides, sometimes circumstances cannot be changed. Nor do I think we can change how we feel simply by willing it. I cannot change my self-hatred into love simply by telling myself that I will do this.

But we can will ourselves to action, and in turn actions can lead to a change in feelings. A simple example is that of relaxation exercises. Practised over weeks, these can lead to mental relaxation, while just willing oneself to unwind would be hopeless. To sum up: forcing others to love us is impossible; forcing self-esteem by willpower is impossible; but forcing ourselves to new behaviour which in turn may change how we feel is possible. Difficult, admittedly, but possible. This is one way forward out of the trap of self-hatred.

By trying to act as if we loved others, we will increase in our own regard. We can start behaving like good friends, without demanding friendship back. I already began to like myself a little when I decided I would try to help others. One of my very first efforts was both absurd and unsuccessful. I was much concerned by the misery of the meths drinkers living on the streets around me, and I decided I would try to make their lives less miserable. In pursuit of this, I took one of the women into a restaurant and bought her a meal. She vomited all over the tablecloth and was too ill or drunk to eat. I had to learn that if I wanted to give meths drinkers food, I should bring them takeaway food which they could eat – if their stomachs accepted it – on the street. I did that woman no good at all. But I remember the day very clearly, because of the feeling of relief and happiness I had after the fiasco. For several days I had felt tense and miserable and self-pitying. That day I had tried to act rightly out of concern for others, and I felt better about myself even though the action had been unsuccessful.

Loving, or trying to love, others is not what I expected. Somehow I thought that warm spontaneous feelings would flow from me, and loving others would be natural and easy. But much of trying to change my own behaviour, and through it my feelings about myself, has been hard work. I have had to try to learn to be silent when I wanted to gossip. I have had to try to stop improving others. I have had to try to be courteous to people I did not like. I have had to try, and this I find very hard indeed, to be the first to apologise: and to apologise without expecting as a right either forgiveness or an equal apology. All this has added up to a unilateral change in behaviour. I have had to give up the idea that others should change first, or the even more persistent idea that if I do the right thing then I am entitled to expect others to do so too.

This programme for better relationships through self-reformation, is far away from the idea of love as natural and spontaneous. It also challenges the assumption that only good relationships are worth having. It is possible that the intimacy of a bad or difficult relationship is physically and mentally better for a human being than no relationship at all.[16] All this hard work on my part, however, has helped spontaneous feeling somewhat. By the sheer practice I've gained through trying to be kinder to others, I think that the motions have become more natural to me. By doing the right thing, I think that the feelings of my heart are very very slowly improving too. I find it easier now, than I did, to love others. Here I must add the rider, that I am still impatient, angry, malicious, childish, and disapproving much more often than I would wish. I do not live up to my own ideals, alas.

For my own part there is one rather subtle trap which often catches me out when I am trying to love my neighbour. It is the temptation to make that love conditional. There is the straight swap: I will love you if you will in return a) love me back, b) be sexually faithful, c) keep a good job and good health, d) give up those unpleasant friends of yours. But quite often we make conditions without even being conscious of them; and we are as fiercely resentful when they are broken as if they had been mutually agreed in the first place. My particular failing is the conditional love of the rescuer. If he marries me, I remember thinking about my first husband, I will *make* him happy. But the poor man remained unhappy as was his right, and I left him. My love had been conditional, but it had been concealed in the virtuous idea of helping him.

It is very difficult indeed to accept that other people have the right to be unhappy, bad, ill, frightened, anxious, emotionally warped, drug-addicted or even downright suicidal. We love them and want them to get well: that is all right. More often, though, we love them in order to cure them and that is all wrong. It is an insult to their individuality, for it means we do not love them as they are. It is also a piece of self-delusion, because even love cannot force change. When those conditions which we have set to our love are not kept, when our loved ones stay unhappy, bad, ill, frightened, anxious, drug-addicted or whatever, then we feel angry. Did I not give him the best years of my life? I made sure she had the best doctors' attention? Why did she not get well after all I've done for her?

There is, however, a danger in the idea of unconditional love.

It has to be practised not just on others, but on ourselves. Occasionally I have driven myself into exhaustion by spending all my time in trying to look after others, and neglected myself. There is also the trap of confusing loving others with a desire to please them. Sometimes unpleasant things have to be said, help has to be withdrawn, or even an action taken which will make the loved one very angry indeed. Often I have neglected to do these things, because I have been frightened of the hurt involved. Or, and I am ashamed of this, I have felt that the result might be the withdrawal of love from me – thus showing, I think, how conditional my own love has been. How to love others is such an enormously complicated subject to examine, that I am only too conscious how badly I do it. The broad principle – that one way to self-love is through love of others – is probably correct but difficult to translate into action, given the confusion of motive and circumstance that surrounds the average encounter. It is often hard to see what is the truly loving action. But whatever my failure, I must love myself uncon-ditionally too – perhaps trying to reform, but not making a proper self-esteem conditional upon it. Faults, idiocies and all, I too am worth loviṅg.

The practice of realistic unconditional love requires enormous self-confidence, and I believe that it also builds enormous self-confidence. To be able to love with detachment, without trying to change a person, is a rare ability: an ability I have often had to fake. But by acting as if I felt it, I have sometimes come to feel it – rather like putting on a happy face which works from the outside in. Part of the inner confidence required is to under-pin risk-taking: one has to be prepared to make mistakes, to be a fool at times, to be let down, and even to be misunderstood. I am enormously defensive and quick to make excuses for myself. On the rare occasions when I have been able to listen to another's accusation without immediately springing to my defence, I have been reassured. What others feel cannot hurt me. A woman once told me that for two years she had disliked the way I rushed hither and thither, always active if not over-active. During that time I had no idea she disliked me; her feelings had done *me* no harm at all. When I make a fool of myself, as when I lend money which I expect but don't get back, I am not harmed either. I don't quite understand why, but if I can act as though I am sure inwardly what to do, without caring if this involves slightly odd behaviour in the eyes of outsiders, then it seems to add to my confidence.

Trying to love others requires a kind of permanent optimism. Many religions advise looking for the good in people, not the bad. This optimism has a common-sensical basis, summed up by the proverb 'Give a dog a bad name and hang him'. Our expectations of people shape how they behave to us. One striking example occurred in the classroom. At the beginning of the school year, teachers were given a list of children who they were told were 'late bloomers', individuals who were showing unexpected signs of improvement. The choice of names was entirely arbitrary. But by the end of the year the children who had been thus classified, had developed accordingly. Their teachers had expected more from them, and had perhaps unconsciously given them more time and attention as a result. [17] Thus what we expect may become a self-fulfilling prophecy. If we look for the best in others, we have a better chance of finding it.

The Quaker founder George Fox advised his followers to set a good example, 'then you will come to walk cheerfully over the world answering that of God in everyone'. 'We are allowed to hate cruelty and meanness,' says a later Quaker writer, 'but we must learn to love the cruel and the mean; we must learn to love those who hurt us; and, a more difficult thing to do, we must learn to love those who hurt others.' [18] Many religions believe that no one is past redemption, that we can at any point change our behaviour for the better. Viktor Frankl, who wrote about his experiences in a concentration camp, once met a certain Dr J. 'the only man I ever encountered in my whole life whom I would dare to call a Mephistophelean being, a satanic figure'. Dr J. had been an enthusiastic practitioner of the Nazi euthanasia programme, making sure that no designated patient in the large mental hospital of Steinhof in Vienna escaped the gas chamber. Many years later Viktor Frankl heard of him again, from an Austrian who had been imprisoned behind the iron curtain in the infamous Ljubljanka prison on Moscow. Dr J., mass murderer, had been there too and had 'showed himself to be the best comrade you can imagine!' reported the Austrian. 'He gave consolation to everybody. He lived up to the highest conceivable moral standard. He was the best friend I ever met during my long years in prison.'[19] At the end of his life, this mass murderer had shown that no individual is all bad. In a religious sense he had perhaps redeemed himself.

Most religions maintain that every human being has a value, and if this is not true, then it is a noble lie. Only this makes sense of the fact that we do not kill our hopelessly insane patients, like the Nazis did. We also keep alive the apparently incurable and the permanently unconscious. 'Every year in Great Britain about four hundred patients are admitted to hospital who remain unconscious for more than a month . . . ' wrote the late Dr Walpole Lewin, a consultant neurological surgeon in the *British Medical Journal.* 'The actual number who remain totally dependent for several years is small. It has been suggested that this is a useless life, unkind and unnecessary and even economically unjustifiable. I have always objected to the word ''vegetable'' because it carries the implication that these patients are not making any further contribution . . . Those working in this field know that doctors, nurses, physiotherapists and others attending these patients gain in their understanding of human life, and the same can be said for the relatives of these patients. In many instances they have been helped to adjust to life and understand sacrifice from the experience of an unconscious patient. No man is an island and whatever we do or not do affects others in society. To very few is given the privilege of knowing that they have made a positive contribution to someone else. To suggest that one necessarily has to be conscious and speaking to make a contribution to others is an unwarranted assumption. There seems little justification for trying to measure the amount of care that should be given to these patients in terms of the economic health of the country. For without moral health there will be no economic health of any lasting duration. We should not lose sight of the fact that it is our responsibilities rather than our rights that are important to society, and this includes respect for the lives of others.'[20] Fortunately we still act in our hospitals as if we believed in every individual's case, even if that value is not immediately apparent.

But if we need to look for the best in people, we must also remain loving when we are disappointed. Our optimism must be balanced by ever vigilant realism. 'Begin each day by telling yourself: Today I shall be meeting with interference, ingratitude, insolence, disloyalty, ill-will and selfishness – all of them due to the offenders' ignorance of what is good or evil', wrote Marcus Aurelius Antoninus, Roman emperor in the second century AD. He goes on to say 'none of those things can injure me, for nobody can implicate me in what is degrading. Neither can I be angry with my brother or fall foul of him; for he and I were born to work together, like a man's two hands, feet or eyelids.'[21] It is a useful mental trick to think of the bad and violent of our society as those who are unable to love: victims of their own inner violence and hatred. For if I am to try to love my neighbour as myself, I must forgive him his vices. To be angry about another person's behaviour is to harm myself, rather than that other person. Inner anger and intolerance are unpleasant emotions, and possibly can even harm our physical health. Compassion may not help its object, but it certainly helps the person who feels it.

Compassion, itself, has to be learned. Small children torture animals till they are helped to experience fellow feelings of pain; slightly larger children often gang up on and bully weaker ones. There is an unfair bias in most human beings to dislike the ugly, the disabled, or the unloved. We prefer those who are beautiful on the outside. We judge by appearances. Indeed when we are shown snapshots of people, most of us will say that the attractive subjects are better spouses, more happily married, have better jobs and are more socially desirable.[22] When photographs of beautiful girls are attached to poorly written essays, the judges tend to award higher marks than when photographs of homely girls are attached.[23] We are biased against those whom we should pity; we may even blame them for their misfortunes. Recall the way that in the obedience experiment, some of the volunteers who administered the electric shocks then argued that their victims deserved such treatment.

One of the horrifying aspects of Buchenwald, reported Christopher Burney, was the way many of the non-Jewish prisoners mistreated the even more wretched Jews who were brought there in convoys on their way to extermination. 'It is impossible for any civilised person who has not himself seen it to imagine that such a lack of charity towards suffering could exist. But for those Jews there was never one kind word.' The Jews themselves 'were annoying in the extreme by their obsequiousness, even to the SS' continues Burney, unconsciously affected himself by the feeling that those who are wretched somehow deserve it, 'and even among themselves they behaved more like animals than men, fighting and even robbing the dead and dying of their clothing. Sensible men would have realised that treatment such as they had endured must inevitably have affected their better natures, and would at least have tried to bring them back to humanity.'[24] We should all, perhaps, at least recognise these complimentary human tendencies to kick those who are already down, and to kow tow to those higher than ourselves, so as to beware of them. I know I feel the latter, and occasionally the former too. Loving others requires the cultivation of fellow feelings with those who are degraded, irresponsible, and even bad. Even evil men and women feel pain, and if they deserve it that does not necessarily ease their sufferings.

While our long-term happiness must lie in the cultivation of the love of others, hand in hand with self-love, I have acquired some handy rules of thumb for dealing with the unhappiness of the moment. Egoism being a form of self-hatred, as Fromm has shown, it is hardly surprising to discover that most of one's small miseries are rooted in self-concern. I have only to bury myself in some kind of absorbing activity to find relief. I am probably most completely happy when entirely concerned with some task like gardening, lovemaking, writing or talking to others. Nor is this just my peculiarity. Researchers have noted that absorption with a task can relieve people of low self-esteem. The focus is taken from self to the task: the burden of self is temporarily forgotten.[25]

The other trick of happiness which I have been advised to practise, is simply to do some act of kindness for others when I am feeling unhappy. This sounds revoltingly pious, like a moral out of a Victorian children's book. A kind of tag from *Froggy's Little Brother* or *Jessica's Last Prayer*; but it works. Self-pity, from which I too often suffer, melts away if I go and see my friend who is imprisoned in Parkinson's disease. My imagined troubles fade into nothing compared with the misery of the illnesses which afflict so many other human beings. Thinking of others, rather like concentration on some task, relieves me of the burden of myself. And once again, this is not just my peculiar quirk. Bernard Rimland, an American psychologist, has published a simple test to measure the link between altruism and happiness. He calls it 'the altruism paradox'. Write down a list of ten people you know best. Next to each name, write down if they are selfish or unselfish. Then go through the names writing down if they are happy or unhappy. Rimland asked 216 students to do this, and when he added up the cases of 1988 people the results were on average clear. The selfish people were unhappy; the altruistic people were happy. 'The findings represent an interesting paradox: Selfish people are, by definition, those whose activities are devoted to *bringing themselves happiness*', he concluded. 'Yet, at least as judged by others these selfish people are far *less* likely to be happy than those whose efforts are devoted to making others happy.'[26]

Rimland's conclusion was 'Do unto others as you would have them do unto you.' My own conclusions are borrowed from Sir Thomas Browne, writing in the seventeenth century. 'Bless me in this life with but peace of my conscience, command of my affections, the love of Thyself and my dearest friends, and I shall be happy enough to pity Caesar. These are, O Lord, the humble desires of my most reasonable ambition, and all I dare call happiness on earth.'[27] If I could live that, as easily as I can write it, then I should be happy indeed.

Our Want of Love

REFERENCES

1 'TV crew filmed as man burned', *Daily Telegraph*, 11 May 1983.
2 Letter, *Daily Mail*, 2 June 1982.
3 'Behind a surge of suicides in young people', Jeannye Thornton, *US News & World Report*, 20 June 1983.
4 Figures from the Office of Population Censuses & Surveys.
5 Lak Bulusu and Michael Alderson, 'Suicides 1950-82', *Population Trends*, vol. 35, OPCS, Spring 1984.
6 'The lost children: where "trolls" flee "chicken-hawks" ', *The Sunday Times*, 2 January 1983.
7 Information from Scotland Yard's Juvenile Affairs Bureau in 1978.
8 'Children in care in England and Wales March 1982', Department of Health and Social Security, 1984.
9 'Children Today', National Children's Home, 1983.
10 Census 1981 press release, Office of Population Censuses and Surveys, 24 May 1984.
11 'Marital status and living arrangements: March 1980', Current Population Reports, Population Characteristics, Series P-20, no. 365, October 1981.
12 M. Rutter and N. Madge, *Cycles of Disadvantage*. Portsmouth, NH: Heinemann Educational Books, 1976.
13 'Record 50 p.c. rise in number of drug addicts', *Daily Telegraph*, 22 May 1984.
14 'Children hooked on heroin', *Evening Standard*, 15 May 1984.
15 Amasa B. Ford and Norman B. Rushforth, 'Urban violence in the United States – implications for health and for Britain in the future: discussion paper', in *Journal of the Royal Society of Medicine*, vol. 76, April 1983, pp. 283-8.
16 'Social Trends 13', Central Statistical Office, HMSO, 1983.
17 'Battered grannies scandal', *Mail on Sunday*, 5 December 1982.
18 Phyllis B. Grodsky and Arthur Weinberger, 'Apartners', *New Yorker Magazine*, 13 December 1982.
19 Fred C. Pampel, 'Changes in the propensity to live alone: evidence from consecutive cross-sectional surveys 1960-1976', in *Demography*, vol. 20, no. 4, 1983, pp. 433-47.
20 Ken Fogelman, ed., 'Britain's Sixteen Year Olds', National Children's Bureau, 1976.
21 James J. Lynch, *The Broken Heart*. Harper and Row, New York, 1979.
22 'Neighbours, what we think of the folk next door', *The Sunday Times*, 12 December 1982.

23   'The 11 million who feel left out', *Sunday Times Magazine*,
      11 December 1983.
24   'Has the quality of life deteriorated since the "good old days"?',
      Newsletter, vol. 2, no. 2, Institute for Social Research, University of
      Michigan, Summer 1974.
25   Tony Whitehead, 'A poor man's Napoleon – or a member of the
      secret police', in *Mind Out*, no. 55, November 1981, pp. 16-17.
26   Walter R. Gove, 'Sex, marital status and mortality', in the *American
      Journal of Sociology*, vol. 79, no. 1, 1973/74, pp. 45-67.
27   Hugh Carter and Paul C. Glick, *Marriage and Divorce*. Cambridge,
      MA: Harvard University Press, 1976.
28   Marsden G. Wagner, 'Getting the health out of people's daily lives',
      in the *Lancet*, 27 November 1982, pp. 1207-8.
29   C.S. Lewis, *The Four Loves*. New York: Harcourt Brace Jovanovich,
      1971.
30   Corinthians 1, the Bible, chapter 13, verses 4-7.
31   William Barclay's translation of the New Testament quoted in Denis
      Duncan, *Love, The Word That Heals*. London: Arthur James, 1981.

First Love

REFERENCES

1   Ernest Jones, *The Life and Work of Sigmund Freud*, Lionel Trilling
     and Steven Marcus, eds., Pelican Books, 1964.
2   Melvin Konner, 'Evolution of Human Behaviour Development', in
     P. Herbert Leiderman, Steven R. Tulkin and Anne Rosenfeld, eds.,
     Culture and Infancy. San Diego, CA: Academic Press, 1977.
3   Peter Paterson, 'A ghost of Christmas past', in the *Spectator*,
     18 December 1982.
4   John Bowlby, *Maternal Care and Mental Health*. New York:
     Schocken Paperback, 1966, 2nd ed.
5   L. Casler, 'Perceptual deprivation in institutional settings', in G.
     Newton and S. Levine, eds., *Early Experience and Behaviour*. Lon-
     don: Charles C. Thomas, 1968.
6   Harry F. Harlow and Clara Mears, *The Human Model*. London: V.
     H. Winston, 1979.
7   Marshall H. Klaus, Mary Anne Trause and John H. Kennell, 'Does
     human maternal behaviour after delivery show a characteristic
     pattern?', in Ciba Foundation Symposium 33, *Parent-Infant
     Interaction*, Associated Scientific Publishers, 1975.

8   John H. Kennell, statement from discussion following 'Evidence for a sensitive period in the human mother', in *Parent-Infant Interaction,* op. cit.

9   Aidan Macfarlane, 'Olfaction in the development of social preferences in the human neonate', in *Parent-Infant Interaction,* op. cit.

10 P. Johnson and D.M. Salisbury, 'Breathing and sucking during feeding in the newborn', in *Parent-Infant Interaction,* op. cit.

11 Dr Genevieve Carpenter, 'Mother's face and the newborn', in the *New Scientist,* 21 March 1974, pp. 742-4.

12 H.R. Schaffer and P.E. Emerson, 'Patterns of response to physical contact in early human development', in the *Journal of Child Psychology and Psychiatry,* vol. 5, 1964, pp. 1-13.

13 M.P.M. Richards, 'An ecological study of infant development in an urban setting in Britain', in *Culture and Infancy,* op. cit.

14 Evelyn B. Thomas, 'How a rejecting baby affects mother-infant synchrony', in *Parent-Infant Interaction,* op. cit.

15 F. Truby King, *The Expectant Mother and Baby's First Month.* London: Macmillan, 1924.

16 Benjamin Spock, *The Pocket Book of Baby and Child Care.* New York: Pocket Books, 1946.

17 Melvin Konner, 'Infancy among the Kalahari Desert San', in *Culture and Infancy,* op. cit.

18 N.G. Blurton-Jones, 'Contemporary child-rearing in evolutionary perspective', in R. Chester, P. Diggory, M.B. Sutherland, eds., *Changing Patterns of Child-bearing and Child-rearing.* Orlando, FL: Academic Press, 1981.

19 Michael Rutter, 'Normal psychosexual development', in the *Journal of Child Psychology and Psychiatry,* vol. 11, 1971, pp. 259-83.

20 Bettye M. Caldwell 'The effects of infant care', in the *Review of Child Development Research,* eds. Martin L. Hoffman and Lois Wladis Hoffman, vol. 1, Russell Sage Foundation, 1964.

21 M. Rutter, 'Separation experiences: a new look at an old topic', in the *Journal of Pediatrics,* vol. 95, no. 1, 1979, pp. 147-54.

22 M.H. Klaus, R. Jerauld, N. Kreger, W. McAlpine, M. Steffa, and J. Kennell, 'Maternal attachment, importance of the first post-partum days', in the *New England Journal of Medicine,* vol. 286, no. 9, March 1972, pp. 460-3.

23 J.H. Kennell, M.A. Trause and M.H. Klaus 'Evidence for a sensitive period in the human mother', in *Parent-Infant Interaction,* op. cit.

24 M.P.M. Richards, 'Possible effects of early separation on later development of children – a review', in *Clinics in Developmental Medicine,* no. 68, pp. 12-32, quoted in F.S.W. Brimblecombe, M.P.M. Richards and N.R.C. Robertson, eds., *Separation and Special Care Baby Units.* Philadelphia, PA: J.B. Lippincott, 1978.

25 P. Herbert Leiderman and Marjorie J. Seashore, 'Mother-infant

neonatal separation: some delayed consequences', in *Parent-Infant Interaction*, op. cit.

26   Barbara Tizard and Anne Joseph, 'Cognitive development of young children in residential care: a study of children aged 24 months', in the *Journal of Child Psychology and Psychiatry*, vol. 11, 1970, pp. 177-86.

27   Barbara Tizard and Judith Rees, 'A comparison of the effects of adoption, restoration to the natural mother and continued institutionalisation on the cognitive development of four-year-old children', in *Child Development*, no. 45, 1974, pp. 92-9.

28   Ronald Davie, Neville Butler and Harvey Goldstein, *From Birth to Seven*, Longmans in association with the National Children's Bureau, 1972.

29   Marcelle Geber, 'The psycho-motor development of African children in the first year, and the influence of maternal behaviour', in the *Journal of Social Psychology*, vol. 47, 1958, pp. 185-95.

30   Burton L. White and Peter W. Castle, 'Visual exploratory behaviour following postnatal handling of human infants', in *Perceptual and Motor Skills*, vol. 18, 1964, pp. 497-502.

31   Leon J. Yarrow, Frank A. Pederson and Judith Rubenstein, 'Mother-infant interaction and development in infancy', in *Culture and Infancy*, op. cit.

32   Rudolph Schaffer, *Mothering*. Cambridge, MA: Harvard U. Press, 1977.

33   Mary D.S. Ainsworth, 'Infant development and mother-infant interaction among Ganda and American families', in *Culture and Infancy*, op. cit.

34   Donelda J. Stayton, Mary D. Salter Ainsworth, 'Individual differences in infant responses to brief, everyday separations as related to other infant and maternal behaviours', in *Developmental Psychology*, vol. 9, no. 2, 1973, pp. 226-35.

35   M. Ann Easterbrooks and Michael E. Lamb, 'The relationship between quality of infant-mother attachment and infant competence in initial encounters with peers', in *Child Development*, vol. 50, 1979, pp. 380-7.

36   Barbara Tizard and Jill Hodges, 'The effect of early institutional rearing on the development of eight-year-old children', in the *Journal of Child Psychology and Psychiatry*, vol. 19, 1978, pp. 99-118.

37   M.L. Kellmer Pringle and V. Bossio, 'Early prolonged separation and emotional maladjustment', in *Child Psychology and Psychiatry*, vol. 1, 1960, pp. 37-48.

38   M.L. Kellmer Pringle and L. Clifford, 'Conditions associated with emotional maladjustment among children in care', in *Educational Review*, vol. 14, 1961-2, pp. 112-23.

39   Anna Freud and Sophie Dann, 'An experiment in group upbringing', in the *Psycho-analytic Study of the Child*, vol. VI, 1951, pp. 127-68.

When Love Goes Wrong

REFERENCES

1   'Boy died after last social worker's call', *Daily Mail*, 26 October 1982.
2   'Drug tragedy mother jailed', *Daily Mail*, 26 October 1982.
3   'Children lived on raw bacon', *Daily Mirror*, 27 October 1982.
4   'Chained to Beam', *The Times*, 7 November 1982.
5   A.D.M. Jackson, 'Wednesday's children: a review of child abuse', in the *Journal of the Royal Society of Medicine*, vol. 75, February 1982, pp. 83-8.
6   Susan J. Creighton, 'Child victims of physical abuse', NSPCC report, 1976.
7   Susan J. Creighton, 'Child abuse', in the *Journal of the Royal Society of Medicine*, vol. 75, June 1982, p. 484.
8   Susan J. Creighton, 'Trends in child abuse', NSPCC, July 1984.
9   NSPCC press release, 7 June 1982.
10   Richard J. Gelles, 'Violence toward children in the United States', in the *American Journal of Orthopsychiatry*, vol. 48 (4), 1978, pp. 580-92.
11   Stephen J. Pfohl, 'The "discovery" of child abuse', in *Social Problems*, vol. 24 (3), February 1977, pp. 310-23.
12   Leroy H. Pelton, 'Child abuse and neglect: in the *American Journal of Orthopsychiatry*, vol. 48 (4), 1978, pp. 608-17.
13   Susan J. Creighton and Peter J. Owtram, 'Child victims of physical abuse, a report on the findings of NSPCC special units' registers', NSPCC.
14   Phyllis Ann Jameson and Cynthia Jeanne Schellenbach, 'Sociological and psychological factors on the backgrounds of male and female perpetrators of child abuse', in *Child Abuse and Neglect*, vol. 1, 1977, pp. 77-83.
15   Selwyn M. Smith and Ruth Hanson, 'Interpersonal relationships and child-rearing practices in 214 parents of battered children', in the *British Journal of Psychiatry*, vol. 127, 1975, pp. 513-25.
16   Melvin Konner, op. cit.
17   George W. Brown, Maire Ni Bhrolchain and Tirril Harris, 'Social class and psychiatric disturbance among women in an urban population', in *Sociology*, vol. 9, 1975, pp. 225-54.
18   Selwyn M. Smith, Ruth Hanson and Sheila Noble, 'Social aspects of the battered baby syndrome', in the *British Journal of Psychiatry*, vol. 125, 1974, pp. 568-82.
19   Margo I. Wilson, Martin Daly and Suzanne J. Weghorst, 'Household composition and the risk of child abuse and neglect', in the *Journal of Biosocial Science*, vol. 12, 1980, pp. 333-40.

20 Jack Oliver, 'Some studies of families in which children suffer maltreatment', in Alfred White Franklin, ed., *The Challenge of Child Abuse*. Orlando, FL: Academic Press, 1977.

21 John J. Spinetta and David Rigler, 'The child-abusing parent: a psychological review', in *Psychological Bulletin*, vol. 77 (4), 1972, pp. 296-304.

22 Selwyn M. Smith, Ruth Hanson and Sheila Noble, 'Parents of battered children: a controlled study', in Alfred White Franklin, ed., *Concerning Child Abuse*. New York: Churchill Livingstone, 1975.

23 Jean G. Moore and Beryl M. Day, 'Family interaction associated with abuse of children over 5 years old', in *Child Abuse and Neglect*, 1979.

24 William N. Friedrich and Jerry A. Boriskin, 'The role of the child in abuse: a review of the literature', in the *American Journal of Orthopsychiatry*, vol. 46 (4), 1976, pp. 580-90.

25 Margaret Lynch and Jacqueline Roberts, 'Early alerting signs', in Alfred White Franklin, ed., *Child Abuse*. New York: Churchill Livingstone, 1977.

26 Margaret Lynch, 'Ill health and child abuse', in the *Lancet*, 16 August 1975, pp. 317-9.

27 Michael Rutter, *Maternal Deprivation Reassessed*. New York: Penguin Books, 1981, 2nd ed.

28 H.R. Schaffer and Evelyn B. Schaffer, *Child care and the family, a study of short term admission to care*, G. Bell, 1968.

29 D.P. Farrington, 'The family backgrounds of aggressive youths', in L.A. Hersov and M. Berger, eds., *Aggression and Anti-Social Behaviour in Childhood and Adolescence*. Elmsford, NY: Pergamon Press, 1980.

30 N. Richman, J.E. Stevenson and P.J. Graham, 'Prevalence of behaviour problems in three-year-old children: an epidemiological study in a London borough', in the *Journal of Child Psychology and Psychiatry*, vol. 16, 1975, pp. 277-87.

31 Carolyn Okell Jones, 'The fate of abused children', in *The Challenge of Child Abuse*, op. cit.

32 Harold P. Martin and Patricia Beezley, 'Behavioural observations of abused children', in *Developmental Medicine and Child Neurology*, vol. 19, 1977, pp. 373-87.

33 Jane Rowe, 'Alternative families', in *The Challenge of Child Abuse*, op. cit.

34 Barbara Tizard and Judith Rees, 'A comparison of the effects of adoption, restoration to the natural mother and continued institutionalisation on the cognitive development of four-year-old children', in *Child Development*, vol. 45, 1974, pp. 92-9.

35 Anthony C. Fairburn, 'Statutory removal of a newborn baby', in *Child Abuse*, op. cit.

36 Leonard A. Rosenblum and Harry F. Harlow, 'Approach-avoidance conflict in the mother-surrogate situation', in *Psychological Reports*, vol. 12, 1963, pp. 83-5.

37 John and Elizabeth Newson, *Infant Care in an Urban Community*.

Winchester, MA: George Allen and Unwin, 1963.
38 Proverbs, the Bible, chapter 13, verse 24.
39 Ross D. Parke, 'Socialization into child abuse: a social interactional perspective', in June Louin Tapp and Felice J. Levine, eds., *Law, Justice and the Individual in Society: Psychological and Legal Issues,* Holt, Rinehart & Winston, New York, 1970.
40 Alfred White Franklin, 'The gentle art of neonatalogy', *Child Abuse,* op. cit.
41 Rudolph Schaffer, *Mothering.* Cambridge, MA: Harvard U. Press, 1977.
42 Margaret Mead, *Male and Female.* New York: William Morrow, 1975.

Friends in Need, Friends Indeed

REFERENCES

1 Sir Thomas Browne, *Religio Medici*, Joseph Rickerby, ed., 1838.
2 Aristotle, *Metaphysics X-XIV,* H. Tredennick and G. Cyril Armstrong, trans. London: William Heinemann, 1969.
3 Michel de Montaigne, *Essais*, John Florio, trans., Everyman's Library, 1965.
4 Robert Brain, *Friends and Lovers.* London: Hart-Davis MacGibbon, 1976.
5 Lillian Faderman, *Surpassing the Love of Men.* New York: William Morrow, 1981.
6 Benjamin Disraeli, *Coningsby.* Oxford, England: Oxford U. Press, 1982.
7 Havelock Ellis, *Studies in the Psychology of Sex,* vol. 2, F.A. Davis, Philadelphia, 1921.
8 Robert Bernard Martin, *Tennyson, the Unquiet Heart.* Winchester, MA: Faber & Faber, 1980.
9 Michael and Eleanor Brock, eds., *H.H. Asquith:·Letters to Venetia Stanley.* Oxford, England: Oxford University Press, 1982.
10 H.C.G. Matthew, ed., *The Gladstone Diaries, Vols. VII and VIII 1869-1874.* Oxford, England: Oxford University Press, 1982.
11 Michael Young and Peter Willmott, *Family and Kinship in East London,* revised edition. England: Penguin Books, 1962.
12 Colin Rosser and C.C. Harris, 'Relationships through marriage in a Welsh urban area', in *Sociological Review,* vol. 9, 1961, pp. 293-321.
13 Graham A. Allan, *A Sociology of Friendship and Kinship.* Winchester, MA: Allen and Unwin, 1979.
14 Geoffrey K. Leigh, 'Kinship interaction over the family life span', in the *Journal of Marriage and the Family,* vol. 44, no. 1, February 1982, pp. 197-207.

15 R.A. Hinde, *Biological Bases of Human Social Behaviour*. New York: McGraw-Hill, 1974.

16 Claire Russell and W.M.S. Russell, 'Kinship in monkeys and man', in *Biology and Human Affairs*, vol. 43, no. 1, 1978, pp. 1-31.

17 Harry F. Harlow and Margaret K. Harlow, 'Effects of various mother-infant relationships on rhesus monkey behaviours', in B.M. Foss, ed., *Determinants of Infant Behaviour*, vol. IV, Methuen, 1969.

18 H.M.H. Wu, W.G. Holmes, S.R. Medina and G.P. Sackett, 'Kin preference in infant Macaca nemestrina', in *Nature*, vol. 285, 22 May 1980, pp. 225-7.

19 Zick Rubin, *Children's Friendships*. Cambridge, MA: Harvard U. Press, 1980.

20 E. Waters, J. Wippman and L.A. Sroufe, 'Attachment, positive affect, and competence in the peer group, two studies in construct validation', in *Child Development*, vol. 50, 1979, pp. 821-9.

21 Colin Brydon, 'From play to talk to trust', lecture at the British Psychological Society, York, April 1982.

22 H.H. Remmers and D.H. Radler, 'Teenage attitudes', in the *Scientific American*, vol. 198, no. 6, June 1958, pp. 25-9.

23 H.J. Locke, *Predicting Adjustment in Marriage*. New York: Henry Holt, 1951.

24. St. Matthew, the Bible, chapter 25, verse 29.

25 Zick Rubin, *Liking and Loving*, Holt, Rinehart & Winston, New York, 1973.

26 Mady W. Segal, 'Alphabet and attraction', in the *Journal of Personality and Social Psychology*, vol. 30, no. 5, 1974, pp. 654-7.

27 Robert F. Priest and Jack Sawyer, 'Proximity and peership: bases of balance in interpersonal attraction', in the *American Journal of Sociology*, vol. 72, 1966/67, pp. 633-49.

28 Vicky Rippere, 'What's the thing to do when you're feeling depressed? – a pilot study', in *Behavioural Research and Therapy*, vol. 15, 1977, pp. 185-91.

29 Gerald Gurin, Joseph Veroff and Sheila Feld, *Americans View Their Mental Health*. New York: Basic Books, 1960.

30 Francis Bacon 'Of Friendship', *Essays,* W. Aldis Wright, ed. London: Macmillan, 1892.

31 Sydney H. Croog, Alberta Lipson and Sol Levine, 'Help patterns in severe illness: the roles of kin network, non-family resources and institutions', in the *Journal of Marriage and the Family*, vol. 34, no. 1, February 1972, pp. 32-41.

32 Eugene Litwak and Ivan Szelenyi, 'Primary group structures and their functions: kin, neighbors and friends', in the *American Sociological Review*, vol. 34, 1969, pp. 465-81.

33 Scott Henderson, D.G. Byrne, P. Duncan-Jones, Sylvia Adcock, Ruth Scott and G.P. Steele, 'Social bonds in the epidemiology of neurosis: a preliminary communication', in the *British Journal of Psychiatry*, vol. 132, 1978, pp. 463-6.

34 Scott Henderson, D.G. Byrne, P. Duncan-Jones, Ruth Scott and Sylvia Adcock, 'Social relationships, adversity and neurosis: a study of associations in a general population sample', in the *British Journal of Psychiatry*, vol. 136, 1980, pp. 574-83.

35 Susan M. Essock-Vitale and Lynn A. Fairbanks, 'Sociobiological theories of kin selection and reciprocal altruism and their relevance for psychiatry', in the *Journal of Nervous and Mental Disease*, vol. 167, no. 1, 1979, pp. 23-8.

36 P. McC. Miller and J.G. Ingham, 'Friends, confidants and symptoms', in *Social Psychiatry*, vol. 11, 1976, pp. 51-8.

37 Lisa F. Berkman and S. Leonard Syme, 'Social networks, host resistance and mortality: a nine-year follow-up study of Alameda county residents', in the *American Journal of Epidemiology*, vol. 109, no. 2, 1979, pp. 186-204.

38 G. Dooghe, 'Characteristics and social conditions of residents in old people's homes', in H.G. Moors, R.L. Cliquet, G. Dooghe and D.J. van de Kaa, eds., *Population and the Family in the Low Countries*, vol. 1, Netherlands Interuniversity Demographic Institute and the Population and Family Study Centre, 1976.

39 Christopher Burney, *Solitary Confinement*. London: Clerke and Cockeran, 1952.

Enduring Love or Sexual Excitement?

REFERENCES

1 Mary Wollstonecraft, *A Vindication of the Rights of Women*. New York: W.W. Norton, 1976.

2 Theodor van de Velde, *Ideal Marriage*. Westport, CT: Greenwood Press, 1980.

3 William H. Masters and Virginia E. Johnson. *Human Sexual Inadequacy*. New York: Little, Brown, 1970.

4 Edward M. Brecher, *The Sex Researchers*. London: Panther Books, 1972.

5 Alex Comfort, *The Joy of Sex*. New York: Simon & Schuster, 1974.

6 Alex Comfort, 'Sexuality in a zero growth society', in James R. Smith and Lynn G. Smith, eds., *Beyond Monogamy*. Baltimore: MD: John Hopkins University Press, 1974.

7 Robert and Anna Francoeur, 'Social sex: the new single standard', in Maggie Tripp, ed., *Woman In The Year 2000*. New York: Dell, 1974.

8 James Ramey, 'Emerging Patterns of innovative marriage behaviour', in *Beyond Monogamy*, op. cit.

9   Moreton Hunt, *Sexual Behaviour in the Seventies.* New York: Dell, 1975.
10 Desmond Morris, *The Naked Ape.* New York: Dell, 1984.
11 Sydney Mellen, *The Evolution of Love.* New York: W.H. Freeman, 1981.
12 Frank A. Beach and Ariel Merari, 'Coital behaviour in dogs', in the *Journal of Comparative and Physiological Psychology*, vol. 70, No. 1, part 2, January 1970, pp. 1-22.
13 Clellan S. Ford and Frank A. Beach, *Patterns of Sexual Behaviour.* (rep. 1951 ed.) Westport, CT: Greenwood Press, 1980.
14 R.A. Hinde, *Biological Bases of Human Social Behaviour.* New York: McGraw-Hill, 1974.
15 Alan P. Bell and Martin S. Weinburg, *Homosexualities.* London: Mitchell Beazley, 1979.
16 'The Mosher survey, sexual attitudes of 45 Victorian women', reviewed in the *Journal of Marriage and the Family*, vol. 44, no. 1, February 1982, pp. 251-3.
17 Shere Hite, *The Hite Report.* New York: Dell, 1976.
18 Margaret Mead, *Male and Female.* New York: William Morrow, 1975.
19 Donald Symons, *The Evolution of Human Sexuality.* Oxford, England: Oxford University Press, 1979.
20 Glenn Wilson, *Love and Instinct.* Middlesex, England: Temple-Smith, 1981.
21 Alfred C. Kinsey, Wardell B. Pomeroy, Clyde E. Martin, *Sexual Behaviour in the Human Male.* Philadelphia, PA: W.B. Saunders, 1948.
22 William H. James, personal communication to author, 1983.
23 William H. Masters and Virginia E. Johnson, *The Pleasure Bond.* New York: Little, Brown, 1975.
24 Letitia A. Peplau, Zick Rubin and Charles T. Hill, 'Sexual intimacy in dating relationships', in the *Journal of Social Issues*, vol. 33, no. 2, 1977, pp. 86-109.
25 Charles T. Hill, Zick Rubin and Letitia A. Peplau, 'Break-ups before marriage: the end of 103 affairs', in the *Journal of Social Issues*, vol. 32, no. 1, 1976, pp. 147-68.
26 Larry Constantine and Joan M. Constantine, 'Sexual aspects of multilateral relations', in *Beyond Monogamy*, op. cit.
27 Celia Haddon, *The Sensuous Lie.* Briarcliff Manor, N.Y.: Stein and Day, 1983.
28 Barbara Thornes and Jean Collard, *Who Divorces?* Boston, MA: Routledge and Kegan Paul, 1979.
29 M. Komarovsky, *Blue-Collar Marriage.* New York: Vintage Books, 1967.
30 J.P. Watson and B. Brockman, 'The work of a psychosexual problems clinic: a follow-up study', in *Eugenics Society Bulletin 14*, 1982, pp. 17-20.
31 James W. Ramey, 'Communes, group marriage and the upper middle class', in *Beyond Monogamy*, op. cit.

32 William H. James, 'Decline in coital rates with spouses' ages and duration of marriage', in the *Journal of Biosocial Science*, vol. 15, 1983, pp. 83-7.

33 Lorna V. Sarrel and Philip M. Sarrel, *Sexual Turning Points*. New York: Macmillan, 1984.

34 Martin Cole, 'Sex therapy, a critical reappraisal', in the *British Journal of Sexual Medicine*, vol. 11, no. 104, January 1984, pp. 18-22.

35 James W. Ramey, *Intimate Friendships*. Englewood Cliffs, NJ: Prentice-Hall, 1976.

36 Gay Talese, *Thy Neighbour's Wife*. New York: Dell, 1981.

37 Alex Comfort, *More Joy of Sex*. New York: Simon & Schuster, 1975.

38 James R. Smith and Lynn G. Smith, Introduction to *Beyond Monogamy*, op. cit.

39 Gilbert D. Bartell, 'Group sex among the mid-Americans', in the *Journal of Sex Research*, vol. 6, no. 2, May 1970, pp. 113-30.

40 Charles A. Varni, 'An exploratory study of spouse swapping', in *Beyond Monogamy*, op. cit.

41 Duane Denfeld, 'Dropouts from swinging: the marriage counsellor as informant', in *Beyond Monogamy*, op. cit.

42 Eugene C. Kennedy and Victor J. Heckler, 'The Catholic priest in the United States, psychological investigations', Publications Office, US Catholic Conference, 1971.

43 Jon Twichell, 'Sexual liberality and personality: a pilot study', in *Beyond Monogamy*, op. cit.

44 Brian G. Gilmartin, 'Sexual deviance and social networks: a study of social, family, and marital interaction patterns among co-marital sex participants', in *Beyond Monogamy*, op. cit.

45 Jeremy Seabrook, 'Teenage suicide', in Monica Dickens and Rosemary Sutcliffe, eds., *Is Anyone There?* New York: Penguin Books, 1978.

Marriage, Divorce and the Disruption of Love

REFERENCES

1 Edward Shorter, *The Making of the Modern Family*. New York: Basic Books, 1975.

2 John Haskey, 'The proportion of marriages ending in divorce', in *Population Trends*, no. 27, Office of Population Censuses and Surveys, HMSO, 1982.

3 'Births, Marriages, Divorces and Deaths for 1981', in the *Monthly Vital Statistics Report*, vol. 30, no. 12, 18 March 1982.

4 'Births, Marriages, Divorces and Deaths for 1983', *Monthly Vital Statistics Report*, vol. 32, no. 12, 26 March 1984.

5   'Duration of Marriage before Divorce', in *Vital and Health Statistics Series 21,* no. 38, (PHS) 81-1916, 1981.

6   Denis Baillon, Nelly Costecalde, Georges Godin and Brigitte Munoz Perez, *La Divorce en France,* tome 1, INSEE, Series D. no. 85-6, 1981.

7   Ferdinand Mount, *The Subversive Family.* Winchester, MA: Allen & Unwin, Inc., 1983.

8   Peter Laslett, *Family Life and Illicit Love in Earlier Generations.* Cambridge, England: CUP, 1977.

9   Lawrence Stone, *The Family, Sex and Marriage in England 1550-1800.* New York: Harper & Row, 1977.

10   Andrew J. Cherlin, *Marriage, Divorce, Remarriage.* Cambridge, MA: Harvard University Press, 1981.

11   John Birtchnell, 'Some familial and clinical characteristics of female suicidal psychiatric patients', in the *British Journal of Psychiatry,* vol. 138, 1981, pp. 381-90.

12   Jack H. Medalie and Uri Goldbourt, 'Angina pectoris among 10,000 men', in the *American Journal of Medicine,* vol. 60, 31 May 1976, pp. 910-21.

13   Hugh Carter and Paul C. Glick, *Marriage and Divorce, a Social and Economic Study.* Cambridge, MA: Harvard University Press, 1976.

14   Michael Rutter, *Changing Youth in a Changing Society*, Nuffield Provincial Hospitals Trust, 1979.

15   'Yo yo children, a study of 23 violent matrimonial cases', the Training Department, NSPCC, July 1974.

16   F. Ivan Nye, 'Child adjustment in broken and in unhappy unbroken homes', in *Marriage and Family Living,* vol. XIX, no. 4, November 1975.

17   Judith S. Wallerstein and Joan Berlin Kelly, *Surviving the Breakup.* New York: Basic Books, 1980.

18   Judson T. Landis, 'The Trauma of children when parents divorce', in *Marriage and Family Living*, vol. XXII, no. 1, February 1960.

19   Ann Mitchell, 'Children's feelings about separation and divorce', Marriage Guidance, Winter 1983.

20   Richard A. Kulka and Helen Weingarten, 'The long-term effects of parental divorce in childhood on adult adjustment', in the *Journal of Social Issues,* vol. 35, no. 4, 1979, pp. 50-78.

21   Charles W. Mueller and Hallowell Pope, 'Marital instability: a study of its transmission between generations', in the *Journal of Marriage and the Family,* vol. 39, no. 1, pp. 83-92, February 1977.

22   Hallowell Pope and Charles W. Mueller, 'The intergenerational transmission of marital instability: comparisons by race and sex', in the *Journal of Social Issues,* vol. 32, no. 1, 1976, pp. 49-66.

23   Peter Moss, 'Patterns of child-care and child-rearing practice', at the Conference on the implications of current demographic trends in the UK for social and economic policy, British Society for Population Studies, 'Occasional Paper 19/2'.

24 Lesley Rimmer, 'Families in focus', Study Commission on the Family, 'Occasional Paper no. 6', 1981.

25 Ruth Inglis, *Must Divorce Hurt the Children*. Middlesex, England: Temple Smith, 1982.

26 'US reports 20% of children reside with only one parent', *New York Times*, 9 August 1982.

27 'Advance report of final divorce statistics', in the *Monthly Vital Statistics Report*, vol. 30, no. 2, Supplement, 29 May 1981.

28 Phone conversation with Divorce Action Group, Dublin, September 1982.

29 Colin Gibson, 'The association between divorce and social class in England and Wales', in the *British Journal of Sociology*, vol. 25, no. 1, 1974, pp. 79-93.

30 Robert Chester, 'Divorce and legal aid: a false hypothesis'.

31 Arthur J. Norton and Paul C. Glick, 'Marital instability: past, present and future', in the *Journal of Social Issues*, vol. 32, no. 1, 1976, pp. 5-19.

32 Robert Chester, 'Sex differences in divorce behaviour', in the *Journal of Biosocial Science*, Supplement 2, 1970, pp. 121-8.

33 'Divorces 1982', in the *OPCS Monitor*, FM2 83/4, 15 November 1983.

34 Sir Roger Ormrod, 'The role of law in marriage', (my notes), paper given at the Survival of Marriage Conference, London, 27 April 1983.

35 Jessie Bernard, *The Future of Marriage*. New Haven, CT: Yale U. Press, 1982.

36 William Congreve, *The Way of the World*. Lincoln, NE: Univ. of Nebraska Press, 1965.

37 Lenore Radloff, 'Sex differences in depression', in *Sex Roles*, vol. 1, no. 3, 1975, pp. 249-65.

38 Phillips Cutright, 'Income and family events: marital stability', in the *Journal of Marriage and the Family*, vol. 33, no. 2, Decade Review, part 3, May 1971, pp. 291-306.

39 Larry L. Bumpass and James A. Sweet, 'Differentials in marital instability: 1970', in the *American Sociological Review*, vol. 37, no. 6, 1972, pp. 754-66.

40 J. Joel Moss and Ruby Gingles, 'The relationship of personality to the incidence of early marriage', in *Marriage and Family Living*, vol. XXI, no. 4, November 1959, pp. 373-77.

41 Lee G. Burchinal, 'Adolescent role deprivation and high school age marriage', in *Marriage and Family Living*, vol. XXI, no. 4, November 1959.

42 Harold T. Christensen and Hanna H. Meissner, 'Studies in child spacing: 111-premarital pregnancy as a factor in divorce', in the *American Sociological Review*, vol. 18, 1953, pp. 641-4.

43 F.F. Furstenberg, 'Premarital pregnancy and marital instability', in the *Journal of Social Issues*, vol. 32, no. 1, 1976, pp. 67-86.

44 Wesley R. Burr, 'Satisfaction with various aspects of marriage over the life cycle: a random middle class sample', in the *Journal of Marriage and the Family*, February 1970, pp. 29-37.

45 Judson T. Landis, 'Length of time required to achieve adjustment in

marriage', in the *American Sociological Review*, vol. 11, 1946, pp. 666-77.

46 Barbara Thornes and Jean Collard. *Who Divorces?* Boston, MA: Routledge and Kegan Paul, 1971.

47 'Divorce, revealed the secret behind every fourth door', *Daily Mail*, 3 June 1980.

48 Audrey Brown and Kathleen Kiernan, 'Cohabitation in Great Britain: evidence from the General Household Survey', in *Population Trends 25*, Office of Population Censuses and Surveys, HMSO, August 1981.

49 Richard Driscoll, Keith E. Davis and Milton E. Lipetz, 'Parental interference and romantic love: the Romeo and Juliet effect', in the *Journal of Personality and Social Psychology*, vol. 24, no. 1, 1972, pp. 1-10.

50 Elaine Walster, 'The effect of self-esteem on romantic liking', in the *Journal of Experimental Social Psychology*, vol. 1, 1965, pp. 184-97.

51 Glenn Wilson and David Nias, *Love's Mysteries*. Somerset, England: Open Books, 1976.

52 Tipsheet for Silhouette Books, 21 August 1979.

53 Jack Dominion, 'Continuity and change of values in marriage', (my notes), paper given at the Survival of Marriage Conference, London, 27 April 1983.

54 Hans J. Eysenck, *'I do', Your Guide to a Happy Marriage*. London: Century Publishing, 1983.

Friendships Between Man and Beast

REFERENCES

1 Sigmund Freud to Marie Bonaparte, 6 December 1936, from Ernst L. Freud, ed., *Letters of Sigmund Freud, 1873-1939*. Hogarth Press, 1961.

2 James Boswell, *Life of Johnson*. Macmillan, 1903.

3 Michel de Montaigne, *Essais*. John Florio, trans. Everyman's Library, 1965.

4 Kenneth M.G. Keddie, 'Pathological mourning after the death of a domestic pet', in the *British Journal of Psychiatry*, vol. 131, 1977, pp. 21-5.

5 W.S. Mason, Sara A. Scott and M.D. Kenney, 'Dogs as monkey companions', abstract in *Group for the study of the human companion animal bond newsletter*, vol. 2, no. 4, November 1981.

6   Aaron H. Katcher, 'Interactions between people and their pets: form and function', in Bruce Fogle, ed., *Interrelations between People and Pets*. Springfield, Illinois: Charles C. Thomas, 1981.

7   C.W. Hume, *The Status of Animals in the Christian Religion*, Universities Federation for the Welfare of Animals, 1980.

8   Genesis, the Bible, chapter 1, verse 28.

9   Peter Singer, *Animal Liberation*. New York: Avon, 1977.

10 Michael Fox, 'Relationships between the human and non-human animals', in *Interrelations between People and Pets*, op. cit.

11 'Profile', Pet Food Manufacturers' Association booklet, 1982.

12 'Pet ownership trends', MRC update, Pet Food Institute USA, Fact Sheet, 1982.

13 Peter R. Messent and James A. Serpell, 'A historical and biological view of the pet-owner bond', in *Interrelations between People and Pets*, op. cit.

14 Juliet Clutton-Brock, 'Man-made dogs', in *Science*, vol. 197, 1977, pp. 1340-2.

15 Charles Darwin, *The Expression of the Emotions in Man and Animals*. Chicago, IL: University of Chicago Press, 1965.

16 Lewis Carroll, *Alice's Adventures in Wonderland*. New York: Macmillan, 1962.

17 N. Bolwig, 'Facial expression in remates with remarks on a parallel development in certain carnivores', in *Behaviour*, vol. 22, 1962, pp. 167-92.

18 James Serpell, 'The personality of the dog and its influence on the pet-owner bond', in A.H. Katcher and A. Beck, eds., *The Human-Companion Animal Bond*, Philadelphia University Press, in preparation.

19 Glenn Wilson and David Nias, *Love's Mysteries*. Somerset, England: Open Books, 1976.

20 Michael Fox, 'Pet-owner relations', in R.S. Anderson, ed., *Pet Animals and Society*. Sussex, England: Balliere Tindall, 1975.

21 Allan Hobson, 'The ethology of sleep', Roche Products leaflet, 1979.

22 J.J. Lynch, 'Social responding in dogs: heart rate changes to a person', *Psychophysiology*, vol. 5, no. 4, 1969, pp. 389-93.

23 Aaron H. Katcher, Erika Friedmann, Peter R. Messent and James J. Lynch, 'Touching pet dogs and changes in blood pressure', *Pedigree Petfoods Magazine*, no date.

24 Erika Friedmann, Aaron H. Katcher, James J. Lynch and Sue A. Thomas, 'Animal companions and one year survival of patients after discharge from a coronary care unit', *Public Health Reports*, vol. 95, no. 4, 1980, pp. 307-12.

25 Susanne S. Robb, 'Health status correlates of pet-human association in a health-impaired population', paper given at the Human-companion animal bond symposium, Philadelphia, October 1981.

26 Survey on the health of dog breeders and owners, Lesley Scott-Ordish.

27 Dorothy Walster, 'Why not prescribe a pet?' *Geriatric Medicine*,

April 1982, pp. 13-19.

28 Keith Webb, 'Four good legs', paper given to the Group for the Study of the Human Companion Animal Bond, Cambridge University meeting, 7 July 1980.

29 Paul Cameron, Carol Conrad, Dave D. Kirkpatrick and Robert J. Bateen, 'Pet ownership and sex as determinants of stated affect toward others and estimates of others' regard of self', *Psychological Reports*, vol. 19, 1966, pp. 884-6.

30 Paul Cameron and Michael Mattson, 'Psychological correlates of pet ownership', *Psychological Reports*, vol. 30, 1972, pp. 286.

31 Aline H. Kidd and Bruce Max Feldmann, 'Pet ownership and self-perceptions of older people', *Psychological Reports*, vol. 48, 1981, pp. 867-75.

32 Lesley Scott-Ordish, 'Motivating factors in animal welfare workers – extension of study to compare dog-owning and non dog-owning households', *Group for the study of the human companion animal bond newsletter*, vol. 2, no. 4, November 1981.

33 Robin Furneaux, *William Wilberforce*. London: Hamish Hamilton, 1974.

34 Larry T. Brown, Terry G. Shaw and Karen D. Kirkland, 'Affection for people as a function of affection for dogs', *Psychological Reports*, vol. 31, 1972, pp. 957-8.

35 R.A. Mugford and J.G. M'Comisky, 'Some recent work on the psychotherapeutic value of cage birds with old people', in *Pet Animals and Society*, op. cit.

36 Peter R. Messent, 'Social facilitation of contact with other people by pet dogs', paper given at the Human-companion animal bond symposium, Philadelphia, October 1981.

37 'Pets as a social phenomenon', report by Petcare Information and Advisory Service, Melbourne, Australia, no date.

38 Peter Salmon, 'The psychology of animal ownership in an Australian environment', given at the inaugural seminar of the Joint Advisory Committee on Pets in Society, 3 September 1980.

39 Sharon L. Smith, 'Interactions between pet dog and family members', digest in *Group for the study of the human companion animal bond newsletter*, vol. 2, no. 4, supplement, November 1981.

40 J.S. Hutton, 'Animal abuse as a diagnostic approach in social work: a pilot study', ibid.

41 J.S. Hutton, 'Social workers act like animals in their casework relations', paper given at the Workshop on Pet Psychotherapy, Imperial College, London, 23 October 1982.

42 Phil Arkow, 'Pet therapy, a study of the use of companion animals in selected therapies', in the 'Humane Society of the Pikes Peak Region booklet', second edition, February 1982.

43 Clark M. Brickel, 'The therapeutic roles of cat mascots with a hospital-based geriatric population: a staff survey', the *Gerontologist*, vol. 19, no. 4, 1979, 368-72.

44 Samuel A. Corson, E. O'Leary Corson, Donald D. De Hass, Regina Gunsett, Peter H. Gwynne, L. Eugene, Arnold and Candace N. Corson, 'The socialising role of pet animals in nursing homes: an experiment in non-verbal communication therapy', preliminary draft of a paper for the International Symposium on Society, Stress and Disease: Ageing and Old Age, Stockholm, June 1976.

45 'Report on the international symposium on the human-pet relationship', at Vienna, October 1983, in the *Society for Companion Animal Studies news-sheet*, no. 8, January 1984.

The Healing Power of Love

REFERENCES

1   Max Glatt, *Alcoholism, A Social Disease.* Kent, England: Hodder and Stoughton Teach Yourself Paperback, 1976.

2   Dr Fraser Watts, 'Need for research into psychotherapy', in *Mind Out*, no. 55, November 1981, pp. 10-11.

3   Susan Milmore, Robert Rosenthal, Howard T. Blane, Morris E. Chafetz and Irving Wolf, 'The doctor's voice, postdicter of successful referral of alcoholic patients', in the *Journal of Abnormal Psychology*, vol. 72, 1967, pp. 78-84.

4   Charles B. Truax et al, 'Therapist empathy, genuineness and warmth, and patient therapeutic outcome,' in the *Journal of Consulting Psychology*, vol. 30, no. 5, 1966, pp. 395-401.

5   Scott Henderson, 'Care-eliciting behaviour in man', in the *Journal of Nervous and Mental Disease*, vol. 159, no. 3, 1974, pp. 172-81.

6   Scott Henderson, 'The social network, support and neurosis', in the *British Journal of Psychiatry*, vol. 131, 1977, pp. 185-91.

7   Charles B. Truax and Robert R. Carkuff, 'Significant developments in psychotherapy research', in *Progress in Clinical Psychology*, vol. 6, 1965, pp. 124-55.

8   P.S. Byrne and B.E.L. Long, 'Doctors Talking to Patients', HMSO, 1976.

9   Jonathan Gathorne-Hardy, *Doctors.* London: Weidenfeld and Nicolson, 1984.

10 Stuart Sutherland, *Breakdown.* London: Weidenfeld and Nicolson, 1976.

11 D.L. Rosenham, 'On being sane in insane places', in *Science*, vol. 179, 19 January 1973, pp. 250-8.

12 David Robinson and Stuart Henry, *Self-Help and Health*. Oxford England: Martin Robertson, 1977.

13 'To the Newcomer', Overeaters Anonymous, 1979.

14 Ernest Jones, *The Life and Work of Sigmund Freud*, Lionel Trilling and Steven Marcus, eds., Penguin Books, 1964.

15 Stanton Peel and Archie Brodsky, 'Addiction is a social disease', in *Addictions*, vol. 23, no. 4, Winter 1976, pp. 2-21.

16 Stanton Peel with Archie Brodsky, *Love and Addiction*. New York: New American Library, 1975.

17 J. Hubert Lacey, 'Compulsive overeating', in M.M. Glatt and J. Marks, eds., *The Dependence Phenomenon*. Ridgewood, NJ: Bogden & Sons, 1982.

18 'Alcohol and alcoholism', report of a special committee of the Royal College of Psychiatrists, Tavistock, 1979.

19 Joan Curlee, 'How a therapist can use Alcoholics Anonymous', *Annals New York Academy of Sciences*, vol. 233, 1974, pp. 137-43.

20 'Another Look', Narcotics Anonymous, 1976.

21 Otto Newman, *Gambling: Hazard and Reward*. London: The Athlone Press, 1972.

22 Overeaters Anonymous, 1980.

23 'Survey of Alcoholics Anonymous in Britain, 1981', the Gen. Service Bd. of AA (Great Britain) Ltd.

24 '1982 Membership, group and contribution data', Eastern United States AA Directory, 1983.

25 'Questions and answers about the problem of compulsive gambling and the GA recovery programme', Gamblers Anonymous, London.

26 James J. Lynch, 'Warning: living alone is dangerous to your health', in *US News and World Report*, 1980.

27 David Robinson, *Talking Out of Alcoholism*. Kent, England: Croom Helm, 1979.

28 Ralph D. Bonacker, 'Alcoholism and Alcoholics Anonymous viewed symptomatologically', in *Mental Hygiene*, vol. 42, 1958, pp. 562-6.

29 Oliver R. Whitley, 'Life with Alcoholics Anonymous', in the *Journal of Studies on Alcohol*, vol. 38, no. 5. 1977, pp. 831-48.

30 'Discussion' in the *American Journal of Psychiatry*, vol. 116, 1959, pp. 49-50.

31 Harrison M. Trice, 'A study of the process of affiliation with Alcoholics Anonymous', in the *Quarterly Journal Studies of Alcohol*, vol. 18, 1957, pp. 39-54.

32 'Who, what, how and why', Narcotics Anonymous, 1976.

33 Ernest Kurtz, *Not God: A History of Alcoholics Anonymous*. Center City, MN: Hazelden Educational Services, 1979.

34 G. Edwards, 'The Puzzle of AA', in *New Society*, 28 May 1964, pp. 10-11.

35 Alcoholics Anonymous, 1976.

36 Eric Berne, *The Mind in Action*. London: John Lehmann, 1949.

37 'A Commitment to Abstinence', Overeaters Anonymous, 1981.

38 'Twelve Steps and Twelve Traditions', Alcoholics Anonymous, 1960.

39 'Survey Highlights', Overeaters Anonymous, 1981.
40 Herbert S. Ripley and Joan K. Jackson, 'Therapeutic factors in Alcoholics Anonymous', in the *American Journal of Psychiatry*, vol. 116, 1959, pp. 44-9.
41 Letter from A.D. Henderson to *New Society*, 'Alcoholics Anonymous', 4 June 1964, pp. 28.
42 Harry M. Tiebout, 'Conversation as a psychological phenomenon', paper given before the New York Psychiatric Society, April 1944.

From the Love of God to the Love of Others

REFERENCES

1 J.Z. Young, *Programmes of the Brain*, Oxford, England: OUP, 1978.
2 Trevor Ling, *Karl Marx and Religion*. London: Macmillan, 1980.
3 Mary Kenny, *Why Christianity Works*. London: Michael Joseph, 1981.
4 Robert Towler and Audrey Chamberlain, 'Common religion', in *A Sociological Yearbook of Religion in Britain*, vol. 6, 1973, pp. 1-27.
5 Conor Cruise O'Brien, 'The little lies that lead on to big ones', the *Observer*, 11 September 1983.
6 Christel Lane, 'Some explanations for the persistence of Christian religion in Soviet society', in *Sociology*, vol. 8, 1974, pp. 233-43.
7 Marcus Aurelius, *Meditations*, Maxwell Staniforth, trans. London: Penguin Books, 1964.
8 Viktor E. Frankl, *Man's Search for Meaning*. New York: Pocket Books, 1980.
9 Elie A. Cohen, *Human Behaviour in the Concentration Camp*. Westport, CN: Greenwood Press, 1984 (rep.)
10 Christopher Burney, *Solitary Confinement*. London: Clerke and Cockeran, 1952.
11 Hilde O. Bluhm, 'How did they survive', in the *American Journal of Psychotherapy*, vol. 2, 1948, pp. 3-32.
12 Mary Craig, 'Maximilian Kolbe', Catholic Truth Society pamphlet, 1982.
13 Monica Furlong, ed., *The Trial of John Bunyan and the Persecution of the Puritans*. London: The Folio Society, 1978.
14 Emmanuel Curtis, *Blessed Oliver Plunkett*. Clonmore and Reynolds, Dublin, 1963.

15   David Boniface and Philip Graham, 'The three-year-old and his attachment to a special soft object, in the *Journal of Child Psychology and Psychiatry*, vol. 20, 1979, pp. 217-24.

16   John Bowlby, *Attachment*, vol. 1 of *Attachment and Loss*. New York: Basic Books, 1983.

17   Leonard A. Rosenblum and Harry F. Harlow, 'Approach-avoidance conflict in the mother-surrogate situation', in *Psychological Reports*, vol. 12, 1963, pp. 83-5.

18   John Bowker, 'Many paths to God', the *Listener*, 3 February 1983.

19   Quoted in M.C. D'Arcy, *The Mind and Heart of Love*. Winchester, MA: Faber and Faber, 1954.

20   'The objective efficacy of prayer', in the *Journal of Chronic Disease*, vol. 18, 1965, pp. 367-77.

21   Gerald Gurin, Joseph Veroff and Sheila Feld, *Americans View Their Mental Health*. New York: Basic Books, 1960.

22   Quoted in G.S. Spinks, *Psychology and Religion*. New York: Methuen, 1963.

23   Barry Blackwell et al, 'Transcendental meditation in hypertension', the *Lancet*, 31 January 1976, pp. 223-6.

24   Chandra Patel, M.G. Marmot and D.J. Terry, 'Controlled trial of biofeedback-aided behavioural methods in reducing mild hypertension', in the *British Medical Journal*, vol. 282, 20 June 1981, pp. 2005-8.

25   Vicky Rippere, 'Behavioural treatment of depression in historical perspective', in S. Rachman, ed., *Contributions to Medical Psychology*, vol. 2. Elmsford, NY: Pergamon Press, 1980, pp. 31-54.

26   Vicky Rippere, 'More historical dimensions of commonsense knowledge: spiritual consolation for the depressed', in *Behavioural Research and Therapy*, vol. 18, 1980, pp. 549-63.

27   Chad Varah, *Danger signs of acute suicide risk, The Samaritans in the 80s*. London: Constable, 1980.

28   Erwin Stengel, *Suicide and Attempted Suicide*. New York: Penguin, 1973.

29   'Suicide and Deliberate Self-Harm', Office of Health Economics, 1981.

30   John Bowker, *Problems of Suffering in the Religions of the World*. Cambridge, England: CUP, 1970.

31   Proverbs, the Bible, chapter 3, verse 12.

32   The Koran, trans. N.J. Dawood, chapter 3, verses, 140-2. New York: Penguin, 1974.

33   The Epistle of St James, the Bible, chapter 5, verse 11.

34   Peter D. Varney, 'Religion in rural Norfolk', in *A Sociological Yearbook of Religion in Britain*, vol. 3-4, 1970-71, pp. 65-77.

35   David B. Clark, 'Local and cosmopolitan aspects of religious activity in a Northern suburb', in *A Sociological Yearbook of Religion in Britain*, vol. 3, 1970, pp. 45-63.

36   Lisa F. Berkman and S. Leonard Syme, 'Social networks, host resistance and mortality: a nine-year follow-up study of Alameda

county residents', in the *American Journal of Epidemiology*, vol. 109, no. 2, 1979, pp. 186-204.

37 Angus Campbell, *The Sense of Well-Being in America, Recent Patterns and Trends*. New York: McGraw-Hill, 1980.

38 Jay Mann, 'Current assumption in sex therapy, part 1', in the *British Journal of Sexual Medicine*, September 1983, pp. 24-8.

39 Leviticus, the Bible, chapter 19, verse 18.

40 Walpola Rahula, *What the Buddha Taught*. New York: Grove, 1974.

41 Ulfat Aziz-Us-Samad, *Islaam and Christianity*, Al Madina Trust, no date.

42 Gospel of St. John, the Bible, chapter 13, verse 34.

43 Edward Schillebeeck, *Jesus*. New York: Random House, 1981.

44 Gospel of St. Matthew, the Bible, chapter 5, verses 43-4.

45 The Second Epistle of St. John, the Bible, verse 10-11.

46 The Koran, op. cit., chapter 107, verse 7.

47 Gospel of St. Matthew, the Bible, chapter 5, verses 23-4.

48 The Koran, op. cit., chapter 2, verse 263.

49 First Epistle of St. Paul to the Corinthians, the Bible, chapter 13, verse 3.

50 Thomas à Kempis, *The Imitation of Christ*, Richard Whitford, trans. White Plains, NY: Peter Pauper Press, no date.

The Abuse of Love

REFERENCES

1 Blaise Pascal, *Pensées*, A.J. Krailsheimer, trans. New York: Penguin, 1966.

2 George Bruce, *The Stranglers*. Essex, England: Longmans, 1968.

3 John Bowker, 'Evil and temptation', the *Listener*, 10 March 1983.

4 Norman Lewis, 'The tribe that crucified Christ', *Sunday Times Magazine*, 15 May 1983.

5 Mary H. Lystad, 'Violence at home, a review of the literature', in the *American Journal of Orthopsychiatry*, vol. 45, no. 3, 1975, pp. 328-45.

6 'The strange world of cults', *Newsweek*, 16 January 1984.

7 Shiva Naipaul, *Black and White*. London: Hamish Hamilton, 1980.

8 David G. Bromley and Anson D. Shupe Jr, *Moonies in America*. Beverly Hills, CA: Sage Publications, 1979.

9 Christopher Edwards, *Crazy for God*. New York: Prentice-Hall, 1979.

10 Susan and Anne Swatland, *Escape From the Moonies*. London: New English Library, 1982.

11 Erica Heftmann, *Dark Side of the Moonies.* New York: Penguin, 1982.
12 Morris Yanoff, *Where is Joey?* Athens, OH: Ohio U. Press, 1982.
13 Gospel of St Matthew, the Bible, chapter 10, verses 34-7.
14 Tim Miles, 'A sinner's revenge', in the *Daily Mail*, 28 February 1984.
15 Karen Armstrong, *Through the Narrow Gate.* New York: St. Martin's Press, 1981.
16 Richard Cottrell, 'Report on the activity of certain new religious movements within the European Community', European Parliament Committee on Youth, Culture, Education, Information and Sport, PE 82.322/fin, 22 March 1984.
17 Marcia R. Rudin, 'Women, elderly and children in religious cults', paper given at the Citizens' Freedom Foundation Annual Conference, Arlington, Virginia, 23 October 1982.
18 'A son's nightmare', *International Herald Tribune*, 18 November 1983.
19 J.Z. Young, *Programmes of the Brain.* Oxford, England: OUP, 1978.
20 Stanley Milgram, *Obedience to Authority.* New York: Harper & Row, 1975.
21 John G. Clark, 'The manipulation of madness', paper presented at

23 H. Perry, *The Human Be-In.* New York: Viking, 1970.
24 David E. Smith, John Luce and Ernest A. Dernberg, 'Love needs care: Haight-Ashbury dies', in *New Society,* 16 July 1970, pp. 98-101.
25 Brian Wells, *Psychedelic Drugs.* New York: Penguin, 1973.
26 Christopher Burney, *The Dungeon Democracy.* London: Heinemann, 1945.
27 Tom Hopkins, *How to Master the Art of Selling.* New York: Warner, 1984.
28 Erich Fromm, *The Art of Loving.* New York: Harper & Row, 1974.
29 Arthur and Cynthia Koestler, *Stranger on the Square.* New York: Random House, 1984.
30 Jill Tweedie, *In the Name of Love.* London: Granada, 1980.
31 Susan Atkins, *Child of Satan, Child of God.* (Logos International) South Plainfield, NJ: Bridge Publishing Co., 1977.
32 R. Emerson Dobash and Russell Dobash, *Violence Against Wives.* New York: Free Press, 1979.
33 Walter R. Gove, 'Sex, marital status and mortality', in the *American Journal of Sociology*, vol. 79, no. 1, 1973/74, pp. 45-67.
34 Erin Pizzey and Jeff Shapiro, 'Observations on violence-prone families', in *New Society*, 23 April 1981.
35 I.D. Yalom and Morton A. Libberman, 'A study of encounter group casualties', in the *Archives of General Psychiatry*, vol. 25, July 1971, pp. 16-30.

Learning to Love

REFERENCES

1 Michael Rutter, Barbara Maughan, Peter Mortimore and Janet Ouston, *Fifteen Thousand Hours, Secondary Schools and Their Effects on Children.* Cambridge, MA: Harvard U. Press, 1979.
2 Janet Nussman and Marianna Burt, 'No room for pets', *The Latham Letter,* vol. 4, no. 4, Fall 1983.
3 Jan Carter 'Strengthening the Individual?', in Alfred White Franklin, ed., *The Challenge of Child Abuse.* Orlando, FL: Academic Press, 1977.
4 'Stress codes to help GPs', *Daily Telegraph,* 31 May 1984.
5 'Assessment and teaching of empathy', the *Lancet,* 14 March 1981, pp. 596-7.
6 Erich Fromm, 'Selfishness and self-love', in *Psychiatry,* vol. 2, 1939, pp. 507-23.
7 Quoted in Dov Peretz Elkins, ed., *Glad to be Me.* New York: Prentice-Hall, 1976.
8 E. Lakin Phillips, 'Attitudes towards self and others: a brief questionnaire report', in the *Journal of Consulting Psychiatry,* vol. 15, 1951, pp. 79-81.
9 John Pickett and Andy Maton, 'Protective casework and child abuse, practice and problems', in *Social Work Today,* reprint from the NSPCC, 1978.
10 William A. Altemeier, Susan O'Connor, Peter M. Vietze, Howard M. Sandler and Kathryn B. Sherrod, 'Antecedents of child abuse', in *Behavioural Paediatrics,* vol. 100, no. 5, 1982, pp. 823-9.
11 Gene R. Medinnus and Floyd J. Curtis, 'Relation between maternal self-acceptance and child acceptance', in the *Journal of Consulting Psychology,* vol. 27, no. 6, 1963, pp. 542-4.
12 Harold P. Martin and Patricia Beezley, 'Behavioural observations of abused children', in *Developmental Medicine and Child Neurology,* vol. 19, 1977, pp. 373-87.
13 Angus Campbell, *The Sense of Well-Being in America: Recent Patterns and Trends.* New York: McGraw-Hill, 1980.
14 Lynn R. Kahle, Richard A. Kulka and David M. Klingel, 'Low adolescent self-esteem leads to multiple interpersonal problems: a test of social-adaptation theory', in the *Journal of Personality and Social Psychology,* vol. 39, no. 3, 1980, pp. 496-502.
15 Carl R. Rogers, *On Becoming a Person.* New York: Houghton Mifflin, 1961.
16 James J. Lynch, *The Broken Heart.* New York: Harper & Row, 1979.
17 Zick Rubin, *Liking and Loving.* New York: Holt, Rinehart & Winston, 1973.
18 Professor E.B. Castle, *Approach to Quakerism.* Indiana, IA: Fountain Press, 1961.

19   Viktor E. Frankl, *Man's Search for Meaning*. New York: Pocket Books, 1980.
20   Walpole Lewin, 'Changing attitudes to the management of severe head injuries', in the *British Medical Journal*, 20 November 1976, pp. 1234-9.
21   Marcus Aurelius, *Meditations*, Maxwell Staniforth, trans. New York: Penguin, 1964.
22   Karen Dion, Ellen Berscheid, Elaine Walster, 'What is beautiful is good', in the *Journal of Personality and Social Psychology*, vol. 24, no. 3, 1972, pp. 285-90.
23   David Landy and Harold Sigall, 'Beauty is talent', in the *Journal of Personality and Social Psychology*, vol. 29, no. 3, 1974, pp. 299-304.
24   Christopher Burney, *The Dungeon Democracy*. London: Heinemann, 1945.
25   Joel Brockner and A.J. Blethyn Hulton, 'How to reverse the vicious cycle of low self-esteem: the importance of attentional focus', in the *Journal of Experimental Social Psychology*, vol. 14, 1978, pp. 564-78.
26   Bernard Rimland, 'The altruism paradox', in *Psychological Reports*, vol. 51, 1982, pp. 521-2.
27   Sir Thomas Browne, *Religio Medici*, Joseph Rickerby, ed., 1838.

Index

abortion, 11, 171
acupuncture, 181
Adam and Eve, 103
addiction, 120-33
adolescents, *see* teenagers
adoption, children, 47
Adventists, 137
affection, 20, 78-9
affluence, 13, 15, 16
Africa, 88
agnostics, 150
AIDS, 75, 81, 83, 86
Alameda County, California, 150
Alcoholics Anonymous (AA), 120,
   123-32, 134, 182
alcoholism, 13; and divorce, 89,
   self-help groups, 120-32, 134;
   treatment of, 115, 116
'altruism paradox', 191
Analysands Anonymous, 132
Anarchism, 155-6
Andrew, Prince, 104
Anglican Church, 136
animal liberation movement, 156
animals, family ties, 59-60;
   friendships with, 100-13, 176;
   mother love, 25-6, 28-9, 36, 38,
   48; pet therapy, 111-13; sexual
   relations, 74-5
Anne, Queen of England, 54
Anniston, Alabama, 9
anorexia nervosa, 116-17
'apartnerships', 16
apomorphine, 115
Apsley, Frances, 54
Aristotle, 51
Armstrong, Karen, 161-3
Asia, 88
Asquith, H.H., 56
astrology, 136
atheists, 150
Augustine, St, 141
Aurelius, Marcus, 145, 189

Auschwitz concentration camp,
   138, 140

babies, child-care methods, 31-3;
   early mental and physical
   development, 27-8, 30-1, 33-5,
   36-7; maternal responses to,
   29-30, 48-50; premature, 45;
   see also children
Babylonians, 88
Bacon, Francis, 62-3, 64, 65,
   130
Bahai faith, 156
Bangwa tribe, 52
baptism, 57
Baptist Church, 137
Bartell, Gilbert, 82
bath houses, 75, 82
battered children, 40-50, 179
battered wives, 44, 122, 172-3
beagles, 74
Beatles, 146
Bedford, 140
behaviour problems, children, 46
Belgium, 65
Bengal, 137, 144
Berg, David, 163
Berlin, 171
Berne, Eric, 129
Bethel, 149-50
Bethnal Green, 57, 58
Betty Ford Center, 125
Bhagwan Shree Rajneesh, 156
Bible, 20, 48, 61, 70, 95, 148, 149,
   150-2, 159
birth control, 11, 44, 83
Blake, Edmund, 54
blood brotherhood, 57
blood pressure, effect of pets on,
   107-8; lowered with meditation,
   146
body language, 169; animals,
   101-2, 105-6